Zaibatsu America

Zaibatsu America

How Japanese Firms Are Colonizing Vital U.S. Industries

Robert L. Kearns

Foreword by Clyde V. Prestowitz, Jr.

THE FREE PRESS
A Division of Macmillan, Inc.
NEW YORK

Maxwell Macmillan Canada
TORONTO

Maxwell Macmillan International
NEW YORK   OXFORD   SINGAPORE   SYDNEY

The Free Press
A Division of Macmillan, Inc.
866 Third Avenue, New York, N.Y. 10022

Maxwell Macmillan Canada, Inc.
1200 Eglinton Avenue East
Suite 200
Don Mills, Ontario M3C 3N1

Macmillan, Inc. is part of the Maxwell Communication Group of Companies.

Printed in the United States of America

printing number
1 2 3 4 5 6 7 8 9 10

HD
2785
· K37
1992

Library of Congress Cataloging-in-Publication Data

Kearns, Robert L.
  Zaibatsu America: how Japanese firms are colonizing vital U.S. industries / Robert L. Kearns.
    p. cm.
  ISBN 0–02–917245–4
  1. Corporations, Japanese—United States. 2. Industrial concentration—United States. 3. Investments, Japanese—United States. 4. United States—Manufactures. I. Title.
  HD2785.K37 1992
  338.8′8952073—dc20   91–35868
                                                          CIP

Contents

Foreword

In the summer and fall of 1991, the discovery that Japan's leading stock brokerages had routinely been compensating large corporate clients for stock market losses created a scandal that reverberated through the world's financial markets. At the same time, major American computer manufacturers such as Compaq and IBM began to consider moving assembly of their newest laptop models out of the United States to Singapore, Taiwan, and Japan. These events coincided with a sudden rash of discrimination suits against their former employers by Americans who had left or been dismissed by large Japanese companies.

The link connecting these phenomena is the nature and practices of the Japanese *keiretsu*, the latter-day heirs of the old, pre–World War I *zaibatsu*. Composed of hundreds of major corporations and financial institutions linked together by stable crossshareholdings, groups such as the Mitsubishi, Mitsui, Sumitomo, Toyota (also linked to Mitsui), and Matsushita groups have become the most powerful business entities the world has ever seen.

This phenomenon of the *keiretsu* would be only an item of limited interest if its impact were limited to Japan, and were Japan not an economic superpower. But, of course, this is not the case. The *keiretsu* system and the Japanese economy of which it is a part have become a powerful force which is transforming the structure of American and, indeed, of world industry. In the continuing discussion of the future of U.S.–Japan relations and of whether or not the United States can compete, it is often said that the United States cannot become like Japan. In fact, it is a certainty that unless we Americans adopt very different policies and structures from those prevailing today, we will inevitably become more like Japan. For Japanese industry will tend to displace U.S. industry and to impose Japanese structures, values, and procedures on the U.S. economy.

It is the story of this extension of the Japanese industrial system into the United States that Robert Kearns tells here. It is one of the most important, if not the most important, stories of our time. For it portends a shift not only of economic but also of political and diplomatic power away from the United States and toward Japan. In some ways the phenomenon may be positive, in that it will continue to introduce more efficient practices into the American economy, and force American business itself to improve. In other ways, however, as the rash of legal actions by ex-employees of Japanese companies indicates, it may be negative and even dangerous.

The possible move of laptop computer assembly out of the United States by Compaq and IBM is a powerful harbinger. This development is rooted in an event that took place in the mid-1980s. It was then that the Toshiba corporation announced a major commitment to the development of flat panel display technology. By way of emphasizing the importance Toshiba attached to this technology, a senior Toshiba executive said that Toshiba was prepared to lose money for many years to achieve a major share of this new market. This was the same company that, along with the rest of the Japanese semiconductor industry, had expanded production capacity by nearly 40 percent in the face of cumulative losses totaling $4 billion between 1984 and 1986. When asked how they can financially justify such investments, Japanese semiconductor executives explain that they do not do Western-style financial analyses because they are not too concerned with financial results—only with achieving long-term market share.

This is a posture that no Western executive or corporation can assume. Even the heads of such powerful companies as IBM, Boeing, Philips, and General Motors cannot damn the financial torpedoes and move full speed ahead to achieve maximum market share regardless of the short- and medium-term earnings consequences. The result is the systematic displacement of American industry from major markets and the increasing dependence of even the most important U.S. corporations on their Japanese competitors.

In the case of flat panel displays, Toshiba, Sharp, and the other Japanese producers launched aggressive efforts in the late 1980s to penetrate the U.S. market. By selling at prices far below what it cost to produce the displays and far below what potential U.S. competitors could afford to charge, the Japanese producers quickly gained market dominance, with IBM, Compaq, Apple, and virtually all other U.S. computer makers becoming wholly dependent on Japan for their flat panel screens. Because selling in a foreign market below the cost of production constitutes illegal dumping under international trade law, the small, entrepreneurial U.S. firms that are actually at the leading edge of flat panel technology filed anti-dumping cases with the U.S. Department of Commerce and the International Trade Commission. These bodies duly concluded that massive illegal dumping was indeed taking place and imposed a duty to prevent it. This ruling in turn led several Japanese producers to announce that they would no longer ship the panels to the United States; U.S. producers were then forced to consider moving laptop assembly offshore in order to obtain the panels. That is to say, Japanese industry has become so powerful that it can exact a price not only from the U.S. industries that have become dependent, but also from the U.S. government, which is put in a position of unintentionally hurting these industries by simply enforcing American law.

The source of this power is the special relationships that bind Japanese corporations to each other and that have been nowhere better demonstrated than in the Japanese financial markets over the past several years. Toshiba and other major Japanese corporations can go flat out for market share and ignore short-term financial considerations because they face little or no risk. There will be no takeovers, no greenmail, no LBOs, and no white knights, because two-thirds of the shares of a Toshiba, or a Sony, or a Toyota are in the hands of other corporations and institutions that are in turn owned on a reciprocal basis. The corporations own each other and are operated not to maximize returns to shareholders, but to minimize risk and thus to maximize long-term earnings. Indeed, there are guarantees against risk. During the latter half of the 1980s, the small number of shares available for trading on the Tokyo Stock Exchange combined with enormous liquidity flooding into Japan to drive share prices to stratospheric levels. As related companies bought and sold each others' shares, prices soared and companies listed on the first section of the Tokyo exchange in 1989 were issuing new equity at virtually zero cost. These funds—which despite all the talk of globalization of world financial markets were not available to firms not listed on the Tokyo exchange—were, in part, placed in broker-controlled investment funds that were used to bid up the stock prices still higher. Companies were particularly anxious to put money into these funds because they all knew what the public only later found out—that the brokers would make good on any market losses. In other words, it was a sure thing.

Not only did the companies know this, but it later became clear that the Japanese government knew it as well. Indeed, the Japanese government was the architect of the system. Having guided creation of the *keiretsu* (*zaibatsu*) in the 1950s and 1960s, it responded to the revaluation of the yen in the late 1980s by pumping up the money supply and pushing interest rates down to historic lows. The objective was to provide enormous amounts of low-cost capital to Japanese industry to enable it to make the investments needed to remain competitive with Western industry even in the face of a sharply falling dollar exchange rate.

Japanese executives can go for market share, dismiss the need for financial analysis and concern for short-term profits, and criticize their American counterparts for shortsightedness because they have a guarantee. Their brokers, the suppliers (of whom they own a part), the distributors (of whom they also own a part), and the government which they largely control will band together to help them over the rough spots. As a senior executive of NEC, a member of the Sumitomo group, told me in 1985: "We know that when we launch a new product or undertake a new project, we will begin with a certain guaranteed level of support because the other members of our group will tend to support us. This is not monolithic, but it greatly reduces our risk." Or as Koji Kobayashi, the former chairman of NEC, told leading Japanese journals in the early 1980s: "We could not have succeeded in getting into the markets for computers without MITI's (i.e., the government's) help."

Many commentators have applauded as Japanese companies have conquered one American market after another. Their high-quality, low-priced goods have been seen as a boon to the American consumer and a much-needed spur to U.S. manufacturers. There has been a tendency to assume that industrial success is entirely a matter of poor or good management and to blame U.S. manufacturers for sloth, greed, and shortsightedness in their so-far losing battle with Japanese industry. Indeed, Robert Kearns himself sometimes falls into this habit.

Although there is no doubt that American managers have made their share of mistakes, and that improvements in their performance have been spurred by Japanese competition, there is also no doubt that most U.S. observers have no concept of the true nature of the competition. Superficially, it may appear from their respective annual reports that General Motors is twice the size of Toyota. Many wonder, therefore, why GM cannot seem to squash the nervy upstart. In fact, however, Toyota is linked to the Mitsui group and in terms of real economic power is probably about ten times the size of General Motors. Some Americans, including Robert Kearns, have criticized the U.S. auto companies for going for profits instead of market share in the 1980s. What these critics fail to realize is that to go for market share requires investment, and in the United States, unlike in Japan, in order to attract the capital necessary for investment a company must have profits, or at least the prospect of profits. No friendly *keiretsu* members or government will provide inexpensive capital just to ensure maximum market share. Thus, even when U.S. management and firms become more efficient, they cannot necessarily withstand the Japanese juggernaut.

The critical point that Robert Kearns makes well and frequently in this book is that the increased efficiency may also come at a price. The essence of the *keiretsu* practice of business is preferential relationships. A Japanese company deals on an at least marginally preferential basis with other members of its group first, then with other members of Japanese industry at large, and finally with foreigners. This is the reason for the tendency of Japanese producers to deal primarily with their longtime domestic suppliers and to bring those suppliers with them when they invest overseas. This is the reason why in order to do business with Japanese companies in the United States, American companies have found they often must enter into joint ventures with the Japanese suppliers of those companies. Thus, whereas in the past it was necessary to agree to a joint venture to enter the Japanese market, it is now necessary to agree to a joint venture to stay in the American market. By the same token, there are increasing signs that management of Japanese overseas subsidiaries tends to remain tightly controlled by Japanese.

The preferential business relationships of the Japanese *keiretsu* pose two major problems in the American context. First, from a strictly economic point of view, they tend to transfer value-added and wealth out of the American economy into Japan. Virtually all studies of Japanese industry concur that there is a much greater tendency for Japanese firms to import parts and services that might be obtained locally from the home country than is the case for other multinationals. Secondly, and more fundamentally, the whole concept of preferential relationships is alien to the American tradition and sense of fair play. As an immigrant nation, the United States operates on the principle that Americans do business on the same basis with all comers. Newcomers get the same treatment as old-timers. If that were not the case, newcomers would not come in the first place, and American society itself would be much more closed and stratified. Reliance on long-term relationships, school ties, and corporate alliances is the antithesis of the openness and the equality of opportunity that we rightly prize. Herein lies the potential danger posed by the extension of the Japanese industrial system into the United States. If some changes are not made to accommodate the very different principles and structures of American and Japanese industry, it is possible—indeed likely—that U.S. industry will continue to be displaced and living standards will continue to decline. It is easy to see how this chain of events could generate a deep sense of unfairness and a bitter backlash.

Robert Kearns has identified this fundamental issue and explains its parameters in *Zaibatsu America*. He also has some important thoughts on how the West can respond constructively. His book is worthy of attention, and is an important contribution to the continuing dialogue on Japan–U.S. relations.

CLYDE V. PRESTOWITZ, JR.

Acknowledgments

While reporting and writing *Zaibatsu America*, I was extremely lucky in the help and encouragement I received as my rough idea grew into a book. Guidance came in many welcome ways from a number of people to whom I am indebted. Some was expected and some a total surprise.

At the outset, especially helpful in getting *Zaibatsu America* moving along were Saville Ryan and Bob Monks. I could not be more grateful for Saville's help and spirited advice and Bob's enthusiasm.

I have also had the good fortune of having Stuart Krichevsky of Sterling Lord Literistic as my agent and Peter Dougherty as my editor—both of whom have helped guide my book to completion with much-valued advice, candor, and patient good humor.

As the book has evolved, John Train has provided insightful comments and the opportunity of meeting his friend and translator Yoshiyuki Zako in Tokyo. I also want to thank Frank Gibney for his advice and many useful leads, George Herrick for his counsel, Bob Schmitz for his assistance, and George Gardner for his efforts on my behalf.

Thanks are also due to the Economic Strategy Institute in Washington and its president, Clyde Prestowitz, for having me as a fellow at ESI during the final stages of my book and giving me the opportunity to spend time with some like-minded fellows there.

Finally, there's my family—Nina, Jessica, and Nicholas—who put up with me and provided me with invaluable advice, support, and understanding as my life became more entwined with *Zaibatsu America*.

1

Welcome to Zaibatsu America

Where Japan Plays Monopoly

The reason the West doesn't do better in competition with Japan is that it is competing with a society that doesn't conduct business but rather wages business—with the intensity and concentration with which it might wage war.

—Edward T. Hall, *Hidden Differences*[1]

We are much like a wealthy family that annually sells acreage. . . . Until the plantation is gone, it's all pleasure and no pain. In the end, however, the family will have traded the life of an owner for the life of a tenant farmer.

—Warren Buffett[2]

Ten years ago Anita Madden's knowledge of the Japanese was pretty basic—like many Americans she knew they made good televisions, Sonys; they put on theatrical performances which were for the most part incomprehensible to Westerners, the Kabuki theater; and they'd bombed Pearl Harbor and we'd destroyed Hiroshima. The Japanese she'd met she liked and that was that. What she and her husband, Preston, knew best was horse-breeding and how to cultivate their lush 1,900-acre bluegrass farm. Raising Kentucky Derby winners was the center of their life and each year in May 2,000 or so guests would fill tents set up on their Polo grounds to celebrate the night before the Derby. It was a genteel, horsey Southern affair.

Now that's changed forever as have the wide-open, gently rolling fields. The Japanese have come and prosperity has taken on a different look. Japanese firms have already invested some $2.6 billion in Kentucky, having built 57 new plants there, the vast majority serving the auto industry. At least 70 percent of them have expansion plans in the works.[3]

Now shopping malls and housing projects are cropping up in fields where thoroughbreds used to blithely amble. Now Japanese businessmen can be found raising champion fillies or bouncing across the verdant, Kentucky terrain in golf carts. Now, even the Maddens have gotten into the act. Two years ago the Maddens' annual party at their Hamburg Place farm had the theme of "A Night on Fujiyama." There were even some Sumo wrestlers, though the Maddens drew the line at serving sushi. Though Preston Madden, whose grandfather built Hamburg Place, remains wedded to his horses, Anita Madden is talking shopping malls and how happy she is to have the Japanese here in the horse business—says Mrs. Madden, "We need them to invest and they couldn't be nicer to do business with. That's it, honey."[4]

Welcome to a patch of "Zaibatsu America." Still little understood, Zaibatsu America is being created as part of one of the largest transfers of capital in history—a transfer of capital of much broader scope, implication and depth than the much-publicized trophy purchase of Columbia Pictures by Sony or the sale of controlling interest in Rockefeller Center to Mitsubishi Estate. On the one hand, Zaibatsu America entails the formation of an almost separate Japanese economy within major sectors of corporate America through a deployment of tightly integrated, fiercely competitive investment that runs from top to bottom of a targeted industry. This book will address the concurrent marriage of the U.S. and Japanese economies and how America will be increasingly influenced by Japan's economic wants and needs which are often distinctly different from America's.

As a result of this singular Japanese strategy—a strategy which gives Japanese corporations unique competitive advantages and traces its roots to the now-outlawed, late nineteenth-century Japanese industrial empires known as the *zaibatsu*,[5] the United States is fast losing control over vital parts of its economic body.

Think of the human body, 98 percent of which is water. The ideal is to keep the whole thing intact and in good working order—sound in body, sound in mind. But some parts of the body are more important to one's survival than others. The brain, the heart, one's ears, eyes, and nose, and the reproductive organs are obviously more vital to one's well-being than a toe or an arm or a full head of hair. The point is that the Japanese, through their own strategic deployment of capital, are gaining a hold on organs critical to America's economic person and not merely its cellulite-laced flab.

This is not a conspiracy. It's the natural extension of Japan's indigenous form of economic growth as Japan's economy takes on new global proportions. What's vital to Japan's economy in the 21st century is also vital to America's. So that as Japanese investment flows into the United States, the form it takes—the economic sectors it targets—frequently mirror the direction and force of the Japanese economy.

Contrary to what some economists claim, it does make a difference what a country makes and who owns its means of production. It is essential for America's economic well-being to continue to have the know-how and the ability to make the most advanced microchips, supercomputers, airplanes, autos and the like. Certainly, the Japanese know the importance of such ownership—that owning a manufacturing base, the ideas that go with it, and the vibrant, creative linkage between the two does make a difference, does add value to an economy, and that retaining manufacturing control of the high-value part of a product is vitally important. Certainly, the Japanese aren't totally self-deluded in tying much of their economic future to the belief that manufacturing creates wealth, spurs inventions, produces higher-paying jobs, nurtures a better educated work force and adds value to many sectors of the economy. As retired Massachusetts senator Paul Tsongas said recently, ''A nation without a manufacturing base is a nation heading towards Third World status.''[6] In this regard, competing against the Japanese for a controlling stake in finance, high technology, autos, a revamped steel industry, machine tools, consumer electronic goods and entertainment is not just a matter of America's private prosperity but also of its public security—especially in the area of high technology. As Zaibatsu America grows and intertwines its roots, the implications of this unprecedented coupling between Japan and America will become more

3

and more apparent. One hopes that the offspring aren't hydra-headed.

Though the term—*zaibatsu*—took on pejorative connotations before and during the Second World War when the Mitsubishi, Mitsui, Sumitomo *zaibatsu* and their ilk—Japan's huge financial cliques of interlocking banks and companies—were closely associated with Japan's war effort,[7] I use it here simply to describe a singularly Japanese form of economic behavior that has its roots in the nineteenth-century Meiji restoration of 1868 and in the prior, feudal Daimyo culture. I prefer using *zaibatsu* to characterize Japan's economic behavior rather than *keiretsu*, the term currently used to describe Japan's huge industrial groupings, because of its historical continuity and implied larger economic and social scope. A *zaibatsu* means quite literally a "financial clique"—*zai batsu*—or as it evolved, a family-dominated holding company, whereas the word *keiretsu* describes a lineage or a group arranged in vertical order—a group which since World War II has come to revolve around its bank and trading company. Ownership of the *zaibatsu* resided in the all-powerful family sitting at the top of the holding company pyramid, whereas now control of a *keiretsu* is shared by member companies connected through interlocking shareholdings. Though in external form a *zaibatsu* and *keiretsu* do differ to some extent, the basic dynamic force underlying the pre- and post–World War II economic structures[8] is the same—the group. Moreover, today's Big Six *keiretsu* have almost the same economic clout as the prewar *zaibatsu*, holding a third or more of corporate Japan in their web of influence.[9] In effect, the new name for such economic endeavors, *keiretsu*, is a bit like the Emperor's new clothes.

Today, forming economic groups bound by interdependencies has become a way of thinking and behaving that is institutionalized in Japanese business and its powerful government bureaucracies. It is a pattern that can be seen as a driving force in the heart of corporate Japan—Tokyo's Marunouchi business district and in the nearby ministries—the all-important Ministry of International Trade and Industry (MITI) and the Ministry of Finance. It is a pattern that can be found giving structure to Japan's high-tech efforts at its mammoth Tsukuba Science City and form to its Technopolis strategy of building high-tech towns throughout Japan so that Japan is in the twenty-first century's technology vanguard. It is a pattern of exclusion, that keeps foreign influences out of Japan and keeps investors as different as retailer Toys 'R'Us and American corporate raider T. Boone Pickens at bay. And it is a pattern of grouping together that will alter very little in Japan, despite America's efforts to force it to change and open up, and also vary little as it is transplanted around the world. For weaving this web of dependencies throughout the Japanese economy and abroad is a consensus of interest among its members, the main threads being money, custom and intimidation. As befits an island culture, such behavior is inward-looking, verging on narcissistic.[10] Such behavior has also nurtured a distinct sense of power and authority where responsibility for decision making is diffused.

It is this clannish *zaibatsu* mentality—with its strong roots running deep and wide in Japan—that gives the pattern of Japanese investment here in America its unique vitality and form. It has meant that Japanese investment in vertically integrated enterprises is becoming a key factor in strategic sectors of the economy in very short order and that Japanese firms are securing a major place in the heartland and Silicon Valleys of American industry, in Hollywood and on Wall Street. It is a pattern that can be seen structuring Toyota, Sony, NEC or Dai-Ichi Kangyo operations in organically similar ways here in America, disparate as their economic endeavors may be. Moreover, it is a pattern that has been greatly reinforced by cheap and infinitely patient Japanese capital—capital that largely as a result of the *keiretsu* system is content with low dividends and long-term growth. When a Japanese corporation has capital flowing through its veins that costs maybe five to ten times less than that of its American competitor,[11] it can flex its muscles much more confidently since it has much greater staying power. This makes it doubly hard for American firms to compete on their own turf against the *zaibatsu* strategy.

This flow of Japanese capital, much of which is financing our domestic budget deficit, underlines and is a symptom of America's slide from preeminence in the world economy. It is the flip side of our huge trade deficit with Japan. It's all the dollars spent on trade—on buying Sony Walkmen, Honda Elites and Fujitsu semiconductors—coming back home to roost under new Japanese ownership to be invested in U.S. government debt or directly in corporate America. While Japan's direct investment in U.S. industry amounted to $70 billion in 1989, it still ranks in number two place behind the United Kingdom's $119 billion in direct investment.[12] However, Japan's investment is now growing at a pace nearly double the U.K.'s, meaning that within a few years its total could exceed the U.K.'s.

Again, Zaibatsu America is not a conspiracy. It's not the result of some nefarious plot. It is a fact of life that America must wake up to, just as it must realize that Tokyo, with seven of the world's ten largest banks, the world's largest stock market and the world's richest security firms, is on the way to becoming the financial center of the world. Japan has already replaced the U.S. as the country with the most net foreign assets. It also is the world's largest lender in international markets. Its banks have more than a trillion dollars in assets outside Japan. Of that, close to 50 percent of all its funds earmarked for foreign investment in manufacturing have been pouring into the U.S.

Evidence of Japan's huge investment in the U.S. is everywhere, coast to coast—from the graffiti-free Kawasaki subway cars that were built in Yonkers and shoot through the granite veins of Manhattan, to Edgewater, New Jersey's Yaohan Supermarket, to Honda Civics made in Ohio, to the City of Chicago's municipal debt sold with the guarantee of a Japanese bank, to ownership of Las Vegas's Dunes Hotel and Casino, to meat importer Zenchiku's $13-million purchase of the Selkirk cattle ranch in Dillon, Montana, to condoms manufactured by Okamoto Industries Inc., in Stratford, Connecticut, to Japanese banks providing more than 20 percent of all the credit in the nation's largest and most populous state, California. Home of the world's largest oil company, the Exxon building on New York's Avenue of the Americas, is owned by Japanese investors, as is the Tiffany building on 57th Street, while 24 of Waikiki's 25 beachfront hotels are now in Japanese hands. It's all part of the $73 billion the Japanese will have invested in U.S. real estate alone by the end of 1990. The Pulitzer Prize-winning play *Heidi Chronicles* got major backing from liquor giant Suntory, which also provided much of the $9 million in financing for hugely successful *Jerome Robbins' Broadway* and the Steppenwolf Theatre's much-acclaimed *Grapes of Wrath*. American superstars Whitney Houston, Michael Jackson and Cyndi Lauper are now singing for Sony Corporation which paid $2 billion to buy CBS Records and subsequently bought Columbia Pictures for another $3.4 billion. Random as some of these Japanese investments may appear, there is nothing helter-skelter about most of them.

The cliquish, exclusionary *zaibatsu*-like pattern of doing business pervades many such investments. Examples already abound in the U.S. They range from subtly interconnected banking and financing arrangements among Japanese banks, the government and corporations, to establishing what has become the hallmark of Japanese industry here—vertically integrated operations in an industry targeted by Japanese corporations, where most every aspect, from financing and construction to suppliers and distribution, is under Japanese control. Japanese manufacturers believe that if such a mode of cooperation and exclusion works in Japan it should work here and thus far, they have good reason to hold on to such beliefs.

When Toyota built its billion-dollar Georgetown, Kentucky, plant it became the latest member of a new, highly efficient Auto Alley constructed in and adjacent to Rustbelt America that, along with the impact of the 1973 Arab oil embargo and the U.S. auto industry's own restructuring, has changed the face of the U.S. auto industry forever. This alley includes all of the major Japanese carmakers and literally hundreds of their parts suppliers. These carmakers have structured their operations here in America so that they retain control over the high-tech, higher value-added portion of their production, while the input of American suppliers and workers is generally of a more routine, commodity type and their jobs are low on learning and high on manual labor. This alley stretches from Mazda's Michigan plant south to Mitsubishi's Illinois facility and Honda's plant in Ohio, on to Toyota's in Georgetown and further south to Nissan Motor Co.'s operation in Smyrna, Tennessee. The result is that Japanese car producers are increasingly making inroads into the U.S. auto market, despite the voluntary, 2.3 million-vehicle lid on annual imports from Japan. By the end of 1990 Japanese automakers had enough U.S. capacity in place to produce about 2 million cars annually. Add in Japanese imports, plus planned capacity additions, and Japan could soon end up with 40 to 50 percent of the largest and richest auto market in the world, while also controlling the higher value-added part of that market.[13]

As a mode of economic behavior, *zaibatsu* has a long history only briefly interrupted at the end of World War II. According to some observers, the four largest *zaibatsu*—Mitsui, Mitsubishi, Sumitomo and Yasuda—were actually structured in a semi-feudal way, modeled along the lines of the old merchant houses that

7

prospered in the previous Tokugawa shogunate. The Sumitomo *zaibatsu*, for example, grew out of a major Japanese merchant house to become one of the largest *zaibatsu* in Japan, controlling some 135 companies in 1945. Since Japan never went through a European-style Industrial Revolution, the major *zaibatsu* are widely credited with turning the country into a modern, capitalist society as Japan gradually opened up to the rest of the world during the latter part of the nineteenth and first half of the twentieth centuries.[14] What the *zaibatsu* structure brought to Japan's push into the twentieth century and what greatly facilitated that speedy transition was a tremendous concentration of economic power in the hands of a few, very aggressive family holding companies, with very close ties to the government and controlling interests in major manufacturers, trading companies and financial institutions. This meant that the Big Six *zaibatsu*, often at the behest of the government, would focus all their energies on a chosen area of development, while competing fiercely among each other.[15] However, along the way the *zaibatsu* came to represent such an awesome concentration of wealth and power, that by the end of the war *zaibatsu* were seen by many as having played a significant role in Japan's imperialistic aggressions.

As Tokyo University professor of Social Anthropology, Chie Nakane, notes in her excellent book, *Japanese Society*, the *zaibatsu* may have been disbanded after the war by the Allied occupation authorities, who outlawed the existence of holding companies in their 1947 Antimonopoly Law,[16] but the principle of their organization survived below the surface as a peculiarly Japanese way of doing business, reaching full flower in today's *keiretsu* bound together by cross-shareholdings.[17] As Professor Nakane sees it, the sort of vertical structure inherent in the *zaibatsu* way of doing business is pervasive in Japanese society, encompassing the home as well as city and business. It is a way of living, a way in which the group is formed in a hierarchy along vertical lines.[18]

The binding force of cliquish *batsu* or factions is so strong in Japan that some observers argue all human relations in Japanese society are based on four kinds of *batsu*: the *keibatsu*, factions based on family and matrimonial ties and the *kyodobatsu*, a group of clansmen or people from the same locality. More influential after childhood are *gakubatsu*, the group of school and university classmates, many of whom one may spend the rest of one's life with, and the *zaibatsu*, factions generally based on monetary relations and not to be confused with the prewar *zaibatsu*.[19] Obviously, such generalizations may be overstatements and inaccurate for many Japanese, but still there is a good deal of truth to the description, especially the idea of the systematic power of the group or factions in Japanese society and the role of group consciousness.

Along these lines Professor Nakane notes that "the criterion by which Japanese classify individuals socially tends to be that of a particular institution, rather than some universal attribute. That such group consciousness and orientation fosters the strength of an institution, and the institutional unit (such as a school or company) is in fact the basis of Japanese social organization."[20] More specifically, Professor Chalmers Johnson points out in his seminal book on modern Japan, *MITI and the Japanese Miracle*, the

> keibatsu and kyodobatsu are part of any large Japanese organization, but gakubatsu is without question the single most important influence within the Japanese state bureaucracy. The cliques of university classmates are inseparable from bureaucratic life, because it is their university degrees and their success in passing the Higher-level Public Officials Examination that set bureaucrats apart from other elites in the society. Gakubatsu also forms the most pervasive 'old boy' network throughout the society as a whole.[21]

Then, too, Professor Nakane says the power of the group is all-pervasive in that "with group-consciousness so highly developed there is almost no social life outside the particular group on which an individual's major economic life depends." As might be expected, each group demands an understood, prescribed form of behavior and loyalty and has little tolerance for foreign ideas or behavior, which it both scorns and fears as a disruptive threat.[22]

While this sudden onslaught of Japanese capital flowing into America and the West has surprised many, it follows the slow evolution of the Japanese economy from insular mercantilism to an as-yet undefined global force. It is the rational consequence of Japan's almost unique trading practices that have allowed it to profit greatly from selling manufactured goods on world markets while keeping its markets virtually closed to similar goods.[23] Therefore, to understand the economic colony Japan is constructing and financing in the U.S., one must look to Japan for much of the explanation. Such understanding is essential to help avoid disputes that are bound to arise between the two superpowers as awareness of, and political questions about, the huge Japanese presence in the U.S. grows. It is a volatile relationship rife with areas of possible conflict, but there can also be creative, synergistic approaches to this relationship that will be beneficial to both Japan and the U.S.

At stake is nothing less than America's economic sovereignty and also the country's technological leadership. To a large extent America is for the first time faced with losing a degree of control over certain rich parts of its domestic economy through direct competition on its own turf. Unlike their European counterparts—British, Dutch and French investors who've been scattering pounds, florins and francs here and there across the land— the Japanese bring more than money. They bring their cliquish way of operating that for the most part excludes outsiders, in this case American firms, from their group's business and a uniquely competitive spirit that has marked their export drive. Add to this an arsenal of almost unlimited cheap financing (though this has changed some in the past year or so), a relatively strong economy at home and government backing, and the U.S. is faced with a formidable economic rival. Moreover, as Japan's economic presence in the U.S. multiplies through direct investment and employing thousands of workers in every state of the union, its political constituency also grows across the land. Then, to nurture public opinion favorable to its interests, corporate Japan spends some $400 million a year employing lobbyists, former U.S. government officials and researchers to get a positive message out in Washington and in state legislative bodies.[24]

The importance of this historic invasion of the U.S. economy— a legacy of the Reagan administration's dollar devaluation and profligate, deficit-producing fiscal ways—can not be underestimated. Zaibatsu America—the declining American economy's burgeoning ties with ascendant Japan—has no precedent in either country's history. The speed with which it is being built is also unprecedented. To a degree Zaibatsu America can be likened to a giant leveraged-buyout of parts of the U.S. economy, financed by extravagant purchases of Japanese products. Unchecked, it will leave future generations tenants rather than landholders, burdened with paying back their parents' debt through a lower standard of living. More will be working in Japanese-owned

10

banks, factories and hotels, having to adapt to Japanese ways. Whether America's debt becomes the junk bonds of the twenty-first century, whether we have entered a Faustian bargain with Japan or whether Japan's economic globalism will push it into a more forceful role in the geopolitical sphere remains to be seen. Certainly, Japan appeared as a rudderless, out-of-control economic superpower during the Iraq War, though Prime Minister Kaifu did finally manage to muster enough support in the Diet to promise $13 billion to help fight the war.

Increasingly, Japan's new global role—a role of leadership that is being thrust on it despite its efforts to retain its low, subservient profile—will include creating policy that will affect the U.S. politically and economically. It is not far-fetched to imagine a time when Japan's powerful Ministry of Finance would have a direct input into U.S. economic policy and could openly influence its course, given the fact that America is becoming increasingly dependent on Japan to finance its debt. It's only natural for a lender, whose loans are growing, to demand a say in the way a corporation or a country's economy is run. Moreover, buying America's debt at break-neck speed gives Japan a great deal of leverage in its negotiations with the U.S. on trade or investment. According to Chalmers Johnson, Japan used a version of this sort of leverage in recent Structural Impediments Initiative (SII) talks aimed at prying open Japanese markets and the *keiretsu* system, so that American firms could more readily do business in Japan. Johnson said the Ministry of Finance threatened that Japan could "cut off" purchases of U.S. debt at any time if the U.S. tried to push it too far in the SII talks.[25] That's leverage—pure and simple.

There is, however, a positive side to Japanese investment in the U.S. economy, besides their continued willingness to buy up America's debt. Japanese direct investment is creating jobs and Japanese management techniques continue to have a salutary effect on American businesses, challenging many American firms to improve their operations or lose out to more efficient competition. In the 1980s Japanese management techniques reinforced the impact of America's industrial restructuring, which when it worked, cut out a lot of the corporate fat and when it didn't, overburdened a company with debt. While a number of companies have caved into the Japanese pressure here, others such as Intel, Motorola, Harley-Davidson, Timken, Eastman Kodak, and Caterpillar have stood their ground, held onto their turf and in some cases, are prospering admirably. In this confrontation there is much to be learned on both sides. The Japanese still have a lot to learn about nurturing creativity and fostering entrepreneurs, while Americans can take a lesson from the Japanese on the basics of manufacturing, motivating workers and converting technology into commercial products.

To champions of foreign investment in the U.S.—and there are many, President George Bush being one—any investment is better than none. However, in many cases a new job created by a Japanese firm in Kentucky may, in effect, be one taken from an aging, mismanaged, import-weakened American plant in Michigan or Ohio—a plant that often slipped into terrible decline in the 1960s and 70s because of shortsighted management that bowed to the demands of shortsighted shareholders and shortsighted, high-priced, non-competitive capital that allowed little to be invested in plant improvement, job training or research and development. In such cases the net gain in national employment is zero. More often than not, the new job will be lower-paying, non-union, and will have been drawn from a largely white population; furthermore, with the new Japanese plant being more efficient, fewer people will be employed there than at the plant it is replacing. If, on the other hand, a Japanese firm buys an existing plant, employment usually declines as the new owner streamlines production.[26] To a degree, the Japanese plants clustered in and around Georgetown are examples of these phenomena.

Supporters of Japanese investment in the U.S. also point out that Japan, along with other foreign investors, owns a mere 10 percent of corporate America, or, according to the Commerce Department's latest estimate, about $1.5 trillion worth of stocks, bonds and land. In recent years, however, Japan's investments here have been growing faster than any other foreign country's. But size of ownership is not the point. The point, as Japan well knows, is what one owns.

Even though the global economy is becoming ever more integrated, it is a fallacy to believe, as Michael Boskin, chairman of President Bush's Council of Economic Advisers, apparently does, that baking a pretzel or building a supercomputer are of equal value to a country's economy. To underline this point about America's manufacturing base, Boskin once asked rhetorically—"Potato chips, computer chips. What's the difference? They're all chips. One hundred dollars of potato chips and one hundred dol-

12

lars of computer chips are both one hundred dollars.''[27] Such superficial judgments are totally off the mark. For one, the sophistication of the work force—from conception of a new silicon chip to its funding and eventual commercialization—far outranks that involved in slicing and cooking potato chips, even when they're manufactured and distributed under the most advanced methods. Also, one can live forever without another bowl of potato chips, whereas in today's world the same isn't true of microchips. While there is nothing strategically important about potato chips, microchips are obviously another matter. It's not just that microchips are the vital parts—the brains—of almost every advanced product America makes, from autos to computers to Patriot missiles, but also in order to remain globally competitive America must have access to the latest chips and not be beholden to Japanese producers who may favor their own countrymen before supplying Americans.

Moreover, if such economic endeavors—manufacturing autos or microchips or VCRs—are so unimportant, why are the Japanese so hell-bent on being globally preeminent in these areas? Does Mr. Boskin, who's been the nation's economic czar as it has slid further and further into the morass of being the world's largest debtor, know something the Japanese don't? Certainly, their own economy's phenomenal success provides ample proof of the merits of keeping these vital economic parts in superb running condition and exporting their unique modus operandi abroad.

Owning a manufacturing base is important to a country's economy in ways other than the quality of jobs provided and the value added. In addition, there is an all-important symbiotic relationship between manufacturing and much of the so-called service economy where one plays off the other and one grows from the other, where creative ideas emanating from design staffs and the shop floor flow back and forth and build upon each other, where one learns by doing. In their book *Manufacturing Matters: The Myth of the Post-Industrial Economy*, Berkeley professors Stephen Cohen and John Zysman correctly argue that

> there is absolutely no way we can lose control and mastery of manufacturing and expect to hold onto the high-wage service jobs that we are constantly told will replace manufacturing. At the heart of our argument is a notion we call ''direct link-

13

age": a substantial core of service employment is tightly tied to manufacturing. It is a complement and not, as the dominant view would have it, a substitute or successor for manufacturing. Lose manufacturing and you will lose—not develop—those high-wage services.[28]

Certainly, Japanese firms well understand this vital interaction of the manufacturing process. Much of Toyota and other manufacturers' success is based on honing this process to a fine degree. Then, of course, the interlocking *zaibatsu* structure is ideally suited to take full advantage of the dynamics of this back-and-forth relationship.

Even Harvard economist Robert Reich, who feels that America's future lies much more in what it thinks—in the way it can "solve, identify, and broker new problems," than in what it is—an accumulation of financial capital still focused to a large degree on manufacturing, concedes that

the idea of "goods" as something distinct from "services" has become meaningless because so much of the value provided by a successful enterprise—in fact, the only value that cannot be easily replicated worldwide—entails services: the specialized research, engineering, design, and production services necessary to solve problems, the specialized sales, marketing, and consulting services necessary to identify problems; and the specialized strategic, financial and management services necessary to broker the first two. High-value enterprises are in the business of providing such services.[29]

However, concluding a recent article in the *Atlantic*, Reich said, "What we own is coming to be far less important than what we are able to do."[30] This just isn't the case—pure and simple. This is the sort of Dr. Pangloss, best-of-all-possible-worlds argument that *BusinessWeek* described as "Robert Reich's Feel-Good Globalism" in reviewing his recent book, *The Work of Nations: Preparing Ourselves for 21st Century Capitalism*.[31] Manufacturing does matter, especially in the real twenty-first-century capitalism of Zaibatsu America.

There can be no better example of what a lack of manufacturing prowess can do than the American consumer electronics debacle. It was bad enough for the U.S. manufacturers, except for Zenith, to quit making TVs, but what happened subsequently as a result of this abandonment is even worse. Though VCRs are an American invention, no American firms make them because they lacked the manufacturing know-how to produce them competitively as a result of forsaking TV manufacturing. It now looks as if this same sad history will be repeated in the multi-multibillion-dollar high definition television market, as American manufacturers slip further backwards down the high-tech, manufacturing-learning curve. America currently has the best digital transmission system for HDTV, but it apparently doesn't have the will or the manufacturing smarts to produce the equipment vital for its success. So even with the best system being American, Japanese consumer electronics manufacturers will most probably take over the market.[32] As Professors Cohen and Zysman warn:

If we lose mastery and control of manufacturing, the high-paying service jobs that are directly linked to manufacturing will, in a few short rounds of product and process innovation, seem to wither away. . . . It is the high-value-added service roles tied directly to manufacturing (whether they are located in service or manufacturing categories) that we must hold and develop if we are to remain a powerful economy.[33]

Making the competitive challenge faced by American firms even more difficult is the fact that the Japanese are going about their chosen task in a distinctly quiet way. Outwardly Japanese executives may be subservient in their dealings in the U.S., but beneath the bow and politesse is a fiercely determined, well-informed businessman. If U.S. firms conduct business, Japanese companies wage business in the old samurai tradition.[34]

While I use *zaibatsu* to broadly describe a Japanese form of cultural and economic behavior, it should not be forgotten that huge *keiretsu* or *zaibatsu*-like conglomerates of co-dependent companies currently flourish in Japan and around the world. *Keiretsu* are not to be confused in any way with much smaller American conglomerates such as ITT or Gulf & Western Industries which came to full flower in the late 1960s. *Keiretsu* differ in size and structure from American conglomerates, being particularly able at providing cheap capital for growth and spreading the economic risk of new ventures over a broad base of companies working in many sectors of the Japanese economy. A *keiretsu* is more than a

15

conglomerate thrown together in synergistic hope, more than a cartel of common interest—it's a living organism, a hierarchical human community, a uniquely Japanese corporate family.

No longer privately held by the *zaibatsu* families, the new *keiretsu* were initially nurtured and formed by banks or trading companies with the government's backing into a network of interrelated activities that now almost mirror the huge prewar *zaibatsu* broken apart during the U.S. occupation. With *zaibatsu* holding companies having been banned, the American ideal was that the individual shareholder would emerge as the all-important investor in corporate Japan. To reinforce this democratic ideal, banks were prohibited from holding more than 5 percent of a company and insurance companies more than 10 percent. It took some time and ingenuity for Japanese companies, whose historic ties had been severed by the war and the subsequent occupation, to regroup along their traditional lines. What corporate Japan eventually came up with was a brilliant solution to its problem—cross-shareholdings, where members of a *keiretsu* own stakes in each other. As Robert Zielinski and Nigel Holloway describe the effect of cross-shareholdings in their new book on Japan's stock market, *Unequal Equities,* it has turned into "the corporate equivalent of blood brotherhood," with Japan Inc. now owning over 70 percent of itself. In 1949, when the Tokyo Stock Exchange reopened, "individuals owned 69.1 percent of all listed shares, securities houses held 12.6 percent, other financial institutions 9.9 percent, non-financial companies 5.6 percent and the government 2.8 percent. Today the situation is almost completely reversed. Corporations own 73 percent, individuals 22.4 percent, the government 0.7 percent and foreigners 4 percent." The reversal of the occupation's shareholder democracy is complete.[35]

The initial aim of these cross-shareholdings was to re-cement many of the old *zaibatsu* ties and to place a company's shares in friendly, stable hands—hands that would not sell out in the event of an unfriendly takeover attempt. Certainly, the blood brotherhood of cross-shareholdings has achieved these two goals admirably but it has also had two other very important effects. It has meant that these blood brothers control much of the Tokyo Stock Market and that they have been able to use these relations to get very inexpensive capital to finance their expansion in Japan and abroad. As a result, cross-shareholdings have proven to be the key factor in today's mammoth *keiretsu* prosperity, where frequently the flow of goods and services in the economy also reflects the pattern of these cross-shareholdings.[36]

There could be no better example of the benefits of cheap equity capital than Sony and the way it financed its acquisitions of CBS Records and Columbia Pictures. Starting in 1987 Sony raised a staggering Y908 billion (or about $6 billion)—the second largest amount of funds any Japanese firm had ever floated on the Tokyo Stock Exchange. Yet the cost of these funds was extremely low. ''Sony's three convertible coupon issues carried a coupon of less than 1.5 percent annually and the dividend yield on shares sold through its two public offerings was under 1 percent. Sony's counterpart raiders in the United States must pay 15 percent or more when they raise their takeover war chest through junk bonds.''[37]

Currently, the six major *keiretsu*—Sumitomo, Mitsui, Mitsubishi, Sanwa, Dai-Ichi Kangyo and Fuyo, which traces its roots back to the pre-war Yasuda *zaibatsu*—directly account for about 27 percent of Japan's assets and 25 percent of its sales, which is pretty much the way it was in the prewar zaibatsu period. These estimates actually understate the scope of their economic presence in many ways. According to Zielinski and Holloway, in the fiscal year ended March 1989 the Big Six *keiretsu* were ''responsible for 58 percent of all listed (Tokyo Stock Exchange) companies sales (excluding financial institutions), 39 percent of net income, and 35 percent of assets.''[38] In terms of pure *keiretsu* size, for example, the Dai-Ichi Kangyo group had revenues of close to half a trillion dollars and is dominated and nurtured by the world's largest bank. For its part, the Sumitomo group, with sales of around $300 billion, has interests in banking, mining, steel, chemicals, machinery, construction, trading, real estate, communications and electronics, to name just some of the areas it is involved in.

There are no hard and fast rules as to how a *keiretsu* is structured, but as *keiretsu* have evolved in corporate Japan two patterns have emerged. Such horizontally connected groups—Mitsubishi, Mitsui, Sumitomo, Fuyo, DKB, and Sanwa—have interests in a wide range of industries that frequently parallel each other. If, for example, Kirin is the beer of choice at Mitsubishi, Sapporo's brew is favored in the Fuyo group and Asahi at Sumitomo, since each of these groups have their own brewers. Smaller than the big six *keiretsu* are the vertically integrated industrial groups—such as a Toyota or Matsushita—where related compa-

17

nies, for the most part suppliers, cluster around a parent company. Most major Japanese companies are linked to one group or another, even if they are not formally part of the super six *keiretsu*. Toyota has ties with the Mitsui group, while Nissan has strong connections with Fuyo. Moreover, other new, vertically integrated groups are forming around Toyota, Hitachi and Matsushita, creating new, smaller *keiretsu* of great economic might. The Japanese government has also encouraged the formation of cartels of small and medium-sized, second-tier firms which share many of the characteristics of the huge *keiretsu*.[39]

Such vertically integrated groups are very different from those encountered in America, where a General Motors management will be calling the shots for their subsidiaries from their plush offices in Detroit and expect little input from their underlings. There you have a direct chain of command, with little interplay. What you have with a *keiretsu* is first of all a difference of size. But, though a *keiretsu* is built in a hierarchy, there is also the idea of interplay in a giant *keiretsu* which, because of its structure, functions on vertical and horizontal lines. Though the cross-shareholdings are circular and seemingly never-ending, a *keiretsu* is perhaps best visualized as groups of vertically integrated companies hanging together and off of a horizontal frame.

There is no corporate entity in the U.S. with the concentration of economic power and scope comparable to a *keiretsu*. The closest the U.S. came to such an economic consortium occurred around the turn of the century, when J. Pierpont Morgan wielded so much economic power that his bank operated as almost an unofficial central banking authority. In 1912, an investigation into Morgan's colossal economic power by Louisiana congressman Arsene Pujo found that he and a handful of New York banks held 341 seats on the boards of 112 major U.S. corporations worth more than $22 billion and that through these interlocking directorates they dominated banking, credit and stock markets in the U.S. In reaction, the Federal Reserve System was created in 1913 and in the ensuing years Morgan's power dissipated, never to be equaled again in the U.S.[40]

One way of imagining how a *keiretsu* works, and how it differs in size and scope from an American conglomerate, is to picture an American *keiretsu* structured along the lines of the Mitsubishi or Sumitomo group. Such a group would be worth close to a trillion dollars. Each of the 30 or so lead companies would own a piece of the other, would do business among themselves, and meet once a month for lunch to discuss matters of common interest and the thousand or so lesser companies that made up their group.

Now just think of what such a setup would be like. It would be as if John Akers (chairman of International Business Machines) Dennis Weatherstone (head of J. P. Morgan), Lee Iacocca (chairman of Chrysler), James Houghton (Corning Inc.'s chairman), August Busch (leader of Anheuser Busch), Richard Mahoney (chairman of Monsanto), Allen Murray (who heads up Mobil), and 15 or 20 more corporate chieftains got together for lunch 12 times a year. Then imagine not just one corporate setup like this but a whole host of them, with six or seven of the largest controlling a third of the U.S. economy. It's the sort of world that would have made J. P. Morgan happy but would have the justice department's anti-trust lawyers working overtime.

Commenting on the power of the Japanese conglomerate structure, long before the term *keiretsu* became widely used, James Abegglen, an expert of Japanese business practices, wrote:

> A conglomerate can channel cash flows from low-growth to high-growth areas and apply the debt capacity of safe, mature businesses to capitalize rapidly growing but unstable ventures. It can move into a dynamic new industry and bring to it financial power that no existing competitor can match. It can increase capacity quickly. The result is that the conglomerate is in a position to dominate a new industry by setting prices so low that existing competitors cannot finance adequate growth. Its costs are so low, compared with the competition's, that it can sell at the going price and earn large profits. In all these senses "Japan Inc." is indeed a conglomerate, a Zaibatsu of Zaibatsu.[41]

As Japan enters the twenty-first century and its financial markets are progressively deregulated and reorganized, the power of these bank-based *keiretsu* will be further strengthened and consolidated. At the center of the *keiretsu* will be a so-called "universal bank" with a scope and power unlike anything seen in America or Europe. For example, when the Fuyo universal bank is eventually formed, it will bond together Japan's third-largest bank and its fourth-largest trust bank, Fuji and Yasuda, with four leading regional banks, three of Japan's largest insurance companies, two

19

leasing companies, fourth-ranking Yamaichi Securities and the leading property developer, Tokyo Tatemono.[42]

Supporting these activities, in some cases directing them and in others interacting with them, is what has been called the "developmental, plan rational state"[43], the combination of Japanese ministries and parliamentary government that has been so instrumental in lifting Japan from the ashes of Hiroshima to its current state of economic prosperity and power. Though frequently denied, the relationship between business and government continues to be extremely close, with both sharing Japan's goal of economic aggrandizement. This symbiotic relationship will continue even after specific areas, such as finance, are progressively deregulated. Even the powerful Ministry of International Trade and Industry, the chief architect along with the Ministry of Finance of the Japanese economic miracle, is set up in a vertical fashion that parallels the cliquish structure of the industries it advises. The cross-fertilization between business and government takes place from the lowest to the highest levels on both sides, with many a ministry bureaucrat having been a classmate of his business counterpart at one of Japan's top universities and therefore, part of the same *gakubatsu*. Populating the highest positions in government and business and moving between the two with ease are graduates of the University of Tokyo and especially of its Law School, the pinnacle of academic achievement in Japan.

The state has been and continues to be invaluable to Japan in times of economic stress, helping it weather two oil crises and more recently the 60 percent rise in the yen—events that would have thrown a less directed society into an economic tailspin. Amazingly enough, even Japanese firms heavily dependent on exports are now reporting record earnings. Through a combination of government direction and impressive gains in productivity, many companies have kept their products competitive on world markets. The expected bankruptcies, mass layoffs and plant closings haven't materialized in the wake of the rising yen. In fact, the Japanese economy managed to register its best growth in 15 years as the yen rose, showing a stunning 5.7 percent growth rate during 1988.[44] Moreover, this growth has continued, with Japan's economy expanding 5.6 percent in 1990.[45] The government also stands behind strategic industry groupings, giving them advice, financing and coming to their rescue when necessary. When the Japanese steel industry recently fell on hard times—partially because the rising yen cut into its profits and partially because it was a mature industry suffering from the problems of world over-capacity, the government encouraged and guided the formation of a steel cartel so that companies could scale back operations and cut out an assigned amount of capacity at the same pace, while laying off as few workers as possible.

While highly productive and energizing, this intimate relationship can also have its less pleasant manifestations. The recent Recruit scandal, which forced Prime Minister Noboru Takeshita to resign, revealed the ugly underbelly of this modus operandi. Recruit, a $3.25 billion, upstart communications and real estate company, sought to assure its future success through giving a number of influential members of Parliament, the Takashita government, the ministries, businessmen, academics and newspaper executives millions of dollars in gifts of stock and cash. Discovery of the scandal has provoked a great deal of public outrage, resulting in over 20 resignations and implicating 140 more, including former Prime Minister Yasuhiro Nakasone and his aides and relatives. What the Japanese public has found particularly galling in the Recruit scandal is how far, wide and high Recruit's trail of calumny led. In a way Recruit can not be faulted for its actions. It was just going about its business the way many other Japanese corporations have in the past, weaving a web of influence within the government and business through well-placed gifts. Unfortunately for Recruit, it got caught at a time when Japan was in a periodic house-cleaning mood, as well as being more exposed to the gaze of the world than in the past.

Besides money, custom and government backing, what holds all these groups together is a dependence between the strong and the weak, the large and the small. As anthropologists Edward and Mildred Hall explain this dependent relationship in their book *Hidden Differences*, the Japanese term *amae* gives an approximate idea of how this dependency works—a dependency or closeness with no negative connotations. "Amae," they say, "is the glue that holds Japanese society together. . . . The crucial point about 'amae' is that one's personal identity is rooted in the soil of one's dependent and interdependent relations to others as a member of a group."[46] As in Japanese society there are virtually no equals in a *keiretsu*, companies rank either above or below another. Consensus, forming up and down the hierarchy, rules the day, with it frequently being difficult to determine who's making decisions. It is this interdependence that gives Japanese companies much of their strength at home and enhances their operations in the U.S.

As with the *zaibatsu*, a chief characteristic of these groups is interlocking shareholding and directorates that help buffer the dangers of risk taking and dissipate the threat of hostile takeovers—a rare occurrence in Japan. Within the *keiretsu* one member will tend to support another, while outside fierce competition rules the day. As a member of an economic group, a firm is normally protected even if it isn't a core company. If a *keiretsu* member gets into financial trouble, as Mazda did in the 1970s with its revolutionary rotary engine,[47] the other members will usually bail it out, though the cost of such support can be a loss of almost any independence. However, such protection doesn't mean that a *keiretsu* group company is shielded from outside competition and can content itself with selling most of its production within the *keiretsu*. A group company knows that a Toyota will go outside the group if the core company doesn't produce and sell its goods very competitively. It is not a relationship that produces much flab.

Such fealty extends beyond national borders to foreign endeavors as well. The U.S. is becoming a case in point, where two Japanese firms may arrive to set up operations here as apparently separate economic entities, while in Japan their ties may run deep. When Toyota or NEC decides to invest billions directly in America they know they will not be alone. They may be in fierce competition with Nissan or Fujitsu, respectively, but they'll also have their supporting camp followers, friendly bankers and usually tacit government support.

Many Japanese corporations also come to invest in the U.S. with a historical advantage, which makes the path to riches much easier. The recent past of the auto, semiconductor, consumer electronics and to a lesser degree steel industries exemplifies this important advantage. Japanese entrée into their market began with a flood of less expensive imports which gained market share at the lower end. Once successful market penetration had been achieved, Japanese manufacturers moved to exporting more profitable products such as custom-designed computer chips or Toyota Camrys. When this happened, the weakened U.S. industry would ask for government protection and get some, as auto, semiconductor and steel producers have.

22

Fearing loss of their market through protectionist actions or responding to U.S. invitations, many Japanese firms then decided to invest directly in America. By then the industry in question probably would have been so weakened by import competition that the Japanese firm could buy in at bargain prices and make very advantageous labor agreements. The competitive advantage frequently doesn't end there. In most cases the U.S.-based Japanese firm eventually had the benefits of an ultra-modern facility, generous state subsidies and cheap Japanese financing. Also its sales and distribution system built up through imports would be in place so that its American production could easily be plugged in to replace that previously supplied from Japan. To preserve any technological lead, a Japanese company will often manufacture the lower-tech content of a car or copier in the U.S., while shipping the high-tech components from Japan.

Recently, the Japanese developed a variation on this pattern that is working to their advantage and can be expected to see wider practice. After years of badgering, the Japanese finally agreed to allow America's beef and citrus producers greater access to Japan. Starting in 1989, Japan began increasing the amount of beef and citrus products it would allow to be sold in its country, with the aim that all restrictions would be lifted by 1991. However, in anticipation of free market access, yen-rich meat and citrus importers, trading companies and wholesalers have been hungrily buying up American beef packers, cattle ranches, feedlots and citrus groves. This means American-owned beef and citrus producers will still have a very difficult time squeezing into the Japanese market. Moreover, Japanese investors can be expected to go on a similar buying spree in America's timberlands and rice fields if the Japanese ever ease access to these restricted markets.[48]

Then too, if Zaibatsu America is the story of an island state creating economic and political islands of influence in the U.S., it should be remembered that the actual corporate moves into the American economy frequently parallel the thrust of the Japanese economy itself. In effect, what the U.S. is witnessing on its own soil are offshoots of Japan's economic flowering already taking hold in various sectors of the U.S. economy.

It is not by chance that much of Japan's recent U.S. investments have been concentrated in the computer, semiconductor, biotechnology, finance and service areas. These are some of the same

23

strategic areas—sectors that are of paramount importance to its long-term economic plans—that the Japanese are emphasizing at home in their efforts to become the world leader in technology in the twenty-first century. In Japan's view, knowledge-based industries will be the greatest source of growth in their and other post-industrial economies. Such high-tech growth is particularly important for Japan since it takes full advantage of Japan's highly educated work force, while reducing the country's dependence on importing raw materials for manufacturing.

Standing behind and helping to orchestrate Japan's move into the next century is ever-powerful MITI, which periodically issues so-called "long-term visions" concerning the future direction of the Japanese economy. After having gone through some dramatic changes in the 1970s that resulted in a more international thrust to its thinking, MITI claims its influence over the economy isn't that great. It's being too modest. All MITI has to do is suggest or nod its head, and industry by and large follows. In its very important 1974 "long-term vision" of Japan's industrial structure, MITI spelled out in detail what a "knowledge-intensive industrial structure" should look like, how energy conservation should be stringently enforced and what a serious threat American protectionism could be. Much of what present-day Japan looks like and is heading for is spelled out in this "vision" and later annually revised versions. With the ground-breaking work of Japanese scientists in the areas of high definition television, superconductivity, supercomputers and telecommunications, the U.S. can no longer complacently say the Japanese are experts at adapting known technology but not innovators themselves.[49]

Such is the competitive threat offered by Japanese firms operating on U.S. soil but it is only part of the challenge confronting America. Zaibatsu America is also the story of Japanese investment in, and growing economic ties with, the U.S. on the more encompassing, more volatile macroeconomic level. It is a level where economic awareness and coordination are desperately needed both here and in Japan, and where stock markets interact frequently on their own and changes in interest rates—often central bank directed—can create massive, disruptive flows of dollars and yen from one country to another. International corporate ties, strong as they are, can be more easily directed and altered than larger economic entanglements, which can take on an uncontrollable life of their own.

24

Of the many legacies of the Reagan administration, the broader ramifications of Zaibatsu America may prove one of the most disturbing and disruptive in the coming decade. Japanese capital, buying up on occasion as much as 90 percent of the new debt floated by the U.S., became the Reagan administration's fiscal "crack," allowing it to claim that economic times have never been better. Thus far, President Bush is continuing in his mentor's ways. The U.S. continues to need ever-larger doses of Japanese and other foreign capital. Financing these excesses has transformed it into the largest debtor nation in the world in less than a decade, with half a trillion dollars currently owed by the American public to foreigners. By the year 2000 the United States foreign debt will reach $3.5 trillion or 32 percent of GNP and a decade later $8.7 trillion or 40 percent if it continues in its profligate ways.[50] Part of the problem with debt is that one is in debt to someone, in this case Japan. Debt signifies a loss of control over one's fate and the more one's debt grows the more one is beholden to someone else. Like the junkie whose life becomes ever more dependent on his dealer, the U.S. is entwined in an economic and cultural web that becomes more and more complex and unpredictable. The recent negotiations concerning the Structural Impediments Initiative with Japan have begun to address some of these interrelated problems, but significant progress is still a long way off.

The U.S. was a debtor nation in the nineteenth and early twentieth centuries, but that debt was used to finance part of the country's unprecedented economic expansion, which in turn created more jobs, a larger economy and more wealth to pay off the debt. Also, its great expansion after the Second World War occurred at the peak of the U.S.'s hegemony, when it was a strong, creditor nation. This time it is a totally different story. Few jobs and little economic expansion are created in this country by overspending on VCRs and Walkmen. Rather, this time round the sort of debt America is building up crowds out productive investment and therefore wastes what small percentage of the GNP America saves. Though it would be unthinkable for the International Monetary Fund to step in and tell the U.S. what to do with its economy as it has with Brazil, Mexico and Venezuela, the time may come when Japan tells the U.S. it will not continue buying its debt unless it mends its spendthrift ways.

It is true it will serve the Japanese ill to make moves harmful to

25

the U.S. economy. Self-interest dictates that they protect their huge investment in the U.S. Moreover, it's hard to imagine where else Japan could put the bulk of its surplus capital other than the huge American economy, though they have been increasing their investment in the European Community. Such behavior is what might be expected in a rational world. However, Black Monday, the unprecedented 22 percent plunge in the Dow Jones Industrial Average on October 19, 1987, illustrated that when panic sets in, rationality goes out the window. Though world markets haven't plunged as dramatically more recently, the fact that the Japanese stock market lost about a third of its value in 1990 again showed that the potential for interactive volatility is still there.

Before Black Monday the United States got a preview, with the near collapse of Continental Bank of Illinois, of how quickly and irrationally world financial markets can behave when fear sets in in Japan. Though unreported at the time, it has finally been learned that America's seventh-largest bank actually failed in Tokyo when Japanese money managers, acting on the basis of a mistranslated press report and without the knowledge of government regulators, pulled their funds out of the bank.[51] The move by the Japanese money managers also underlined a problem Japanese investors face: until recently Japan's huge institutional investors have operated using portfolio managers with quite limited experience in international finance. This shortage of well-trained investment managers and analysts is expected to continue as Japan's financial service sector burgeons with new funds to invest. Sanwa Bank reckons that Japan is producing fewer than 250 qualified securities analysts a year, compared with more than 1,000 a year on post-crash Wall Street.

However, it took the historic 508-point drop in the Dow Jones Industrial Average on October 19 to provide the painful proof of just how vital and potentially volatile these ties with Japan have become. Initially it was thought that computer-led program trading based in Chicago triggered the fall, which wiped out $1 trillion in stock market value in one harrowing day. However, after months of research, Nicholas Brady, head of the presidential task force investigating the plunge and now secretary of the Treasury, concluded that huge Japanese insurance companies ignited the selling when they started to lighten up on their United States Treasury holdings because of uncertainty over the course of U.S. interest rates under the new head of the Federal Reserve, Allan

Greenspan.[52] Despite being the source of the drop, the Japanese stock market fell less than other markets because the powerful Ministry of Finance pressed the Big Four security houses—Nomura, Daiwa, Nikko and Yamaichi—to support the market. The potential for another such plunge remains.[53]

Adding further potential volatility to Japan's huge holdings of U.S. Treasury issues and securities is the fact that all this wealth is concentrated in very few hands. Japan's financial clique—its huge banks, insurance companies and securities firms—has very few members. While there are over 14,000 commercial banks operating in the U.S., Japan has only 158. This concentration of economic power also exists in the life insurance and securities business. In the latter case, Japan's Big Four stock firms do 60 percent of all stock trades. This means that just a few institutions—as illustrated in Continental Bank's recent plight—acting in unison can dramatically affect world financial markets in just a few hours.[54]

How the U.S. public will react when it becomes apparent that a major U.S. economic decision has been dictated by Japan's economic needs may be hard to predict. Much will depend on the state of the U.S. economy at the time, but there can be little doubt that this could occur. Our economies may be together in the same boat of co-prosperity but it could be Japan, who's gaining ever greater economic, if not political, leverage in the world, who will be setting the course to a greater degree in future years. With the U.S. dealing from a weakened position and Japan from growing strength, there are a number of areas of potential conflict.

To help avoid conflicts it is important to understand that the Japanese presence in the U.S. is uniquely Japanese in form and scope. It bears only superficial resemblance to the massive American economic invasion of the European Community in the 1960s and 70s. Therefore, if understanding Japan's cultural, social and economic needs was important when Japanese exports to the U.S. were the key issue in the U.S.-Japan economic relationship, it is even more important now that the U.S. and Japan are developing greater dependencies.

The way a Japanese businessman conducts his business at home and abroad is a reflection of his history and culture, just as an American businessman's practices reflect his societal background. The *zaibatsu* tradition didn't evolve in a vacuum, nor did America's veneration of business schools and a Harvard

MBA. It's not by chance that government-directed capitalism has thrived in Japan, while a free market environment has prospered in the U.S. Still, for the most part, when the U.S. government directs policy affecting Japan, it continues to ignore Japan's different ways, expecting the Japanese to behave as we do.

The differences between the the two countries are as basic as how the two educate their populace and how they view the relationship between economics and politics. Since frequently one's behavior—be it economic, political or social—is greatly influenced by one's upbringing and education, it is of paramount importance for Americans to understand where the Japanese are coming from when they make a move and vice versa. Being raised in Tokyo can give a person a different sense of self and space from growing up in San Francisco or Chicago. School is where Japanese children are first rigorously taught the strict rules of conformity, intimidation and the need to excel in the context of a group. Children thus educated don't need to take a great leap in imagination to adopt the group ways of the *keiretsu* when they get down to the business of being a bureaucrat or making money. Being part of a clique and being loyal to it is second nature by then.

If the U.S. values spontaneity and spunk, the Japanese respect conformity and power. If survival of the fittest holds any sway in Japan, it is survival of the fittest group. In Japan most men or corporations don't act on their own. Consensus, which doesn't necessarily mean endorsement, precedes action in Japan. Action frequently precedes agreement in the U.S., which is one reason there are so many attorneys in the U.S. and so few in Japan.

As far as politics are concerned, the Japanese and Americans are also miles apart. In general Japanese politics follow the dictates of economic priorities, while in the U.S. economic issues are frequently settled by political will. In Japan, the strategic goals of the country are economic not military. The reverse is true in the U.S., though it may be changing a little.

If the U.S. is basically still for a free-wheeling, free market—a laissez-faire economy—if it favors free trade over trade barriers, the Japanese, who come from an almost unified and isolated island culture, have consistently chosen an opposite course of economic action to spur their phenomenal economic growth. The idea that the consumer and his sometimes spendthrift ways should be the key to economic growth as in the United States has found little currency in Japan until recently. For the most part the

28

Japanese live too poorly to be so rich. Americans live rich to become poor.

It is for such cultural and economic reasons that the Japanese view our growing ties with them very differently than we do. To them the interdependence has come about as a natural evolution in the burgeoning economic relationship. It is the tacit assumption made by the Japanese when they enter a deal that it has the potential of becoming something larger. Though the interdependence of the two economies does not surprise them, their rapid ascendancy in this relationship does.

The Japanese are of two minds concerning their relationship with the U.S. and the world, having been content to let the United States take the economic and political lead since the end of World War II. Until the past decade, Japan really had little choice in the matter, but that has changed dramatically as the country has grown into an economic superpower. On the one hand, many Japanese feel they are being thrust into a prominent role they are not ready for and do not wish. For many Japanese, pragmatic economics take precedence over politics and therefore they'd prefer to stay out of the world political arena as much as possible. Making money and dominating certain targeted markets will suffice for them. They also would like to keep as low a profile as possible, because they realize there is little to be gained from having public attention focused on their economic involvement in the U.S. Being anonymous, melding in with the crowd and not sticking out, is, of course, a Japanese trait taught from childhood on.

However, there is a growing awareness within and outside Japan that the country's economic preeminence requires it to assume a larger, more responsible role in the international political sphere. Defining this new identity is no easy task for the Japanese. Just as Japan feels at times inferior and at other times superior to the rest of the world, its push for a greater world political role is frequently countered by rampant, flag-waving chauvinism. The United States is ambivalent about Japan's fence-sitting. We do and we don't want them to be more assertive and we tend to treat them with a sort of double standard. For the most part the U.S. would like Japan to pay more for its global role while the U.S. continues in its political and military leadership role. The ambiguous nature of the relationship between Japan and the U.S. was brought home when Japan sought a larger part in ameliorating the third world debt crisis and created a relief plan which was first rejected by the U.S., and then adopted as the "Brady Plan," named after Treasury secretary, Nicholas Brady. Moreover, the problems inherent in such a vague political alliance and international identity were dramatically underlined when Premier Kaifu's government hemmed and hawed about raising support for the Persian Gulf War, with the effect that when Japan finally promised $13 billion for the cause towards the end of the War, it looked niggardly at best.

While maintaining a low profile in the U.S., Japanese investors have been actively building a political constituency in Washington and throughout the nation's 50 states, spending hundreds of millions on lobbying. The influence of their lobby has already been seen in Japanese efforts to mute U.S. trade retaliation under section 301. It will become more evident as the work force employed by Japanese firms in the U.S. grows. The Japanese, it must be remembered, are well aware of the political leverage they have purchased with their investment here, and they don't want their efforts to backfire. It is not by chance that Japanese firms have been politically astute in negotiating particularly attractive deals with states seeking to have their factories, or that no state has been able to attract more than one Japanese auto firm.

The Reagan administration, in dealing with Japanese-American economic relations, had no policy at all and concentrated its energies on trying to patch together a contradictory strategy to turn the course of the trade deficit.[55] It never really confronted Zaibatsu America and neither has Congress for that matter. Rather than admitting the gradual loss of our economic independence, the U.S. continues to harangue the Japanese about trade issues and how they should transform their economy into a more consumer-oriented one like ours. At the same time we ignore Japan's admonitions to rein in our budget and trade deficits, and the fact Japan is providing our economy with vital, monetary sustenance. Nor does the United States give Japan credit for the remarkable ease with which its economy has digested the ever-rising yen and the economic changes the country has already put in place to give American corporations greater access to Japan's market—efforts that have been largely stifled because of the keiretsu-hold on Japan's goods distribution system.

As a result of this self-deception, this clinging to old myths, the U.S. continues to pay little attention to the political and economic implications of Zaibatsu America and has failed to formulate a policy to deal with it. In Japan, the major players are already in place, in the U.S. they have yet to emerge. In this country there are no counterparts to MITI and the Ministry of Finance—the two ministries widely credited with creating the Japanese miracle and currently the dei ex machina directing the thrust of Japanese investment in the U.S. If the President and Congress aren't dealing with Zaibatsu America in any coherent fashion, neither is the Treasury, the Commerce Department or the State Department. On the rare occasions that these government departments confront the issue they tend to give out conflicting signals that the Japanese can, for the most part, ignore. Development of some rational, up-to-date policy regarding U.S. economic relations with Japan is still far away. Without any policy the relationship will be volatile and crisis-prone, a potential loss situation for both sides.

When President Bush moved into the White House, he found policy toward Japan so confused and uncoordinated that many U.S. officials said they could not figure out how it was made or why economic concerns were regularly subordinated to military and political objectives. This sorry situation has been graphically underlined in the continuing disputes over the development of high definition television and the building of the new FSX warplane, and in the confused efforts to come up with a competing American strategy on semiconductors, supercomputers and superconductors.

In some ways, the Bush administration appears more attuned to the situation than the Reagan administration, though it is still giving out mixed signals. Certainly, Secretary of State James Baker is well aware of the importance of Japanese-American relations since, as secretary of the Treasury in the Reagan administration, he was a major proponent of the declining dollar, a seminal factor in the birth of Zaibatsu America. The yen can now buy nearly twice as many dollars as it could in September 1985, when the Group of Five Finance Ministers, including Baker, met in New York to plot the dollar's decline. While the lower dollar has helped make America cheap pickings for the Japanese, it has done little to cut Americans' thirst for Japanese products or to boost America's exports to Japan significantly—the dual goal of the devaluation exercise. In getting involved in the SII talks and holding a special, April 1990 meeting with Prime Minister Kaifu in California, Bush did manage to emphasize the importance of the nation's economic security and raise trade and investment issues to a much higher level of decision making within the government than previously. But after the drama of the meeting, negotiations appear to have retreated back into mostly fruitless bickering. Despite some assurances to the contrary, it is doubtful that either nation will alter its internal affairs to any great degree to accommodate the other.

While the U.S. government has manifested an incredible nonchalance about the Japanese investment challenge here, states are another matter—a fact of life Japanese investors are fully aware of. States such as Kentucky, Indiana and Illinois have been falling all over themselves to attract Japanese investors through near giveaway programs that few but the most successful domestic company would be offered. States, like humans, tend to favor the new boy in town. To the naive observer, it might almost seem as if we have been giving key sectors of the economy to the Japanese at bargain prices. To others, it looks as if some states are out committing fratricide.[56]

As far as corporate America is concerned, its reaction to Japanese competition and investment in the United States has been inconsistent and, for the most part, ill-timed. At one extreme are steel companies that have welcomed Japanese investors with open arms while vehemently fighting Japanese steel exports to the United States. National Steel, Inland Steel, Wheeling Pittsburgh and U.S. Steel are all of this ilk. At the other extreme are American corporations that are beating Japanese corporations who are fighting them in their own backyard—companies such as Motorola, Caterpillar, Black & Decker, Emerson Electric and Harley Davidson. Then there are the U.S. semiconductor producers, who after seeing the industry they created pirated away by the Japanese, launched strong protests against massive Japanese export dumping in the U.S. and the concurrent lack of access to the keiretsu-dominated Japanese market. Out of these protests was born one of the more positive moves towards confronting Zaibatsu America. With the formation in 1987 of Sematech, a consortium for semiconductor manufacturing research, a group of beleaguered manufacturers representing 80 percent of the U.S. chip-making capacity and the Defense Department launched a long-range effort to keep the U.S. semiconductor industry globally competitive. Though the effort has had its successes thus far, it is too soon to tell how it will fare in achieving its goal.

Given the massive growth of Zaibatsu America, the potential areas of dispute with Japan are many. Conflicts can arise on both the micro- and macroeconomic levels and will be exacerbated when either the Japanese or American economies fall on hard times. Though trade is a secondary issue in this book, superseded in importance by Japan's investment in the U.S., the two may overlap in the eyes of the administration, Congress and the American public. It is entirely possible that if the U.S. government can't resolve a trade issue with Japan, it will retaliate by placing restrictions on Japanese investment in the U.S. The same could be true for disputes over the role of the dollar and yen in global markets, the military burden of protecting Japan and Japan's closed markets.

What if the U.S. falls into a recession, the dollar declines to 100 yen (from its present 140 yen) and Japanese investors escalate their purchase of American real estate, or become aggressive acquirers of U.S. companies? Or what if interest rates rise to a point where a number of firms burdened by debt from a leveraged-buy-out face bankruptcy or Japanese takeover at bargain prices? Or what if the economy takes a nose-dive, unemployment hits double-digit levels and Nissan, Toyota, Mazda and Subaru lay off thousands of workers at their U.S. facilities while keeping domestic Japanese workers on the job? Or what if Japanese companies step up efforts to gain market share from their weakened U.S. competitors during an economic slide? Or what if the U.S. starts slipping into a recession and the Fed wants to lower interest rates to stimulate the economy but can't, because it must keep interest rates high to attract and keep Japanese investors servicing our debt. The economy declines further and what if . . . ? These are just a few of the "what if's" in Zaibatsu America and though it's difficult to predict America's reaction to some of these situations, given the widespread xenophobia shared by many Americans regarding the Japanese, it would probably be pretty unpleasant.

The first thing America and Japan should do is openly confront Zaibatsu America and begin a dialogue at the highest government levels, looking into all its ramifications. The two countries must ask themselves who they want to be in this relationship, how both countries can benefit from this marriage of convenience and how destructive conflicts can be averted. There is a bit of this going on in the SII talks, but clearly not enough. This is especially true for America, since it has much more to lose than Japan does in the creation of Zaibatsu America.

Out of this self-searching, America will have to develop policy to deal rationally with Zaibatsu America. Such policy will have to address the issue of Japanese investment in the U.S. at the federal, state and corporate levels. It is patently ridiculous and self-destructive to have Commerce, State and the Treasury Departments working at cross-purposes by devising policies that contradict one another. At the outset of the Reagan administration, there was a quite popular proposal to combine the trade functions of the Treasury, Commerce and State Departments in one super trade agency to correct the weaknesses inherent in the present system. The idea was that the administration would speak with one voice when it came to trade rather than with three. However, bureaucratic turf wars between the three departments and Congressional objections quickly killed the proposal. Such an agency should be set up to monitor foreign investment in the U.S. An interagency Committee on Foreign Investment in the United States was created 16 years ago, but its purview is national security and it's been largely toothless.

The most immediate problems Washington should address are the domestic and trade deficits and the lack of a strategy to strengthen key industries' competitive position vis-à-vis Japanese corporations operating in the United States. Washington and American business must decide how corporate America can best compete against Japanese firms operating in the *zaibatsu* way here in America. When threatened, America should also protect and nourish its technological infrastructure, the lifeblood of its most profitable industries. Remember, the Japanese now dominate the world market for VCRs, color TVs, and Fax machines—all products invented by Americans—and are even assembling them at U.S. plants. It would be more than a pity to see this defeatism repeated in other areas such as HDTV. It would be a disgrace.

The trend towards lower expenditures on research and development and capital investment in the U.S. must be reversed, especially in light of Japan's dramatic expansion in this area. According to a recent report by the Washington-based Council on Competitiveness, Japan out-invested the United States for the first time in 1989, spending $549 billion to modernize and expand its industries, compared with $513 billion by the U.S. In effect Japan, with a smaller economy and work force, was spending twice as much per worker as the U.S., a disturbing trend that should not be allowed to continue.[57] New developments are al-

34

ready coming out of Japan's Technopolis strategy that are bound to have an effect on how the Japanese presence in telecommunications, autos and financial services is felt in the U.S. during the coming decades. Increasing R&D and capital expenditures can be achieved, in part, by encouraging Americans to save more through a change in tax laws. America's rate of savings, which declined to less than 3 percent of gross national product in 1988 from around 8 percent in the 1950s and 60s, was less than half of thrifty Japan's.[58]

America will also have to better educate its youth so they can work and live competitively in the twenty-first century. This is true for people who'll be working in either the manufacturing or service sectors of the economy. As technology progresses, America's youth will have to develop greater math and verbal skills, whether they are working in a highly mechanized factory or a computerized office.

At the state level, the courting of Japanese investment should be conducted in a saner manner. Tennessee should not have to give away the house to attract Japanese investment as it did with Nissan. States should avoid pitting one state against another in the chase for foreign investment, as happened when state after state threw down the red carpet in an effort to attract Toyota. States should not make deals with Japanese investors that they would not make with an American firm. It makes little sense to have Illinois give Mitsubishi hundreds of millions of dollars in benefits to set up a joint venture with Chrysler in Bloomington and then be miserly to Sears, its largest employer, when the mass merchandiser announced plans to relocate its corporate headquarters.

American firms should study the Japanese with the same vigor and tenacity the Japanese have used in analyzing corporate America, if they are to hone their lost competitive edge. The same can be said of American students, since for every American studying in Japan there are 10 to 12 Japanese studying here in the U.S. Certainly, the Japanese—with their quality circles, their just-in-time inventory management, their competitive drive for market share, and their ways of building productivity and worker loyalty—have set an example worth emulating. American firms, however, can't do the impossible. If they attempt to transform themselves into Japanese clones, they probably won't succeed. They should be open to change, willing to adapt while keeping their American character. They should go back to their roots, re-learn how to motivate workers and how to adapt technology to commercial endeavors, and remember a corporation is made up of people, not abstract accounting concepts. They can also learn from firms that have successfully held their own in the wake of Japanese investment in their markets. Protecting American firms from the Japanese challenge in the U.S. is not the answer, though the government can help American firms compete more success-fully.

Japan, for its part, must confront its new prominence swiftly and intelligently. It can not continue to reap the rewards of its economic prowess without taking a more responsible position in the world. It must abandon its narcissistic, insular ways and work fiercely to give American firms better access to Japanese markets. Using its habitual delaying tactics, promising to give more than it actually plans and ignoring the need for structural change in its society will become a less-and-less politically viable route. Just beneath the surface each country's populace harbors a good deal of prejudice against the other and if Japan doesn't change its ways quickly, that prejudice could be transformed into action with regrettable consequences, such as hasty protectionist legisla-tion aimed at Japanese trade and investment that could set off Japanese retaliation.

There could be no better example of this lack of balance in Ja-pan's relation with the U.S. than the way foreign investors are treated in the two countries. While in America the door is wide open and the welcome mat spread out to meet Japanese inves-tors, U.S. investors wishing to set up operations in Japan still have to fight their way day after day. To a large degree only the hardiest and most tenacious American firms—the IBMs and McDonalds of the world—have made a place for themselves. It is true that many of the barriers to foreign investment in Japan are a matter of custom and that Japanese companies have to compete in the same environment. However, one of the greatest impedi-ments to U.S. investment in Japan is the keiretsu system which effectively shuts the door on many U.S. firms wishing to do busi-ness in Japan,[59] whether it be exporting to Japan or investing there. In the former case, Brookings Institute senior fellow Robert Lawrence, says his recent analysis indicates that "producer 'keiretsu' relationships are a significant barrier to the entry of for-eign products into Japan" and that if it weren't for the collusive, *keiretsu* impact, Japan's imports would be greater by tens of billions of dollars annually.[60] U.S. firms, like the Japanese, also have to cope with an antiquated and inefficient distribution system and a highly protected agricultural sector. Because of the political clout of Japan's 20 million shopkeepers and its 11 million farmers, change and opening up has come slowly to these two key areas of the economy. While opening up Japan's markets—giving much greater access to foreign products and investment—should be greatly sped up, such gains may only come slowly unless Japan and America face up to the reality of Zaibatsu America.

Japan and the United States must work towards a greater global equilibrium in which Japanese investment in the U.S. is more in balance with America's presence in Japan and the two economies are more in sync. We tell the Japanese they live too poorly to be so rich and that they should lessen their saving and increase their consumption. The Japanese, with good reason, tell us we are living beyond our means, that we must cut back and that we should save more and invest those savings in productive investments. There's truth in both statements, but repeating such exhortations does little good unless both countries work towards better coordination. In America's case, it should get its own debt-ridden household in order before exhorting Japan to be more like it. It would seem that reaching greater symmetry between the two economies might be easily achieved. However, realizing this goal may be one of the most difficult tasks facing our two societies.

2

Auto Alley Zaibatsu Style

No member of the industry, no matter how strong, can afford to overlook the challenger, whose name—Toyota Motor—is rapidly coming to be both celebrated and feared. . . . This year Toyota will sell around 125,000 cars in the U.S.; next year it expects sales to exceed 200,000.

—*Fortune*, December 1969[1]

The whole idea of daring to export our products to the U.S. was like an impossible dream. It was only our strong desire to do so that supported us. Still, the first ten years were filled with nothing more than continuous humiliations and setbacks. . . . But we succeeded in getting our foot in the door little by little.

—Seisi Kato, former chairman of Toyota Motor Sales Co.,
commenting on export efforts begun in 1958[2]

I t's early February, 1987, and the road from Lexington to nearby Georgetown, Kentucky, is slicked with freezing rain and snow. Erratic, muddy tire tracks lead the way to cars and trucks thrown askew along the side of Route 75. Except for the occasional driver slowly plowing along, traffic has all but halted.

Outside Georgetown, an easy-going college town of horse-breeders and tobacco farmers where well-kept eighteenth- and nineteenth-century houses line East Main Street and change used to come slow, fourteen huge construction cranes loom. They seemingly strut across the 1,400-acre plant site at the command of Ohbayashi Construction Corporation, standing as proud as the town's Second Empire-style, courthouse steeple. Here, sequest-

39

ered in one of the most beautiful parts of America, Japan's largest auto producer is building a $1-billion, 3.7-million-square-foot auto factory, that will produce on U.S. soil as many Toyotas as the company exported from Japan just two decades earlier. Blizzard or not, work continues.

"Toyota—Our New Old Kentucky Home," says the sign greeting visitors to the site. Toyota is in high gear to get 10 percent or more of the world auto market and at least that much in the United States. It's all part of Japanese automakers' push to gain as much as 50 percent of the U.S. car market[3] in "one of history's great transfers of wealth and power."[4] The importance of this transfer cannot be underestimated, since the U.S. auto industry remains one of the country's greatest sources of wealth and work, not to mention the all-important technological innovation it spawns. There is no time to waste—no pausing at the crossing. Toyota's Georgetown plant will be ready just in time. So, too, will the nearly 60 Japanese auto parts facilities being set up around the state by Japanese suppliers to help Toyota and other Japanese auto producers feel at home in their new Auto Alley. So, too, will the Japanese banks, insurance companies, construction firms and car dealerships that make up Toyota's entourage. Toyota's whole economic infrastructure of *zaibatsu*-like interlocking dependencies is swarming in, in droves.

Here, the unique *zaibatsu* pattern of doing business is close to blossoming and will soon be in full flower. Here new roots of Zaibatsu America are forming, spreading and intertwining. Here Toyota is following a pattern of exclusivity and vertical integration—this keeping the best part of the meal, the high value-added, most profitable portion of production, for oneself. Here, as University of Notre Dame economist Candace Howes points out, Japanese firms buy the most mundane parts from American producers—the door handles, tires and such that can be used interchangeably on several vehicles, while supplying the real, high-tech, value-added heart of the car—the parts that drive the car and give it its character—from its own sources in Japan.[5] Here, like other Japanese auto producers, Toyota has chosen a site of relative prosperity, low unionization rates and few blacks.[6] Here, such employment and sourcing practices suggest the Japanese presence is "not being translated into new skills for U.S. managers, production workers, skilled trades and suppliers."[7]

It is a pattern of operation that gives Toyota a special competitive force. Inherent in the pattern is great flexibility of production, where model changes come with ease and dominance through vertical control both here and in Japan. It is a form of vertical integration that must be distinguished from the old, General Motors-style operations where orders came from the top, traveled down the line and the troops did as they were told. Back in Japan Toyota can, and does, put the squeeze on its close family of suppliers, expecting them to constantly improve their products and lower their costs, but the relationship is much more fluid, with ideas traveling back and forth between Toyota and its suppliers, who take active roles in the design of new products from conception to final production and are party to the evolution of a Camry or Lexus. By and large its American suppliers are not treated similarly. It is this complex exclusionary pattern that is being repeated in other parts of the economy and up and down Routes 55, 65, and 75, the main arteries of Japan's Auto Alley running from Michigan to Tennessee. Already plugged into these arteries are Honda, Mitsubishi, Nissan, Subaru, Isuzu and a pack of 240 or so Japanese-controlled auto parts suppliers who give a new meaning to the term "local content," in that possibly close to 90 percent of the parts and components that go into cars manufactured in the U.S. by Toyota and its brethren "come from Japan or Japanese owned suppliers with factories in the U.S."[8]

The point is that these companies have not flocked to America on their own. The leaders have come in a fiercely competitive group, each with its own special crew of groupies bound to each other through interlocking shareholdings and a long history of inter-company sales. They already have their own support system that gives them unique strength—a strength in numbers and more. They don't have to depend on the kindness of strangers in a foreign land, though even the strongest usually benefit from generous state aid. Greasing the way in Toyota's case is $325.4 million in aid and subsidies to be paid for by Kentucky's citizenry as a welcoming gesture to Japan's most successful and richest automaker.[9] It's a very different sort of competition, with a unique dynamism that can be seen in different stages of development elsewhere in the American economy. Here, in Auto Alley, what one sees is the *zaibatsu* pattern being played out in full, having been matured and refined for decades in Japan before being exported to the U.S.

In the auto industry's case, America's manufacturing base is not being hollowed out. It's being displaced and rebuilt right here, as Japan's young and vigorous automakers build a separate auto economy within the U.S. Unlike the U.S. consumer electronics industry, which, except for holdout Zenith, is for all intents and purposes Japanese, or the domestic steel industry, which has all but fallen into Japanese hands, the American auto industry is still battling Japanese producers to remain the dominant force on its own turf. As Japanese plants open—at the invitation of American automakers, states, and government officials—U.S. auto plants will ironically topple one by one. The U.S. auto market may be the biggest in the world, representing 4 percent of GNP and embracing a staggering 14 to 15 percent of the U.S. economy when its broad reach across the economy is added in, but there's only room for so many to feed at the table. For many American producers' plants and those of the weaker Japanese auto firms that have set up production here, the decade of the 1990s will prove the last supper.

"I think you have to remember an American firm is not competing against a Japanese company as an individual but against a company as a member of a group," says Michael Kane, executive director of the U.S.-Japan International Management Institute at the University of Kentucky. Kane, a keen, if dispassionate observer of Japanese economic and cultural mores, gained much of his knowledge working for IBM in Japan and studying Japanese firms' behavior in Kentucky and the rest of the U.S. Kane is not criticizing the Japanese so much as just stating facts he feels Americans should be aware of and frequently aren't. "In Japan there are strong vertical ties within an industry. There are industrial groupings that limit competition at different levels." According to Kane, the philosophy in these groupings is that individual companies sacrifice much of their profit to the leading company, whereas American companies are out for themselves and out to profit as quickly as possible. Says Kane, "culturally we have nothing in common with this system. The Japanese business system is an outgrowth of Japanese culture just as ours is."[10]

It is precisely this sort of relationship that Federal Trade Commission chairman Janet D. Steiger described in testimony at a House Judiciary Committee hearing in May 1990, when she revealed that the FTC was investigating potential anti-trust violations by Japanese transplant auto and parts manufacturers through a *keiretsu* system. Her description of the system is an apt definition of operating in the *zaibatsu* way. In fact, others giving testimony at the hearing said the "so-called 'Japanese Miracle' had been accomplished by the reformation of the Japan prewar 'zaibatsu'" and that such economic behavior could also be found in the U.S. According to the FTC's Steiger, a *keiretsu* can be defined as "an interweaving of companies through equity exchanges, interlocking directorates, intra-group financial commitments, joint research and development efforts and membership in exclusive management councils or clubs. In the auto industry, these relationships are usually between manufacturers and their suppliers." This is a fitting account of what is going on in Kentucky and other parts of the country.

Used to being surrounded by over 100 suppliers as part of its centralized operations in Toyota City, Japan, Toyota doesn't travel light nor does it leave home lightly. Since it's number one at home and one of the richest companies in the world with over $20 billion in cash—it's often referred to as the Toyota bank—it let Nissan, Honda and other Japanese auto producers build plants in the U.S. first, in effect to test the waters. Also before starting its own operation from scratch, Toyota took a test run at Freemont, California, in a moderately successful joint venture with General Motors. Though Toyota denies that it asked any of its group companies to follow it to America, Toyota obviously likes to do business with a familiar Japanese face and in familiar surroundings. Certainly, such fealty is already very much in evidence around Georgetown on this wintry day.

Directing construction of the plant from its office at the site is Ohbayashi Construction Corporation, a member of the Sanwa Bank group and the fourth-largest construction company in Japan. Though Ohbayashi does not belong directly to the so-called "Toyota group" of companies—a designation Toyota uses frequently to describe its large family of closely affiliated firms, and one which is readily understood in Japan—the Sanwa connection forms a strong link between Toyota and Ohbayashi. Sanwa Bank is a major shareholder in both companies, being the third-largest share owner in Toyota with 5 percent of its shares and the fourth-largest in Ohbayashi with 3.9 percent. This is just the beginning of the burgeoning Japanese network.[11]

While Japanese engineers work and plan in Ohbayashi's site office here, taking their orders from Toyota City and Tokyo, faxes flow fast and furious between Georgetown and Japan, with directions and answers spewing from the thin, plastic lips of the machines. The plant itself is to be a smaller, "mirror image" of Toyota's Tsutsumi car plant at Toyota City, as manufacturing manager Mike Dodge later explains it. The guts of the operation—the machines that drive the factory—will be Japanese, arriving on the Japanese export flotilla and then trucked to Georgetown. A grey-and-yellow, 2,300-ton-capacity transfer press from Komatsu, robots by Kawasaki and Toyota forklift trucks will populate the 36-inch-thick plant floor that will measure over half a mile long. Over 200 Japanese robots will be making 4,000 welds on each Camry, checking body openings and lifting and placing batteries in the cars. Even the company cleaning its immaculate aisles will be Japanese owned, though eventually an American firm will take over the job. And the same yellow tricycles seen at Toyota City, with their covered, square storage box in the rear, will be making the rounds, carrying necessary small parts and manuals, while following colored routes laid down with Tsutsumi's design in mind.

By May 1988 the first Camry will have rolled off the line and four months later Georgetown will be in full production. Waiting to take delivery of Georgetown's production are 1,081 Toyota dealers that have been selling Toyota's Japanese imports in the United States for years. Since Toyota's American distribution system is already well entrenched, channeling Georgetown's production of Camrys into Toyota's selling organization and the heart of America is an easy trick. It's not like starting from scratch. As Georgetown Camrys begin to be seen on the nation's highways, workers will have begun building a neighboring engine plant, modeled after Toyota's Kamigo plant, to produce on U.S. soil its very popular 16-valve engine. Plant general manager Russ Scaffede refers to Kamigo as "the mother plant," and again the major production equipment is Japanese. Again Ohbayashi is directing construction of this so-called "power-train" facility that in the early 1990s will build Toyota's lightweight, powerful and versatile 4-cylinder, 16-valve engines—engines that are far ahead of anything being mass-produced by America's Big Three automakers. The engine is yet another example of a design developed by the American producers but first nurtured into mass production by the Japanese. Like VCRs and Fax machines, Japanese auto producers seized the design and ran with it, creating a perky, fuel-efficient, technically advanced engine that gives Japanese auto producers a new, challenging lead, even though American automakers are now improving the quality and durability of their cars. Still, in the 1990 model year only GM will offer a multivalve engine for use in the United States—and only as an option on several models.[12]

Soon the construction cranes will have quit the site and in their stead will stand the newly completed Toyota plant, a utilitarian edifice with about as much character as your basic Toyota Corona—a study in grey efficiency ready to do battle in the 1990s. Within the plant are all the understated trappings of successful Japanese management. The office floors are open, with one department melding into another. What offices there are, are simple at best, with none of Detroit's rich paneling and heavy mahogany desks. Outside there are no executive parking spaces. This is Japanese corporate democracy transplanted to Kentucky. Managers do their work coatless and tieless, while workers labor along the production line in small, egalitarian groups and form quality circles here and there to hone the process of their work to perfection. The Toyota motto posted around the plant—"quality today, success tomorrow"—appears to be taken to heart. Certainly, Georgetown Camrys are selling well.

As manufacturing manager Dodge—a gregarious, lifetime car man, sporting a blue sweater with Toyota seal—leads a visitor around the immaculate plant, one can't help but admire what Toyota's built here. In and of itself it is a microcosm of what's right with Japanese auto production and what's wrong with the U.S.'s. It provides a graphic illustration of why "a brand-new assembly plant in this country has enormous advantages over a facility that has been in operation for 20 years."[13] The plant's new, the workers are novices trained by Toyota at Kentucky's expense, and the money used to build the facility is relatively cheap—just to name three factors giving Toyota the upper hand. The Georgetown work force, many of whom Dodge knows on a first-name basis, numbers a little over 3,000 and in contrast to many of its American counterparts, is relatively young and lean. Workers average 32 years of age and are non-union, with wages and benefits about 80 percent of the industry average. Picked from 100,000 applicants, 95 percent of the work force comes from Kentucky, with 25 percent women and another 13 percent minorities. Such a work force has many advantages: youth makes the tough work of assembling a Camry easier and faster and means workers do not demand an over-structured workplace and can adapt. Also, such a young work force doesn't present the huge, costly pension liabilities American auto manufacturers have to contend with in dealing with their older workers. Then according to Dodge, who worked for years at Chrysler and then Volkswagen of America before joining Toyota, the company just didn't build a super-robotized plant—a mistake some American counterparts such as GM made in trying to go high-tech full tilt. Georgetown, Dodge said, is "state-of-the-art but not leading-edge." As with the 16-valve engine, Toyota tends to take a process and patiently refine it so that improvements come step by methodical step and are cumulative. The stroke of genius is rare and not expected. Finally, as a result of these and other factors, the brand-new Georgetown plant is already building a car that equals or betters those produced in Japan in terms of quality. It also reached targeted production of 200,000 Camrys a year and quality levels ahead of schedule. And then pulling the whole Georgetown operation together are the Toyota groupies—the Toyota family parts suppliers, bankers and the like who've come from Japan and set up camp near and far in the three years it's taken to get the plant going.

Toyota's American *keiretsu* is now very much in place en masse, having spread its net throughout Kentucky from Lexington to Paris to Elizabethtown and beyond. The Toyota family of companies is now more than ever a formidable force that can't be overlooked in the 1990s. As University of Washington professors Kozo Yamamura and Ulrike Wassmann noted in an article entitled, "Do Japanese Firms Behave Differently? The Effects of 'Keiretsu' in the United States," auto *keiretsus* such as Toyota's are indeed different. As Yamamura and Wassmann conclude:

> Price competitiveness is more easily attained by "keiretsu" auto parts producers than by non-keiretsu firms (including all foreign firms): their long-term trading relationship with an automobile producer enables the "keiretsu" auto parts producers to realize economies of scale, cost reductions due to "learning by doing" and several other significant advantages in producing these products bought by "keiretsu" automakers on a consistent and long-term basis . . .
>
> In short, the long-term trading relationship in crucial ways "integrates" the activities of "keiretsu" firms. There is little incentive for Japanese automobile producers to incur the added

costs necessary in dealing with non-"keiretsu," especially foreign suppliers of auto parts unless price, quality, or other terms of transaction offered by non-"keiretsu" suppliers are sufficiently superior to justify the costs. However, the longer the "keiretsu" relationship has been maintained and the better "integrated" the intra-"keiretsu" activities, the less likely this is to occur.[14]

What this has meant, is that when Japanese transplants such as Toyota go shopping for parts they buy

hardware (door handles, etc.), soft trim, plastic trim, glass, batteries, mufflers, tailpipes, tires, wheels, brake parts, seats and windshield wipers from U.S. manufacturers. These parts all have in common that they are relatively easy to manufacture, require little engineering, are generic in nature—the same parts can fit on several vehicles—and the identity of the vehicle is not defined by these parts.

In contrast, the real heart of the vehicle—the engine, transmission, suspension, steering and electronic controls, are complex, engineering intensive and difficult to manufacture. They are integral to the identity of a vehicle. . . . These components are not being built in-house by the transplant assemblers, nor are they being sourced from outside suppliers in the U.S. They are being designed and for the most part manufactured in Japan.[15]

Making their "new old Kentucky home" in Lexington are branches of three of the world's largest banks—Mitsui, Sanwa and Tokai. In fact, Mitsui and Sanwa are next-door neighbors in Lexington, having their respective offices at 773 and 772 Corporate Drive. Mitsui's and Tokai's ties with Toyota are particularly close. The two are Toyota's two prime banks and its largest shareholders, holding 5.3 and 5.1 percent of Toyota's shares, respectively. Then, too, Japanese banks are much closer to their major customers than their American counterparts, frequently acting as advance men in site selection, plant financing and state aid when a Japanese company moves into the U.S. Back in Japan, Toyota is also a member of each bank's elite group of friendly companies. Toyota is represented as an observer in the *Nimoku-kai* or second Thursday conference of top chairmen and presidents of the 24 leading Mitsui group companies and is a member of the Tokai group's *Wakaba-kai*, a cluster of some of Japan's largest companies who have joined together to exchange information. Fellow members of the *Wakaba-kai* include Japan's largest retailer and supermarket chain, Daiei Inc.; the country's second-largest securities firm, Nikko Securities; and a leading fleet operator, Seino Transportation.

Looking for auto insurance? No problem. Two Toyota-affiliated insurance companies, providing major auto insurance in Japan, have also found a "new old Kentucky home" in Lexington. There's Chiyoda Fire and Marine Insurance Company, a medium-sized non-life firm in which Toyota is a 40.6 percent shareholder, while neighboring Tokai Bank also has 4.9 percent. And then there's Taisho Marine and Fire, a member of the Mitsui group whose ties with the Toyota group go both ways. Toyota owns 2.1 percent of Taisho, while Taisho holds 2.5 percent of Toyota. In the latter case, the small ownership percentages understate the strength of the ties to the Toyota *keiretsu*.

Toyota's ties that bind go well beyond these. There are now a number of Japanese companies located in Kentucky and nearby states that are very used to doing business with Toyota in Japan, whether they are officially members of the Toyota group or not. Executives here and in Toyota City repeatedly deny that they asked them to come along for the ride, but the point is that whether Toyota did or didn't, they have come to America in droves, expecting to do business with Toyota. Certainly, Toyota hasn't told them not to come and does plan to do business with them. To a large degree they are companies that have taken rather mundane, albeit essential products—gas lines, gaskets and such—and refined them to a point where they hold many proprietary qualities and have achieved an enviably high level of quality. They are also the sort of products that have higher profit margins and higher technological content as compared with nuts-and-bolts, commodity-type products. They're just the sort of products American producers claim they can make as well as the Japanese and the Japanese say they can't. At least a few of these companies began their corporate life in the 1950s and 1960s as joint ventures in Japan with American auto parts firms—bonds that were eventually abandoned in some cases. These companies manufacture the sort of defect-free products Toyota, Nissan and Mitsubishi expect. The object of these companies is twofold: to continue their traditional relationship with their Japanese customers in the U.S. and to develop new ones with U.S. automakers.

Just a short distance away from Toyota Motor's plant on Cherry Blossom Way is Trinity Industrial Corporation of America, an early Japanese transplant to Georgetown. Trinity's specialty is making paint-finishing equipment. Trinity is a Toyota affiliate—Toyota owns 30 percent of Trinity's parent's shares. Over in Franklin, Kentucky Franklin Precision Industry Inc. is setting up its business dealing in auto parts—carburetors, valves and so forth. Franklin's parent is Aisan Industry, a Toyota group company in which Toyota has a 24.5 percent interest. Toyota affiliate Toyoda Automatic Loom has another 22.1 percent of Aisan. Looking for some one-piece aluminum wheels? Go no further than Paris, Kentucky, where Central Light Alloy Co. will have plenty in stock. Its parent, Central Motor Wheel, is a major supplier to Toyota in Japan and a member of the Toyota group, with Toyota having 60.4 percent stake in it.

Then there are others who have found Kentucky, with its non-union traditions, a good place to do business and who apparently plan to sell their wares up and down Auto Alley if they follow the pattern of their sales back home in Japan. Ichikoh Industries Ltd. has around 100 people in Shelbyville, Kentucky, working on and polishing its rear- and sideview mirrors. Back home Nissan and Toyota are Ichikoh's biggest customers, buying 58 percent and 16 percent of its production, respectively. But then this might be expected since Nissan owns 22.4 percent of Ichikoh's equity and Toyota 8.6 percent. Making a big splash in Morgantown, Edmonton and Scottsville, Kentucky, is Sumitomo Electric Wiring Systems, which employs some 1,350 people at the three locations working on wiring systems for cars. A member of the huge, number three-ranking Sumitomo industrial group, Electric Wiring is an independent auto parts supplier selling to all the major auto manufacturers in Japan.

Toyota Motor's ties to Japanese steel producers are again much more important than at first apparent. Toyota officials proudly tell anyone who asks that it buys 60 percent of this key product from Armco, Inland, bankrupt LTV and National Steel—all major American steel producers, that have been battered by Japanese imports, plagued by short-sighted management and out-maneuvered by low-cost, domestic mini-mills. It purchases the remaining 40 percent directly from two Japanese firms, the world's largest steel producer Nippon Steel and Japan's third-ranking Sumitomo Metal, a key Sumitomo group member.

But the point is that all four of the U.S. producers supplying Toyota have very strong Japanese connections, which include joint ventures, sharing technology and direct Japanese investment. It is also not an exaggeration to say that almost all the new machinery seen in steel mills around the country is Japanese. Moreover, the Japanese producers are now benefiting from lower industry-wide wages resulting from concessions made in the 1980s by the United Steelworkers of America in an effort to be more competitive with foreign producers such as Japan. The result is that Japanese steel producers are exerting greater and greater control over the production of the steel that Toyota and other Japanese transplant auto and parts producers buy in the U.S. And if in most cases the Japanese steel producers don't have majority ownership, they do exercise great influence over the financing of new production and the new technology so essential to making U.S. steel producers more competitive.

Kawasaki Steel Corporation of Japan has a 49.5 percent stake in Armco Inc.'s Eastern steel-making division, Armco Steel Co. L.P.[16] At LTV its Japanese partner is Toyota supplier Sumitomo Metal, which has invested $280 million so far in two joint ventures with the beleaguered company.[17] National Steel's relationship with one of the world's five largest steel producers, Japan's NKK Corporation, goes back to August 1984 when NKK acquired a half interest in National from its parent National Intergroup.[18] Then in April 1990, NKK became the first Japanese steel company to have a majority stake in a major U.S. steel producer, when it said it would increase its ownership of the nation's sixth-largest steel firm to 90 percent.

However, the most dramatic Japan-U.S. relationship to emerge thus far in the steel industry is that between Toyota Motor's other direct Japanese supplier, Nippon Steel, and Inland Steel, America's third-largest steel producer and one that is generally regarded as the best-managed and most viable in the industry. Inland, one of the most vociferous critics of Japanese-imported steel during the past decade, began exchanging technology and research with Nippon in 1981. It subsequently used the relationship to access cheaper Japanese capital to finance joint ventures. The two companies have been involved in two joint ventures costing about $1 billion that produce steel designed to meet the tough quality demands of Toyota and other Japanese transplants. Then in December 1989, the two said Nippon would buy a 13 percent stake in Inland for $185 million. This was the boldest move until then by a Japanese steel producer in the U.S., but others are expected to follow Nippon's lead,[19] as exemplified by NKK's 90 percent ownership of National Steel announced in 1990.

As might be expected, such distinctive corporate behavior is not confined to the U.S. alone. Rather chauvinistic Japanese businesses can be found setting up similar exclusionary spheres of influence in the European Community, the Far East and Australia. Recently, Michigan State University Economics professor Mordechai Kreinin spent some months in Australia surveying and comparing the habits of 20 Japanese, 22 American and 20 European firms that had set up operations there. What he found was that most American-owned subsidiaries were completely Australian-managed and largely autonomous, while 80 percent of their European counterparts had local management and a great deal of freedom. "By contrast, the Japanese-owned subsidiaries tend to be tightly controlled by their respective parent company." Professor Kreinin said that strong control from Japan and the presence of local Japanese management limited the "autonomy of the subsidiary in making purchasing and sourcing decisions"; and that the Japanese parent influenced many decisions, "either directly or through the Japanese management team in the subsidiary."[20]

The Japanese also differed from their American and European counterparts in the ways they sourced their manufacturing equipment and purchased materials. American firms operating in Australia sourced their capital equipment from all over the world, while European subsidiaries had no dominant supplier, buying their equipment from the United States, Japan, the United Kingdom and several other European countries. However, the Japanese subsidiaries operated as Toyota has in Georgetown, buying as much capital equipment as they could in Japan. Fifteen of the 20 Japanese subsidiaries surveyed by Kreinin had 80 to 100 percent of their equipment shipped from Japan and according to a so-called list of "intended purchases" filed with Melbourne's Industrial Supply Office, Japanese subsidiaries "always intended to source in Japan."

When it came to submitting their purchases to competitive bidding on an international scale the Japanese subsidiaries took a similar insular approach. Three-quarters of the firms, including nine with over 500 workers, did

> not use international competitive bids and most said that they never even considered doing so. In most cases they go directly to Japan and buy Japanese equipment, either from the parent company or from its traditional suppliers in Japan. To the extent that bidding is used it is confined to Japanese suppliers. On the rare occasion that a lower foreign bid is received, the Japanese supplier would match that offer. Often the Japanese ''adviser'' in the subsidiary plays a role in nudging the sourcing decision towards Japan and in general some subsidiaries feel a subtle pressure to buy from traditional Japanese suppliers.

American firms, on the other hand, were totally democratic in the purchase of their manufacturing machinery, paying no attention to the country of origin. ''Nor,'' according to Kreinin, ''was it ever hinted or suggested by the parent company that preference should be given to American equipment.'' The Europeans? They behaved much like the Americans, submitting their purchases to international bidding, though perhaps to a somewhat lesser degree.

Visiting Georgetown, it's not hard to see that Japanese firms are behaving similarly in the U.S. though it may vary state by state. What Professor Kreinin is describing is part and parcel of the zaibatsu way of doing business and, as Professor Kreinin sees it, the way Japanese companies are doing business in Australia is a good gauge of how they operate around the world—just as it's a good gauge of how American and European firms function outside their own markets. ''As most companies in this survey are subsidiaries of giant multinational enterprises,'' Kreinin says in his report, ''this disparity between American and Japanese buying behaviour is representative of parent and sister companies world-wide.'' Indeed, the European Community, which is also being populated by Japanese auto transplants, is beginning to see a pattern similar to that seen around Georgetown. Major component suppliers, ''Nippondenso and Calsonic, which belong respectively to the Toyota and Nissan control spheres, have made important forays into Europe.''[21]

Along these lines, Harvard Business School professor Michael

Porter, author of *The Competitive Advantage of Nations*, noted some time ago that the way Japanese firms operated internationally gave them a sort of double whammy, in that when they travel abroad they take their most prized, proprietary resources with them. In a paper presented to a conference sponsored by the Center for Japanese Studies at the University of Michigan, Porter pointed out that "the U.S. facilities of Japanese companies are heavily tied into global manufacturing systems, and so are the suppliers that are following Japanese companies into the U.S. market. There is a heavy reliance on Japanese technology, a heavy reliance on Japanese components and a heavy reliance on the companies' total international networks. These are not stand-alone investments in the U.S. like the ones U.S. companies have tended to make in foreign countries."[22]

Toyota's multibillion-dollar push to transplant manufacturing in the U.S. may have been provoked by American protectionist pressures and sped on by the dramatic rise in the value of the Japanese yen. But it must also be seen as part of Toyota's and Japan's global push for selected market domination. In his 1990 New Year's Day message, Toyota president Shoichiro Toyoda said globalization was beginning to "take on real meaning for Toyota," noting that Toyota had begun "joint production with Volkswagen in West Germany, resumed manufacturing in the Philippines," announced two manufacturing plants in Great Britain to cost over $1 billion, planned to add truck manufacturing to its NUMMI joint venture with General Motors and started full-scale production at Toyota Motor Manufacturing Canada. Underlining this new thrust on Toyota's part, the company's overseas production of cars and trucks grew over 100 percent in 1989 and is expected to increase at least 30 percent in 1990. Japanese firms such as Toyota are moving from mercantilism to a globalization of their operations, but as seen at Georgetown this globalization is on their own indigenous terms. Building an Auto Alley in the world's richest and most developed nation is a form of colonization that has not been seen before. Georgetown, Marysville, Ohio, and Fort Wayne, Indiana, are not outposts in the Amazon or Africa.

Going international Japanese style is something very different from what its already established, global competitors are used to. As in the U.S., over-capacity and cut-throat competition will be the rule of the day in the global auto markets of the 1990s. According to Vincent Sarni, chairman of PPG Industries, a major supplier of glass and coatings to the auto industry, the global industry faces "wrenching adjustments and shrinking margins. There can be no doubt that the 1990's will test the industry's ability to adapt as never before. In the market-place the Big Ten [the leading U.S., Japanese and European auto groups] face the commercial equivalent of war and we know that some of the combatants are faced with capital spending needs that weigh heavily on their ability to stay on the field."[23]

Going international Japanese style can also create some ironic and compromising situations for a country where Japanese companies set up operations. This happens when the host country—the U.S. or the European Community—tries to define national borders in past terms, when it attempts to say "we" and "they" in terms of the way "we" and "they" used to behave. "I think what the Japanese are doing is integrating themselves into all of the major economies so that you can't do damage to Japan without doing damage to yourself," said University of Kentucky professor Kane. What Professor Kane is saying is that corporate Japan is already so entangled in the economic fiber of America or Europe, that politically attacking Japanese practices can be like shooting oneself in the foot. When the U.S. Congress tried to sanction Toshiba for selling strategic military equipment to the Russians that seriously imperiled the stealth and secrecy of America's fleet of nuclear submarines, it ran into some unexpected, powerful opposition. Many of the companies lobbying against sanctioning Toshiba turned out to be American competitors: among the strongest supporters of Toshiba were Tektronix, Inc., Apple Computer, Inc., Sun Microsystems, Inc., Hewlett-Packard Co., American Telephone and Telegraph Co., and Compaq, Inc., all of whom depended on Toshiba as a supplier of components and feared their supply would be cut off as a result of harsh sanctions.[24]

Or, the U.S. administration can get into the sort of nonsensical situation where it is speaking with two tongues, such as tacitly supporting voluntary restraints on imports of Toyotas and other Japanese cars, while pushing for unrestrained exports of U.S.-produced Toyotas to the European Community. President Bush's special trade representative, Carla Hills—the get-tough lady who said she was taking a crowbar to trade negotiations with Japan in order to pry open its markets to U.S. goods—recently found herself in such a situation, vehemently protecting Japanese transplant-produced cars from European Community trade restrictions. To American trade negotiators, a Toyota Camry with a 16-valve engine produced at Georgetown is an American car when shipped to Europe. However, to European negotiators a Toyota is a Japanese car, whether it's produced in Toyota City or Georgetown. In point of fact, a Georgetown Camry is a bit of a mutt, albeit a tough, alert and healthy mutt with a dominant Japanese bloodline and genes. The same, of course, is also true for so-called "Made in America" cars produced by the Big Three, though here the lineage is mostly American. About the only pure-breds being produced around Georgetown are those four-legged creatures gamboling about the Kentucky bluegrass.

Back on Cherry Blossom Road though, the constant refrain is how American Toyota is becoming. Though Toyota Georgetown is run by a Japanese and 70 or 80 Japanese advisers can be seen about the plant helping workers, on a recent visit, which included interviews with six members of Toyota Georgetown's management, not one Japanese was introduced. An effort is made to emphasize how down-home the operation is—how Americans have adapted to Japanese ways but retain their American character, how Georgetown is, as senior vice president Alex Warren put it, run with a "blend of the best of American and Japanese methods."

Given the high quality of the Georgetown Camrys, the same may be true of the blend of parts used to construct the car. However, Warren and other officials are very short on details as to who actually supplies Georgetown with parts. All that Toyota's managers will say is that in terms of value the Camrys rolling off the production line are currently 60 percent American and that their goal is to increase local American content to 75 percent. Other than naming the four American steel firms from whom they purchase flat-rolled steel for their fenders, hoods and other essential products, few specifics concerning their "just-in-time" inventory suppliers are forthcoming. Moreover, as has been seen, the term "American content" takes on a new meaning when much of it is produced or controlled by traditional Japanese suppliers that have set up shop in the U.S. and includes depreciation, transportation and even the cost of mowing the lawn in Georgetown. According to a 1989 Government Accounting Office report, Japanese automakers have reached 51 percent local content, as compared to an average of 87 percent for the Big Three.

But the problem goes beyond this and the fact that Japanese-American content is coming from factories that are displacing older, established U.S. production. Particularly worrisome is the fact that American firms are also being cut out from selling high-tech, high-margin products to Japanese transplants—products that are essential for keeping the U.S. economy alive. Much of the engineering, the intellectual content in a Toyota Camry, is Japanese; the brawn and the commodity-type products that also go into the makeup of a Camry are American. Over the long term this is not a good position for America to be in. Just look at the U.S. steel industry and ask where all of the innovation comes from—Japan.

In February 1990, Marc Santucci, president of ELM International, a well-known firm that specializes in auto industry consulting and research, told a hearing sponsored by the Commerce Department that "in a survey done in 1989 of approximately 1,100 tier one suppliers, all of which supplied the Big Three, only 235 supplied at least one Japanese auto maker." Included in the survey were four Japanese automakers that also produced a car for one of the Big Three. Moreover, Santucci pointed out that almost half the firms in the U.S. supplying Japanese transplants are in fact transplants themselves and that "most of the parts supplied by U.S. firms are low value, low technology parts." He also noted that when Boston University professor Susan Helper surveyed over 900 American-owned, tier-one suppliers, she found that "for the most part American companies who sold 'high-tech' parts to the Japanese did so through a joint venture with a Japanese supplier."

Frequently such joint ventures are not particularly successful arrangements for the U.S. partner. University of Michigan professor Vladimir Pucik, an expert on the auto industry, is one such skeptic. In a speech given at a conference, Pucik said "today's joint venture fever is really a symptom of the industry's competitive problem; it is not a solution. The joint ventures that have emerged recently have all too frequently represented a desperate attempt on the part of the American manufacturers to find a way around their competitive disadvantage. They are generally purely defensive in nature and they tend, when directed at the Japanese market, to exchange market access for technology."[25] As Harvard professor Robert Reich warns, ''Although the joint venture may be profitable for the American partner in the short term, in the long term it may leave the American partner vulnerable. It may give the Japanese a significant beach-head in the U.S. market.''[26]

Japanese transplant auto producers will counter that the problem is the poor-quality U.S. parts and that it takes time—at least two to three years according to Toyota—before a U.S. parts producer can become a supplier and that most U.S. producers don't persevere to meet their exacting standards. Consultant Santucci counters that such arguments wrongly stereotype all U.S. companies as inferior to their Japanese competitors and that according to his firm's analysis U.S. firms have spent on average four years attempting to get Japanese business. ''This does not reflect an industry that doesn't try,'' Santucci told the Commerce Department hearing.

Moreover, if many U.S. auto parts producers are being selectively cut out of the best business—being given the table scraps—they also face other competitive pressures. A first-tier Japanese parts producer that sets up operations in the U.S. to supply Japanese transplants will benefit from economies of scale and its traditional familiarity with its major customers. The importance of the latter can not be underestimated. As Santucci noted in an interview, a Japanese auto supplier that also supplies a producer in Japan will be able to spread his costs globally, charging the costs to maybe 200,000 parts manufactured in the U.S., another 100,000 made in the European Community and maybe 1 million in Japan. This is a great advantage that University of Kentucky professor Kane said can spell disaster for the smaller to medium-sized U.S. parts producer that can't benefit from this global mass. It also means that a Toyota or Hitachi located in Harrodsburg can source parts from around the world and that if there are protectionist pressures that might affect supplies from Japan, they can be sourced from plants in the Far East.

Discussing this global advantage, Harvard's Porter said,

While U.S. auto companies once had a tremendous opportunity to convert global positions into a competitive advantage, I do not believe that they have [now]. U.S. companies have been competing with what I call country-centered strategies. They have European operations that by and large have been detached, unconnected and uncoordinated with what is going on in the U.S. U.S. companies typically run their operations in other parts of the world as separate units—sometimes selling under a different brand name—and these units have a high level of local autonomy.

Japanese companies have global strategies. When they invest in a foreign country, they invest in a way that leverages the overall system to the greatest extent possible. They achieve high levels of coordination between subsidiaries in different countries. Where parts are made, where assembly takes place, where engines are produced—all that is thought through in terms of a global manufacturing system. Product line choices are not made based on only one market but on the ability to sell those products in other markets around the world.[27]

This is where Georgetown fits in in terms of the American market and also in Toyota's global strategy. At least some of the peppy, 16-valve engines that will be produced at Georgetown will be shipped abroad or at least until Toyota's U.S. production has reached a point where it can consume all of them. Such an interweaving of global interdependencies extends to Toyota's major suppliers and is one reason why American competitors are being systematically shut out. This is part and parcel of the *zaibatsu* pattern in operation globally, a pattern of control that can be seen in full force in and around Toyota City, Georgetown's and Toyota's womb.

———

Teruyuki Hanabusa, the Japan-based manager of Toyota's North American operations, is obviously taken aback by the question. A vigorous, controlled man, sporting dark-rimmed aviator glasses—the antithesis of Detroit's bloated bureaucrats—has to pause and think a bit. The question: what Toyota has learned from its American operations? For a moment he fiddles with his card case in silence, tapping it on a huge conference table filling an antiseptic meeting room above the company's exhibition hall in Toyota City. Below, the company's triumphs are chronicled, as a sort of digital auto-clock ticks off the 65,305,903rd, then 4th . . . Toyota produced. Not far away on the main floor a line of Toyota's ever more efficient and lighter engines is displayed and a sign above a map of the world proclaims: ''Toyota . . . cars to love, the world over." Finally Hanabusa gives an answer through an interpreter that can be seen as realistic or arrogant depending on one's view of what the U.S. might offer.

"I cannot find any concrete examples right now," responds Hanabusa, a graduate of the prestigious Waseda University. Apparently realizing how his answer may sound, he then lamely talks about how American people make decisions regarding job promotions and the choice of suppliers in a "very fair way." That's it. That's about all he has to say on the matter, as he discusses Toyota's expansion plans for North America. No two-way street here. America's not on Toyota's learning curve.

Admittedly, Toyota entered the 1984 NUMMI joint venture with GM to produce cars in Freemont, California, as a sort of tutor for GM, with one aim of the project being that GM learn better and more productive labor practices from Toyota. And it has been decades now that Japanese auto producers have been taking the lessons of Edwards Deming—lessons until recently shunned by Detroit—to heart. But considering the fact that Toyota has been selling some of the most popular cars in America for decades, that it has been producing Chevy Novas and Corollas in the California joint venture with General Motors for close to a decade, that it has already invested over $1 billion in its Georgetown plant and that it plans to double its Georgetown car capacity to 400,000 Camrys a year, one might think creating such a large presence in the U.S. would have also been a learning experience for Toyota—an experience in which Toyota gained not just profits but also knowledge which it could bring back to Japan and use.

A look around Toyota City, though, gives a good explanation why this hasn't been the case—why Hanabusa drew a blank when asked what Toyota had learned in the U.S. In a way Toyota's distinct pattern of entering the U.S. can be seen as a classic example of character determining the course of one's action. The point is Toyota didn't move to the U.S. to learn but to bring as much of its own, highly successful modus operandi to the U.S. as it could. Conducting one's business in the *zaibatsu* way as Toyota does here tends to exclude the influence of external factors rather than embracing them. As one sees at Georgetown, creating a "mirror image" in Kentucky was not limited to building the new plant along the lines of Tsutsumi and filling it with Japanese equipment. Such an attitude may sound provincial and arrogant, but when you've worked for decades honing your manufacturing methods and it's worked as well as it has for Toyota, then you're loath to pick up foreign ways. Maybe it's also just being smart.

In Toyota's 1989 Annual Report, Eiji Toyoda and Shoichiro Toyoda, chairman and president, respectively, and descendants of Toyota's founder, discuss just such qualms about manufacturing abroad in terms of an inability to establish their unique labor practices on foreign turf. They claim what they feared most in setting up shop abroad was "a worker whose face we could not read—whose heart was a mystery to us. When the time came for us to make a wholesale structural shift and move our manufacturing overseas, this was our greatest fear. We had developed a very finely tuned production system. What would happen if we turned it over to him?" To make their point, a burly American worker scowls defiantly at the reader from a picture on the facing page. However, they say such fears proved to be "nonsense," and smiling from the following page are a group of five American workers, including a black and a woman, all wearing Toyota Motor Manufacturing's red T-shirt. "For our first half-century we thought of ourselves as a Japanese company. . . . Now we think of ourselves as a world company," say the Toyodas. Now that Toyota has found its way of doing business travels better than expected, globalization is a big word around the once-hesitant Toyota—but its own form of globalization and keeping the Toyota family together. And if it's learned one thing that Hanabusa didn't mention, it's that it can deal with labor worldwide.

Still Toyota City, located in the middle of Japan, is the center of the world for Toyota—the place from which Japan's most prolific automaker and its largest corporation's prosperity and momentum are sprung. This is where it invented its much-emulated formula for just-in-time inventory delivery or *kanban*, and perfected its quality control. It is a place of constant motion, teeming with activity not unlike the proverbial ant hill. Trucks, weaving in and out of traffic, dash to deliver engines, wheels, mufflers, bolts, switches, hoses as needed. On factory floors workers perform the tough calisthenics of Japan's economic miracle—lifting fenders with balletic precision, keeping time with robots flexing their motorized arms, and inspecting, inspecting and inspecting for defects. At the Tsutsumi factory, the progenitor of the Georgetown plant, a new Toyota—a Camry, Corona or Lexus 250—drives off the factory's flexible body line every 60 seconds bound for Tokyo or beyond. In Toyota's old Japanese home everyone is dancing to the same tune and there is no doubt who sets the beat—Toyota.

This is Toyota's cocoon in which the *zaibatsu* way of doing business is encapsulated—its narcissistic existence enshrined. If the pattern seems at times diffuse in and around Georgetown, there's no mistaking it here. Toyota's factories and those of the Toyota group of companies sprawl in all directions as one drives down from Nagoya, a rich manufacturing city of about 2 million, lying between the old and new capitals of Japan, Kyoto and Tokyo. At Toyota City and in the surrounding Aichi prefecture everyone belongs to the group or they don't belong. It is a place where weaving the web of mutual dependency comes naturally. Unlike rival Nissan's operations which are sprinkled throughout Japan, virtually all of Toyota's manufacturing operations are located in this area. So too are the majority of the major Toyota group suppliers, many of whom have also made their way to the U.S. Here you can find the headquarters of Nippondenso, one of the older members of the Toyota group which now produces air conditioners, windshield wipers and gauges for instrument panels at three plants in the U.S. employing about 2,000 workers; or, Aisin Seiki which manufactures automotive windowframes and brake components in Seymour, Indiana; or Toyoda Gosei, whose TG Corporation subsidiary makes steering wheels, side moldings, plastic parts and gears in Perryville, Missouri. And these are just a few examples of the many Toyota group companies who've followed Toyota to America.

Toyota City, which was called Koromo until it adopted the automaker's name in 1959, is the ultimate company town, complete with dormitories for single employees and company housing for married couples, a huge sports center with an indoor pool, tennis courts and two gymnasiums, and a 403-bed Toyota Hospital. It's as if General Motors had located almost all of its auto plants, workers and suppliers in one town such as Flint, Michigan, which is, however, today a sad contrast with its Japanese counterpart. Toyota's paternalism extends far beyond Toyota City. For unmarried employees working in Tokyo it provides cheap housing and it also operates inexpensive resort houses in scenic spots in Japan for vacations. Like the company that controls it, Toyota City is somewhat provincial and conservative—a city little visited by foreign tourists. Though it was a major producer of silk in the earlier part of the century, with silkworms spinning their cocoons on thousands of mulberry trees here, it has no sense of luxury. It is a workers' town of down-to-earth values, where Toyota likes to encourage the idea that workers are members of a family, albeit a corporate family. There is nothing of pastoral, bucolic Kentucky here. For greater diversity there is Nagoya, a town offering the variety of expensive foreign goods found in the rich, provincial manufacturing cities of Europe. And from there Tokyo is only a two-hour ride away on the bullet train. At Toyota City, its lean, young, scarce workers are encouraged to be "practical and avoid frivolity." The company's pervasive work slogan is *Yoi Shina, Yoi Kangae* (Good Thinking, Good Products)—a phrase that can be adopted on the production line or in quality circles, where groups of five to ten workers meet frequently to find ways of improving the product and work environment.

Toyota's fetish for quality—what the *Financial Times* called its "relentless pursuit of perfection" in an article of April 20, 1990, on the production of its new luxury car, the Lexus—goes a long way back with Toyota to the nineteenth century. And if there's one thing they know around here it is machines, how to constantly improve them and how to make them hum. Toyota traces its roots back to Sakichi Toyoda, a poor carpenter's son born in 1867, the year before the Meiji restoration. Sakichi, as it turned out, had a remarkable mechanical genius and as Japan began her great modernization, Sakichi grew up to become one of his country's foremost inventors, earning 84 patents for new inventions during his lifetime and founding a whole group of companies out of which Toyota and its affiliates grew.

At the age of 30 Sakichi invented his most famous machine, an automatic wooden loom that did not depend solely on human power and let a worker handle two or three looms at once. Besides increasing productivity, the loom was equipped with a totally new, quality control device that allowed the loom to stop when a thread was dropped or ran out, thus assuring the consistency of its woven goods. The device is still used on today's looms and in concept, it is not unlike a key manufacturing principle Toyota introduced in the production of autos and eventually much copied by other automakers. Just as the loom stops when a thread is dropped, Toyota's auto assembly line comes to a halt after a worker signals through pulling a rope that he's found a defect or has a problem that he can't correct. Sakichi continued to improve his looms, introducing more efficient and less expensive models, just as today Toyota continues to refine the performance of its autos and engines and demand similar cost-cutting and efficiency measures from its suppliers. Soon, with financing from the Mitsui *zaibatsu*, Sakichi was able to establish Toyoda Automatic Loom Works in the Nagoya area, the firm from which the Toyota group of companies has sprung. Moreover, Toyota's close relationship with the Mitsui companies continues to this day, with Mitsui Bank being its largest shareholder.

Sakichi's eldest son, Kiichiro, was cut from the same cloth as his father. After graduating from Tokyo University with a degree in Mechanical Engineering, he invented a loom that was so simple and efficient that it was called the "Magic Loom" and sold worldwide.[28] Despite the Toyodas' worldwide success in building looms, the father and son wanted to branch out. Inventors thrive on new challenges and, given their mechanical genius, it's not surprising that they were intrigued by autos. This was the jazz age and much of the 1920s' glamour was associated with fast, sleek cars. Even the conservative Toyodas must have been tempted. Ironically, most of the passenger cars in Japan at the time were American, since both Ford and General Motors had assembly plants there and together dominated the market. Kiichiro, however, had a dream—to manufacture an all-Japanese car. With this in mind Kiichiro traveled in America and Japan to study auto manufacturing there. In 1929 he got the money to bring this dream to reality after Sakichi sold all the manufacturing and sales rights to his loom, except for Japan, China and the United States, to Platt Brothers Ltd., a leading British loom manufacturer, for £100,000.

Sakichi, who apparently had great faith in his eldest son's ability, generously gave Kiichiro the £100,000 as seed money to begin building a Japanese auto. Borrowing machinists and workers from the loom assembly line when he could, Kiichiro worked on building an experimental engine and in 1934 he set up his Auto Department inside the Toyoda Automatic Loom Works. The following year he produced his prototype vehicle and on August 28, 1937, the Toyota Motor Company was established, with its headquarters and new plant in Koromo. The first car to roll off the line was a rather clunky-looking AA sedan and Toyota was in business.

Stories vary as to why it was named Toyota rather than Toyoda.

According to some accounts, the name emerged from a contest to choose a new name for the company, whereas Toyota claims Kiichiro chose it "to place the emphasis on its new contribution to Japanese society, rather than on its family origins." But the most plausible explanation seems to be that a mistake was made in writing the Toyoda name when the company was registered—a somewhat ironic turn of events, given Toyota's obsessions with quality, defect-free products.

The road to Toyota's current prosperity, however, has not always been an easy one. Soon after Toyota got its start as a fledgling auto company, Japan went to war with the United States. For Toyota this meant that as the war progressed materials were harder and harder to get and the products it could produce were more and more makeshift. Some of the trucks it built had no radiator grills, wooden decks and seats, breaks only on the rear wheels and a single headlight. Many were also pieced together and recycled from wrecked or worn-out trucks. Then, at the war's end, it faced a very uncertain future, having 3,000 employees, bomb-damaged plants and no business. Moreover, Japan's economy, if that's the right way of describing it at the time, was in chaos, with very few people having enough money to buy food much less contemplate the purchase of a truck or car.

Still, Toyota was not a company that gave up easily. Then, as today, it was driven with the tenacity of an inventor who won't give in. Under Kiichiro's leadership, Toyota decided to concentrate on manufacturing small cars, so that it would not compete directly with American carmakers who were focusing their efforts on medium and large-sized cars. In any event, a small, fuel-efficient car, such as the one Toyota developed with a top speed of 54 miles an hour, was about all most Japanese could afford at the time. Unfortunately for Toyota, its labor relations weren't as felicitous as they are now and when the Japanese economy fell into a recession in the 1949–50 period, Toyota was faced with a liquidity crisis and the need to lay off 2,000 workers. In April 1949, Toyota's in-house union, the Toyota Labor Union which continues to represent Toyota workers today, launched its one-and-only strike to date, after Toyota failed to meet its regular payroll, cut salaries and threatened dismissals. Relations between Toyota and its workers deteriorated to the point where Toyota was talking about bankruptcy and dissolving the company. However, a settlement was reached in June 1950, only after the union agreed to the worker layoff and Kiichiro and his entire executive staff resigned en masse. Since then Toyota has never had a strike, but it should be remembered that the familial relations that have prevailed at Toyota and other Japanese companies since the mid-1950s are a relatively new phenomenon. Prior to World War II there were frequent labor conflicts in Japan between autocratic corporations and their workers. The 1920s were filled with labor disputes, as was most of the decade after World War II. The labor harmony seen today in Japan emerged only in the 1950s, as a result of pressure from corporations and the government to quell unrest. Since then what's changed are Japanese corporations' attitudes and treatment of their workers, and the realization that hard-working, cooperative and intelligent workers are a company's major asset. Also by and large, Japanese labor has been working in an expanding industrial market where unemployment is low and workers in high demand and thus expensive. This is certainly true at Toyota City, where the supply of young workers is scarce and as many expensive jobs as possible are being replaced by robots whose number is growing at 10 percent a year.

Toyota showed the same pluck when its first entry into the U.S. market ended as an utter disaster. In July 1958, it started exporting the Toyota Crown to the U.S., only to find that the Crown, with its puny engine, was totally unsuited to the sort of long-distance, high-speed driving Americans liked. Within three years the Crown—a great success in Japan and Toyota's first attempt to export one of its cars to any market—was withdrawn. But Toyota persisted.

In 1965 Toyota had its first big hit, the $1,700 Corona, a car engineered with the American market in mind and one that paved the way for the Japanese invasion of the U.S. auto market. Now, more than two decades later, Toyota is the number one foreign car bought by Americans in the U.S., with U.S. sales reaching 945,353 vehicles in 1989.[29] Kiichiro died less than two years after he and his fellow executives departed en masse, so that he never saw his dream of building an all-Japanese auto manufacturer reach unimagined proportions. Though he never returned to run the company, his family has been involved with it ever since.

Large and international as Toyota has become in a little over five decades, it is still a family-run company, run out of a family-controlled town. Structurally, Toyota doesn't conform to the classic *zaibatsu* setup where it would sit at the top of a group of

companies, having absolute power over their fate, deciding what
direction they should take, whom they should deal with and who
should be excluded from their financial web. In such an arrangement the actual direction may be given in subtle ways, while the
lines of power may appear to be direct. At Toyota, control is exer-
cised by the company in more indirect ways, but in and around
Toyota City there is little question as to who's calling the shots—
who's running the show—Toyota. The ties that bind, as might be
expected, are cross-shareholdings, while the major puppeteers
are members of the Toyoda family.

Besides having Sakichi's nephew Eiji Toyoda as chairman of
Toyota, there's Toyota's president Shoichiro Toyoda, who is Sakichi's grandson and Kiichiro's son. In addition, direct members of
the Toyoda family or in-laws hold key positions in Toyoda Automatic Loom Works, Toyota Trading, Toyoda Spinning and Weaving, Nippondenso, Aisin Seiki, Toyoda Gosei and Toyota of
America, and these are just a few of the Toyota group companies
in which Toyoda family members have important positions. In a
recent *Financial Times* survey of the world car market, the paper
said in discussing the Toyoda family

> not surprisingly, the Toyoda family's influence on the group
> is pervasive, and it has, for the most part, been an influence
> towards the provincial virtues of caution and frugality. Toyota
> is above all a deeply conservative, provincial enterprise.
>
> No one would accuse the Toyodas of being frivolous. Al-
> though wealthy by any definition, they do not figure in the
> latest Fortune list of billionaires. Shoichiro is reportedly the
> wealthiest, with assets, mainly Toyota shares, valued in ex-
> cess of $300 million. The Toyodas tend not to hold large quan-
> tities of group company shares in their own right. Rather,
> control is established through large interlocking stakes held by
> the major companies in each other.[30]

Sounds like a familiar story—wonder where they learned it? At
the top is the Toyota Motor Co. which has a major stake in all
of the group companies. Toyota's holdings of group companies
generally range from about 20 percent of a company's shares, as
is the case with Nippondenso or Toyoda Automatic Loom, to as
much as 50 percent or more as with Central Motor Wheel or
Kanto Auto Works, a car assembly operation. In addition, major

shareholders in Toyota, such as Mitsui and Tokai Banks, Nippon Life and Toyoda Automatic Loom, will also hold significant blocks of Toyota group companies. For example, Toyota Machine Works, a major supplier of power steering apparatus, crank and camshafts and machine tools to Toyota and Toyota group companies, has over 40 percent of its shares held by Toyota, Mitsui Bank, Mitsui Trust & Banking, Tokai Bank and Nippon Life—all familiar faces around Toyota City. However, the ties that bind the Toyota group together are even more complicated than implied so far, since group companies also hold shares in each other. For example, Toyoda Tsusho, the Toyota group's main trading arm, owns 45 percent of Toyoda Kako, a manufacturer of auto carpets and interior accessories, 3 percent of Toyoda Iron Works and 2 percent of Toyoda Gosei. In turn, Toyoda Tsusho's major shareholders are the usual cast of characters, including Toyota, Mitsui and Tokai Banks and Toyoda Automatic Loom. So everyone is scratching everyone else's back.

Such cross-shareholdings and interlocking family ties give an added dimension to the gathering of companies that have sprung up around Toyota. Of course, these companies are beholden to Toyota, not just because of cross-shareholdings and the frequent presence of a Toyoda family member in a key corporate position but also because Toyota can make or break many of these companies, especially those elite suppliers who only deal with Toyota. Control, however, is only part of the picture. Such a situation creates a joint sense of purpose, where everyone is in the same boat. Since many have been with Toyota since the beginning, there is also a continuity of experience, which means that many matters don't even have to be discussed before a decision is reached or a common goal defined. As with a group of people who set their sights on completing a joint task or share a common belief, the group frequently will take on a life of its own—an energized momentum that is greater than the parts. Members of a group can also play off each other and in the process expand their own understanding and direction. Information is shared—particularly information about the competition—so that more members of the group play with a full deck. Given the Japanese penchant for collecting and sharing seemingly random information about any subject almost ad infinitum, they might be expected to suffer from information overload but they apparently don't. Actually pinpointing the genesis of an idea or decision or mistake is frequently difficult in such a situation. The risk of launching a new car, for example, is shared on a broader basis with suppliers, just as the benefits of a successful product are. This is why Toyota will share the intimate details of its future plans with its major suppliers, expecting them to contribute significantly to design and cost improvement of the products they produce for Toyota. There is not the destructive waste of the adversarial relationship so typical of American car manufacturers vis-à-vis their suppliers, where the advantages of a long-range relationship are most often sacrificed to short-term profits.

Discovery is not made in isolation but is progressive, where all the little steps forward add up. If Japanese automakers are currently producing some of the most versatile and efficient mass-produced engines in the world, it isn't because of a single stroke of genius. American auto manufacturers started on an equal footing with the Japanese, on a level playing field, but fell behind. Japanese automakers such as Toyota were determined to make a better engine. For Toyota much of its particular skill is a matter of refining and refining. This was Sakichi's lesson. His quality control device for stopping a machine that dropped a thread was an inspiration but he didn't stop there. He kept improving his loom, making it cheaper and more versatile. The lesson has not been lost on Toyota or its suppliers. The Tsutsumi plant—upon which Georgetown is modeled—is old, having been built in 1970, but it is constantly being updated through massive investment in new equipment.

But there is another, very important reason why so many Toyota family companies have made their Japanese home near the Tsutsumi factory and the older Motomachi and Takaoka plants, all of which produce passenger cars. Their proximity gives added force to a chief ingredient of Toyota's success—its highly efficient and much-copied *kanban* or just-in-time method of handling inventory. Invented by Kiichiro Toyoda and developed over the years by Toyota in conjunction with its suppliers, just-in-time means what it says—it means Toyota suppliers supply what Toyota wants when it wants it. This may seem like a simple, logical way of going about one's business, but for it to work in something as complicated as assembling a car from literally thousands of parts, it must be orchestrated with the utmost precision or it can easily get bogged down at a huge cost. Managing so many diverse parts is not unlike weaving, but it means dealing with many more variables. To make its just-in-time system work—that is have just as much inventory on hand when needed and not more—Toyota took a rather unconventional approach, according to Taiichi Ohno, a former executive vice president who was intimately involved in developing the production methods in the 1950s. "We had given a lot of thought to how best to run such a system," Ohno said. "But it was only when we reversed our thinking and considered the production process in terms of backward flow that the solution became apparent."[31]

In practice, just-in-time operates somewhat like a modern supermarket, where shelves are filled by Pepperidge Farm or Coca-Cola bottling deliverymen as they're emptied of cookies and sodas by store customers. This is not surprising since Ohno took much of his inspiration from the American supermarket, with the idea that the customer really directs or pulls the groceries through the system with his or her purchases. In a way it's a straightforward, eminently reasonable concept, positing the customer as the prime motivator, but for many American companies it's been a revolutionary idea that's been hard to assimilate. Looking at the production process in terms of the flow back from the customer is in many ways the antithesis of mass production—the antithesis of Henry Ford's dictum that the customer can have any color car as long as it's black. It goes far beyond the idea that the customer is always right, for implied in just-in-time is a more flexible production process where products can be varied and produced in batches, where a plant doesn't have to be dedicated to producing one model of car or truck and where introduction of new models can be sped up. Also, a plant running under such a system can break even, because of its flexibility, at a much lower level of production than the classic American factory that can only make money running near capacity. Just-in-time with the customer always in mind is also much better suited to today's economy, where markets are frequently fragmented and many successful products are tailored for and sell to segments of a market.

Along the Tsutsumi plant production line, workers and robots have a small supply of parts near them and this supply is replenished as needed. What just-in-time avoids is having suppliers deliver their products when they've completed them, regardless of when Toyota might need them. The result is that Toyota, unlike American auto producers in the past, doesn't have to warehouse huge amounts of inventory for weeks or months at great expense.

American auto producers have in recent years adopted and adapted the just-in-time delivery with varying degrees of success, Ford probably being the most proficient at this endeavor thus far. Such a system is also ideally suited to Japan where space and land—even in Toyota City—is at a premium and its use for storage costly. Some might say wasteful.

It is this just-in-time configuration of the Toyota group plants that one sees driving around Toyota City in a bulky, black, company Toyota equipped with individual seat massagers and heaters. Being near to Toyota's main plants is apparently an essential part of being a key just-in-time supplier. Toyota has two primary supplier groups: its so-called *Kyoho-Kai* includes 176 auto parts manufacturers, some of which are subsidiaries and affiliates, and its *Eiho-Kai* which embraces 57 plant contractors and manufacturers of molds and gauges. The vast majority of *Kyoho-Kai* parts companies, or some 136 manufacturers operating in and around Toyota City, are therefore called *Tokai Kyoho-Kai* after the district where Toyota has its headquarters.[32]

The *Kyoho-Kai* and the *Eiho-Kai* groups are the top of the heap and for the most part get at least 60 to 70 percent of their business from Toyota. Each company, in turn, uses 20 to 60 secondary suppliers and subcontractors that total an estimated 4,000 in Toyota's case. Though the latter group's economic ties to Toyota are important, the relationship obviously isn't as close. In hard economic times, it is this broad group that serves as a sort of shock absorber for Toyota, bearing the brunt of whatever cutbacks occur at the top.

As Dodwell describes the three-tiered relationship, it is similar to a pyramid, with Toyota at the top, the primary suppliers in the middle and the secondary, tertiary subcontractors at the bottom. Such a tripledecker relationship is not unique to Toyota, but is shared by other major Japanese automakers such as Nissan or Mitsubishi. Also typical of such an arrangement is a situation where Toyota or Nissan pretty much controls design and production of the high value-added, high-tech proprietary parts that differentiate a carmaker, whereas the third tier of companies perform more of the labor-intensive, grunt work.

In practice, Toyota or Nissan will have four sources of supply: its own in-house production, affiliated suppliers, suppliers more closely associated with other automakers, and independents, not intimately connected to one auto group. Normally, an automaker will make about 25 percent of its components and parts in-house, concentrating on engines, engine parts and body panels. Affiliated companies such as those in Toyota's *Kyoho-Kai* group will join Toyota in the early stages of developing products and features that will distinguish its cars from Nissan's or Honda's. Electronic components and transmissions, which carry Toyota's own distinctive stamp, fall in this category. Bottom-tier companies that supply more labor-intensive, commodity-type products will usually operate under long-term contracts that specify price reductions of from 1 to 10 percent a year. From the independent parts producers, Toyota or Nissan or Honda will purchase the sort of parts that benefit from large-scale production, require a good deal of technological input and could prove prohibitively expensive for one automaker to produce in-house. NGK spark plugs, Akebono brakes and Kayaba Industry shock absorbers are products manufactured by independents and used by all the major Japanese automakers. In the case of Akebono, its long-term customers Nissan, Toyota, Isuzu and Hino Motors also have major stakes in the company.

Given the highly successful support system Toyota has built up in and around Toyota City, it's not hard to see why it hesitated for so long to stray from the unique security there. But then a number of factors combined to make Toyota's setting up operations in the U.S. almost inevitable.

First of all, as America's trade deficit with Japan began to mount in the mid-1980s almost on a monthly basis, protectionist pressures rose in tandem to virulent levels. Much of this anti-Japanese sentiment was directed at its autoproducers since Americans—especially the young to young middle-aged, the people with the right consumer demographics—were buying Toyotas, Nissans and Hondas as quickly as they could be unloaded on the West Coast. Moreover, it appeared many of these buyers might be lost to Detroit forever, since by the mid-1980s a number of these buyers were driving their second or third Japanese import, thus manifesting to Detroit a disturbing loyalty to the high-quality, low-cost cars. Quite naturally, the most vociferous protectionists venting their anger at Japan were American automakers and their workers. Eventually, with aid and pressure from the U.S. government, the Japanese to save face agreed to limit the number of cars it would export to the U.S. to a little over 2 million a year. Such protectionism managed well can help revive an industry, but in wrong hands it can turn into what University of California professor Chalmers Johnson called the "acquisition of unearned rent."[33] Guess what American auto producers did?

For a moment, American auto producers appeared to have the upper hand in their own market. By limiting Japanese exports to the U.S., the only way the Japanese producers could increase their American market share would be to set up production in the U.S., and the Americans knew Japanese producers could never make it in the U.S. if they had to compete on an equal footing with them. Or, at least that's what they'd said for years: the reason the Japanese were able to produce a car for $600 to $700 less than Detroit was cheap labor, cheap capital and a cheap yen. Then the U.S. Treasury secretary, James Baker, gave the U.S. auto industry another gift: the 1985 Plaza Agreement whose aim—largely fulfilled in the following two years—was to boost the value of the yen and the currencies of other major industrial nations in relation to the dollar. The idea behind the move, in the case of the yen, was that as the yen rose Japanese exports such as cars would become more expensive and less competitive in the U.S. This, at least, was the chief stated goal of the finance ministers of the U.S., Great Britain, France, Japan, and Germany, who met in September 1985 at New York's Plaza Hotel in an effort to change America's trade imbalance.

But then American auto producers largely blew what brief, little advantage they had over the Japanese. They greedily and shortsightedly raised their prices, thus giving the Japanese room to raise theirs as the yen rose. And they have continued in these ways, again aggressively raising prices in August 1990 despite a weakening economy and record market-share gains by Japanese automakers.[34] Also, as in the past, they underestimated their Japanese competition's ability to adapt to adversity and drastically cut their costs. Here, again, the benefits of the *keiretsu* system came into play, in that the yen shock could be absorbed throughout a Toyota or a Nissan's group of companies. In addition, the appreciating yen boomeranged as few had expected, making moving production to, and investing in America all the cheaper for the Japanese. Rather than being set back by the rising yen and protectionist pressures, Toyota and other Japanese firms found opportunity in adversity and ran with it.

As if the appreciating yen and protectionist pressures weren't enough to lure Toyota's manufacturing prowess to the U.S., there were forces in play making the move to Georgetown almost inevitable. Toyota was used to competing with its archrivals Nissan, Mitsubishi and Honda on an equal footing and all three of them either had U.S. production in place or were planning it. Toyota realized that if U.S. protectionist pressures continued, it might end up at a competitive disadvantage if it didn't have local production. Toyota knew that the only way to stay in top competitive form was to compete against the other top three Japanese producers on all fronts. Then representatives from scores of states were all over Toyota, competing with tax breaks, outright grants and incentive packages it could hardly refuse.[35] Realizing that it had the upper hand, Toyota played one state against another so that competing states would up the ante. And when the race had narrowed down to Kentucky and Tennessee, Toyota made it clear that it would settle in the "neighboring state" of Tennessee unless it came up with the best incentive package.

Kentucky, which was still smarting from having lost General Motors' Saturn plant to Tennessee, finally beat out the other 34 competing states with an offer that is costing the state an unprecedented $325.4 million over 20 years to help the world's third-largest auto producer feel comfortable in its new Kentucky home. As part of the lure for Toyota, Kentucky bought the 1,400-acre Georgetown site for $12.5 million and allocated $20 million for site preparation. However, costs to level the site escalated to $43.9 million. In addition, Kentucky agreed to spend $47 million on highway improvements, $65 million for Toyota employee training and $5.2 million for Toyota families' education. Included in the education package is a 20-year commitment by the state to provide a so-called "Saturday" tutoring school for the children of Japanese Toyota employees and a 10-year commitment to run an English language class for Toyota employees. However, the biggest cost of all will be the $166.7 to $224 million in interest paid over 20 years on federal and state tax-exempt Economic Development Bonds used to finance the Georgetown project.[36]

To put Georgetown's cost in perspective, it's worth comparing Georgetown to some of the other projects built along Auto Alley. According to the Center for Business and Economic Research at the University of Kentucky, excluding bond interest costs Kentucky is spending approximately $49,900 per worker to create the 3,000 jobs at Georgetown. By comparison, neighboring Tennessee spent about a fifth that amount or $11,000 per employee to attract Nissan to Smyrna, while Michigan provided Mazda's Flat Rock facility benefits of $13,850 per employee and Illinois $33,320 of incentives for each of Chrysler-Mitsubishi's workers. Even attracting GM's $5 billion Saturn plant to Spring Hill, Tennessee, only cost the state $26,660 per worker in incentives or little more than half the Georgetown package.[37]

Though Kentucky's munificence became a heated election issue while the Georgetown plant was being completed—especially since it was being built in the most prosperous part of the state— debate over Georgetown has abated and many Kentuckians appreciate it for the magnet it has been. Gene Royalty, head of the Kentucky Cabinet for Economic Development, has been involved in recruiting many of the Japanese firms that have settled in Kentucky and he's ecstatic about the trend. According to Royalty, an energetic former furniture dealer and banker from Harrodsburg, at the beginning of 1990 Japanese firms had invested $2.6 billion in 57 manufacturing plants which at full production will employ 16,377 people earning $340 million annually. Of the 57 new plants, the vast majority make auto parts or equipment related to producing new cars. Royalty said the new plants and workers will generate $48.5 million in state taxes a year and an additional $18.5 million of taxes at the local level.[38] Royalty thinks the Japanese bonanza is about the best thing to happen to the state since Colonel Sanders started frying chicken some years ago.

"I think the relationship with Japan has been great. They have the money and want to come where the market is. We're being very international. At least 70 percent of plants are expanding or plan to. It speaks well for our work force. Japan bashing is not nearly as popular here as in Washington," Royalty said, speaking in his spacious office atop the marble-clad Capital Plaza in Frankfort. As Royalty explained it, Kentucky is now one of the "top five states" in the U.S. in terms of Japanese investment. "The real winner in all this are probably the young people of Kentucky. It's a learning process for both nations."

Some people learn faster than others and at the moment the U.S. seems to be a slow learner, not that it hasn't been warned. Think of it this way. It's as if a Japanese prefecture offered a prosperous GE or GM a quarter of a billion dollars in aid to set up operations in Japan after their TVs or cars had already surfeited the market. At the peak of the states' Japanese feeding frenzy a few years ago, Tokyo-based management consultant and author

James Abegglen, who founded the Boston Consulting Group's Japanese office, very intelligently warned:

> Japanese factories in the U.S . . . have this absolutely new plant with the latest, most efficient equipment—the newest technology. They'll have a young flexible labor force, and if there's a union, it will be more accommodating.
>
> I think one of the consequences—and I don't think the states know them—is the Japanese factories will shut down U.S. capacity. The irony is that you have all these states here in Tokyo hustling to put plants in the United States that will close down [older] capacity.[39]

Or, as economist Candace Howes points out in a similar vein:

> Close scrutiny of the phenomenon suggests that as Japanese car manufacturers build new plants, they displace hundreds of thousands of well paid autoworkers and suppliers in older industrial regions while creating far fewer jobs at lower overall wages. States battle for job opportunities which redistribute income from older minority workers in declining regions, not primarily to workers in less developed regions, but to the profits of Japanese firms.
>
> The widely praised "transfer" of Japanese skills and techniques is deformed by the reluctance of Japanese firms to look beyond their traditional supplier families and their own skilled workers and managers in Japan.[40]

———

It's four years since Toyota, together with Kentucky's helping hand, leveled this rocky pasture and began construction here. Since 1987 the U.S. auto industry has also been transformed forever. In 1989 Japanese transplants produced 22 percent of the cars built in America—an incredible 53 percent increase in just one year, while by the end of 1990 Japanese auto manufacturers producing cars in the U.S. and Japan had taken over 32 percent of the new car market—including cars built by the Japanese and sold by the Big Three.[41] During the decade of the 1980s General Motors, still the world's number one car producer, has seen its U.S. market share decline drastically about 10 percentage points, to a shade higher than 35 percent at the end of 1990 from around 45 percent in 1980.[42] The eight assembly plants that the Japanese built in the U.S. during the 1980s have put precisely that many Big Three car factories out of business in the 1987–90 period.[43] Also during that same period, about 20,000 auto assembly workers have lost their jobs, while an estimated 11,000 new jobs have opened up in Japanese transplants.[44] The same pattern has been true in the auto parts industry, where local Japanese-owned production has displaced that of older U.S. plants. And as the U.S. auto industry continues its sales slump on into 1991, the Japanese producers, dealing from the strength of healthy balance sheets and still profitable operations, are announcing expansion plans while U.S. producers confronting billions of dollars of losses accelerate plant closings and layoffs. For the truth of the matter is that while a new Japanese plant may bring prosperity to Kentucky or Tennessee, it is progressively meaning unemployment and dislocation in other parts of the country where the U.S. auto industry still holds sway. And these cutbacks come on top of the plant closings and layoffs wrought by Japanese exports to the U.S.

"Competition will be the *Nightmare on Elm Street*," Robert B. McCurry, executive vice president of Toyota's U.S. sales organization, said while discussing Toyota's plans to more than double its American car- and truck-building capacity by 1995. Toyota's goal is to boost its total sale of cars and trucks in the U.S. from imports and domestic production to 1.5 million units a year by the middle of the decade from a little less than 1 million in 1990. McCurry's reference to the particularly gory *Elm Street* movie may be apt, for as he noted "there are too many players in a volatile market."[45] His October 1989 announcement is also pretty cheeky, since it came at a time when the Big Three were cutting production because sales were already slowing. But then part of the *zaibatsu* way of doing business is to heighten the attack for market share when a competitor or competitors show signs of weakness. What with its doubling its Georgetown capacity and building three new factories in Japan, Toyota is certainly following this strategy. And it is also broadening the line of cars it sells Americans to include its luxury Lexus, so that its impact on domestic

American producers is even greater. Commenting on this pattern of aggressive capital investment to gain a competitive advantage, Masaru Yoshitomi, director general of Japan Economic Planning Agency's research institute, said: "It has happened before and I suspect we are seeing it again. Pioneering companies try to make investments during a recession, usually to reduce their labor costs. And in most cases it has worked."[46] In such an environment there are no handouts, no charity to outsiders. Market share lost is lost, in most cases, for good.

Globally, the picture isn't any more encouraging even though the international operations of the Big Three have been their major profit centers in recent years. In 1960, GM, Ford and Chrysler together built more than half of the world's cars. Today, they account for less than a third of the world's output.[47] John Casesa of Wertheim, Schroeder & Co. predicts that by the year 2000 Japan's gains in the U.S. and Europe will give its automakers 40 percent of global sales up from 28 percent today, while Detroit's share will drop to 28 percent.[48]

The thing that's different is that, as the Japanese auto producers' presence in the U.S. has burgeoned, it has also changed. American producers may have greatly increased the quality of their cars as all of the Big Three are wont to say in their ads. During 1990 GM spent millions telling Americans in somewhat boring and embarrassing ads how much it had improved the quality of its cars, while Chrysler chairman Lee Iacocca hit the road to promote the idea that consumers preferred his cars to Japan's. Certainly, Georgetown has good reason to be proud of the quality of its Camrys, just as GM, Ford and Chrysler should be pleased with the quality gains they've made. But as American producers have come closer to equaling Japanese auto producers on quality, Japanese automakers have sped ahead of their American competitors on other planes such as product development and technology.[49] Besides broadening the line of cars they sell in the U.S., so that they now offer a full price range of cars, Japanese firms have set up design and engineering centers here so that they can manufacture cars specifically for the U.S. market. Moreover, Japanese transplant carmakers can still manufacture cars for about $700 less and in less time than their U.S. competitors.[50]

"There is no question that there will be a U.S. automobile industry," says University of Michigan's professor Vladimir Pucik, "it's just that the owners will be different."[51] This is not an extreme, far-fetched statement. Think of what happened to the U.S. consumer electronics industry. Televisions, VCRs and stereos are still manufactured in the U.S., but except for struggling Zenith, a few Koreans, and French investors, the plants' owners are Japanese.

3

Tinseltown
and Tin Pan Alley

If you don't want Japan to buy it, then don't sell it.

—Akio Morita, Sony chairman[1]

Hollywood, unlike Detroit, has found a product that the Japanese can't improve upon.

—Roberto Goizueta, head of Coca-Cola Co.,
former owner of Columbia Pictures[2]

It's probably the first time anyone looked at rocker Cyndi Lauper and thought software. Hardware maybe. Cyndi Lauper looks and acts tough as nails. But software?

Yet, there she stood—red fishnet stockings, grey, yellow, orange and neon green miniskirt, yellow spiked hair with a few black Dalmatian spots—a vision of rock stardom happily smiling from Akio Morita's well-tailored, grey-suited embrace. Software was very much on the Sony Corporation chairman's mind. Software, that is, of the entertaining kind: the CBS records, videos, discs and tapes Cyndi Lauper makes that drive the VCRs, stereos and CD players Sony produces—Sony's hardware.

By the time the picture of Ms. Lauper and Morita's sweet embrace made it to the cover of the *New York Times Magazine* in September 1988,[3] marrying software with hardware—American entertainment with Japanese electronics[4]—had been a prime pursuit of Morita's for more than a few years. It was a hot pursuit that would soon take him to Hollywood where he again would display his yen for companies whose name begins with C—namely Columbia Pictures—as another partner to fulfill and add synergy to his grand design for Sony.

"Sony and CBS Records, What a Romance!" was the title of the *Times* cover story telling how Sony, after long, arduous negotiations, had bought the world's largest record company, CBS Records, from CBS Inc. for $2 billion. The sale came only a few days after the Black Monday crash knocked Wall Street to its knees. Audacious as the October 1987 purchase of CBS Records was, it was just the beginning of an incredible buying spree in the U.S. that would have Sony spending about $6 billion in all in less than two years. "After we acquired CBS Records I thought, now we have become the largest maker of music software in the world. And Sony is the largest video hardware company. So why don't we have video software? Ever since, my mind has been set on making an acquisition in video software . . . ," Morita said of his all-encompassing design.[5]

It is a design that, if it works, will give Sony and its followers such as Matsushita a dominant position in electronic entertainment and possibly computer hardware in the decades to come. Taken to the extreme, such a design could mean that Sony and Matsushita's market position will become so large that U.S. entrants will be excluded from their own market. "Marrying the medium and the message" in Marshall McLuhan's famous phrase,[6] also gives Sony a fast running start in the multibillion-dollar high definition television field—a field that will be a prime sector of electronics-driven growth in the twenty-first century and one in which the near moribund U.S. consumer electronics industry has a chance of regaining much lost ground. The U.S. has the technology—perhaps the leading technology—and the vast American market giving it the potential of being a major factor in HDTV, but it must marshall its forces now so as not to replay past debacles such as the loss of the consumer electronics industry to Japanese firms. Sony, Matsushita and the rest of Japan's electronics giants, with the aid and goading of the Japanese government, are already running full speed ahead in the development of HDTV. Moreover, a European consortium of companies backed by the European Community is also in the fast track. Given the chance the U.S. has in this area, losing out in this vital area would be a disgrace. Forming a business-government consortium to back U.S. development of HDTV should be a national priority. Commenting on the U.S. government's lack of support for HDTV development, MIT dean Lester Thurow said, "If the administration persists in this attitude, the U.S. could be a second-or-third rate industrial power in the year 2000, and President Bush will be remembered as the Herbert Hoover of industrial competitiveness."[7]

To position itself as an entertaining electronics giant, with major, global stakes in developing electronic markets, Sony is establishing a new stage in its distinct *zaibatsu*-like way of doing business in the U.S.—a way which on the surface looks very different from that practiced by Toyota and other Japanese firms operating in the U.S., but in substance is very similar. Sony, in effect, is much further along in creating a distinct presence in the U.S. than many of its compatriots. A key to gaining a dominant position in the hard and soft business of entertaining people is the *zaibatsu*-like vertically integrated structure Sony is building along Morita's monumental plans. It's a long, long-term bet on Morita's and Sony's part, but the payoff could be huge. And even if all the hoped-for synergy doesn't work out, investing in the American entertainment industry is a very good place to put one's money. Sales of American entertainment software have been growing at an annual rate that is the envy of most domestic industries, and it is one of the few American wares sold worldwide that accounts for a trade surplus—a surplus amounting to $8 billion a year, only outranked by aerospace.[8]

Along the way to achieving its goal and assembling its entertainment package, Sony would pick up Columbia Pictures for $3.4 billion and Guber Peters Entertainment Co., producers of such hits as *Rain Man* and *Batman*, for close to $500 million in an extremely messy and litigious acquisition.[9] And also along the way Sony's entertainment foray would attract a number of Japanese investors following Sony's lead and a number of vociferous detractors. Besides giving new meaning and scope to the concept of corporate vertical integration—notwithstanding Ms. Lauper and Morita's embrace which suggested a more horizontal leaning, Sony's purchase of CBS Records and Columbia Pictures also offers classic examples of the contrast between Japanese long-range planning and American business's short-range goals.

"Twenty years from now history will prove us right,"[10] said an obviously delighted Morita after buying CBS Records. Equally pleased at the time was CBS president, Laurence A. Tisch. His gratification was more immediate. Tisch no longer had to dither about what the cyclical and often unpredictable records division might do to quarterly earnings. He could just put Sony's cash in dependable U.S. treasuries.

Buying up some of America's stellar cultural assets was a bold move even for someone who'd grown up before the war in Nagoya's "rich man's street," a rich kid, from an old-rich, sake-brewing family, living across the street from the Toyodas of Toyota—tennis courts in both back yards, butlers at the door and chauffeur in driveway; someone who'd almost flunked out of school on several occasions because he spent so much time studying the magazine *Wireless and Experiments* and tinkering and tinkering, trying to build his own electric phonograph so he could hear his own voice; someone who began his business career inauspiciously in a bombed-out Tokyo department store, attempting to manufacture a rice cooker that ran either too hot or too cold but never just right. It was a bold move even for someone who ended up producing the world's first transistor radios and eventually gave the world the Walkman. So the man whose last name, Morita, means "prosperous rice field" and his first, Akio, "enlightened" or "uncommon," had come a long,[11] long way to hug Cyndi Lauper, who'd come all the way from Brooklyn to make it big on the cover of *Rolling Stone* and the *New York Times Magazine*. By the time he'd finished his $6-billion spending spree, he'd also proven he could do pretty much what he wanted to do with impunity—even write a book highly critical of America, *The Japan That Can Say No*—and, damn the torpedoes, go full speed ahead. He'd also totally transformed the weight and balance of Sony, making it in some ways more American than Japanese.

With their purchase of CBS Records, Cyndi Lauper wasn't the only bit of software Morita and Sony were getting for their $2 billion. Along with Ms. Lauper, Sony got a company with an illustrious past dating back to the late nineteenth century when its first recording stars were John Philip Sousa and the U.S. Marine Band, to the jazz and blues greats of the 1920s, 30s and 40s—Duke Ellington, Bessie Smith, Billie Holiday, Count Basie and Benny Goodman. It was also Columbia that in 1948 introduced the first $33\frac{1}{3}$ r.p.m. long-playing or LP record that was to revolutionize the recording industry. It meant that now-deceased Columbia artist Leonard Bernstein could record whole symphonies on one LP and the cast of *My Fair Lady, West Side Story, South Pacific* or *A Chorus Line* could do the same. Then there was CBS Records' huge stable of superstars, running from the Rolling Stones, Bob Dylan, Simon and Garfunkel, Aretha Franklin, Bruce Springsteen, the Byrds, and Barbra Streisand, to Billy Joel, Gloria Estefan and Michael Jackson. On top of all this highly talented software, Sony got a management, led by flamboyant CBS lawyer Walter Yetnikoff, that wanted to work under Sony rather than tightfisted Laurence Tisch of CBS, a man more interested in the bottom line than the frequently quixotic business of running a record company. If CBS Records' divorce from CBS was far from friendly, verging on acrimonious at times, its marriage with Sony appeared at the time just what Yetnikoff was looking for. Less than three years after the CBS Records-Sony merger Yetnikoff left the record company, apparently fed up, though he departed $20 million richer.[12]

Sony, however, was just beginning its romancing of American firms. A few weeks shy of Black Monday's second anniversary and its purchase of CBS Records, Sony announced the biggest Japanese takeover yet—the $3.4-billion purchase and assumption of $1.2 billion in debt of troubled Columbia Pictures from Coca-Cola Co. Sony's purchase of CBS Records had been controversial, but the stir it created was minor compared with the commotion that brewed up after the Columbia Pictures deal was announced.[13] Columbia Pictures may have been having operational problems, but what it offered Sony was an entrée into movie making and an incredible library of 2,700 films that includes *Lawrence of Arabia, On the Waterfront* and *Bridge on the River Kwai*—all made in Columbia's glory days. Other than such recent hits as *Ghostbusters 2* and *When Harry Met Sally,* Columbia's studio operations had been floundering despite Coca-Cola's efforts to turn them around. Sony also got some 260 television properties that include "Designing Women" and "Jeopardy."

Some may not think of "Jeopardy" or *Ghostbusters 2* as national treasures, but such fare does represent a portion of American culture that is seen, sold and enjoyed around the world, accounting for a multibillion-dollar annual trade surplus. They are a very vital part of the heart and soul of America, just as Detroit and Pittsburgh make up the guts of the American economy and Silicon Valley the brains. They are also an essential part of America's "Pop Culture" that pervades almost all walks of American life.

Even trashy American sitcoms and game shows are frequently far superior to their Japanese counterparts, which are often produced with a remarkable lack of sophistication. So it's not surprising that Sony and other Japanese firms have made forays into Hollywood and Broadway, though by and large on a much smaller scale than Sony. C. Itoh & Co., Suntory Ltd. and Tokyo Broadcasting Systems Inc. formed a consortium to invest $15 million in MGM / UA Communications Co. to help produce three movies,[14] while Fujisankei Communications group provided former Columbia Pictures head, David Puttnam, with $10 million to make pictures.[15] Then just a month and a half before Sony made its move into Tinseltown, Victor Company of Japan (JVC), the Matsushita Electric Industrial Co. subsidiary that created the VHS video format used worldwide, signed a contract with Hollywood producer, Lawrence Gordon, under which the giant consumer electronics company provided the producer or co-producer of *Field of Dreams, Die Hard* and *48 Hours* with over $100 million to make movies.[16] At the time the JVC deal was announced the company told the *Financial Times*, "We thought there might be problems in buying a big studio. We wanted to be sensitive to the feeling in the U.S. We feel that we have very much to learn about films, so we think that this is quite a good deal."[17] Taking a similarly cautious stance was Seiichiro Niwa, senior managing director of JVC. Commenting on Sony's Hollywood gamble—and the deal is certainly not without its risks, Niwa said: "Hollywood is America's most representative art. . . . If a French company bought Tokyo's Kabuki theater, Japanese would object."[18]

Matsushita's diffidence didn't last very long. The Osaka-based archrival of Sony, known for its Panasonic, Technics and Quasar brands and a somewhat plodding management style, began negotiations in late September 1990 for the acquisition of MCA Inc., owner of Universal Pictures, MCA Television, Geffen Records and publisher, G. P. Putnam's Sons. By the end of November the deal was completed for $6.1 billion,[19] making Matsushita's acquisition of MCA the largest ever made by a Japanese firm and giving it a lineup similar to the one Sony had assembled. Matsushita's goal in acquiring MCA is apparently similar, in that it wishes to combine its hardware with MCA's software which includes a 3,000-film library with such blockbuster titles as *E.T.* and *Jaws*. The acquisition is not without its ironies, since it was MCA who in the 1970s fought the sale of home VCRs all the way to the

U.S. Supreme Court, lost and has now been taken over by the world's largest producer of VCRs, Matsushita.[20] The MCA-Matsushita merger is also bound to heighten the already fierce competition with Sony in HDTV and videodiscs. While $6 billion plus is a huge sum, Matsushita, which is about twice the size of Sony, could have paid for it out of its cash accounts without any outside financing if it had chosen to. As of March 1990 Matsushita had $12 billion in cash and another $13 billion in short-term securities.

Discussing the competitive fears the Sony and Matsushita deals have engendered, *BusinessWeek* writer Neil Gross said, "At first blush, such arguments may seem overblown. Japan, after all, is no threat in entertainment. Hollywood is hardly Silicon Valley. And America wrote off consumer electronics more than a decade ago. But the media/technology conglomerates Sony and Matsushita envision constitute a new model of vertical integration. Unlike any existing companies, these two will control both the medium and the message in what the Japanese call the New Information Age."[21] Then, less than a month after the MCA-Matsushita deal was revealed, another major Hollywood-Tokyo deal was set. Walt Disney Co. said that a partnership of Japanese investors and banks would put up close to $1 billion to finance most of its future films. One of the deciding factors in hooking up with the Japanese investors was a lower cost of capital than that offered by its former American investors, Silver Screen Partners.[22]

Sony, for its part, certainly wasn't inhibited by qualms similar to Matsushita's initial fears. In fact, soon after announcing the Columbia Pictures deal, Morita said he'd expected some of the heated reaction it provoked though he hadn't anticipated that it would become as virulent as it did. Speaking at a special meeting of foreign journalists in Tokyo, Morita conceded "Hollywood has a special meaning for American people. Movie stars have a special meaning for American people. We may have to face strong criticism."[23] Morita's comments proved to be quite an understatement. Anti-Japanese sentiment that had been smoldering as Japan bought up more and more of America burst into flame when the Sony-Columbia deal was announced. In early October 1989 when *Newsweek* magazine polled Americans about the transaction, 43 percent felt it was a bad thing while only 19 percent said it was a good thing. Moreover, 52 percent of those polled said

Japan's economic power posed a greater threat to the U.S. than the Soviet Union's military might.[24] Congress, taking its lead from the public, was also up in arms, with U.S. congresswoman Helen Delich Bentley urging the Bush administration, a staunch supporter of foreign investment in the U.S., to investigate the anti-trust implications of the deal—to no avail.

Still others claim that if Federal Communications Commission regulations adopted in 1970 didn't prohibit the TV networks from owning and syndicating the programs they broadcast, the major networks would have been lining up to buy a Columbia Pictures or an MCA since it would give them vertical control over their programming and the multibillion-dollar rewards of TV reruns now collected by Hollywood studios and independent producers.[25] As it was, MCA apparently attracted no suitors other than Matsushita, even though their merger talks were public knowledge for well over two months before the deal was consummated. Commenting on the lack of suitors, Lazard Frères & Co. managing partner and MCA board member Felix Rohatyn said, ''I had not gotten one telephone call.''[26]

Fueling the anti-Japanese and anti-Sony feeling was the unauthorized publication of *The Japan That Can Say No* that Morita wrote with right-wing politician Shintaro Ishihara. Copies of the book were making the rounds on Capitol Hill and across corporate America just around the time the Columbia deal was revealed. In the book Morita and Ishihara contend Japan has reached a level of technological and economic independence and superiority that gives Japan the right to say no to American demands it finds unreasonable. Though much of what Morita said in the book about America and American business practices was not new—Morita had long been on record for saying that corporate America was largely to blame for its decline, coupling his criticism with Ishihara's gave it a whole new spin. It was not the first time Morita had made statements such as ''we Japanese plan and develop our business strategies 10 years ahead, while Americans seem to be concerned only with profits 10 minutes from now.''[27] But to find Morita's strong, outspoken statements appearing in a book where Ishihara says that Japan in a pique could cut off sales of strategic semiconductors to the U.S. and instead sell them to the Soviet Union was indeed a shocker. In a similarly inflammatory vein, Ishihara suggests in a section entitled ''Racial Prejudice Is at the Root of Japan Bashing'' that ''during the Second World War Americans bombed civilian targets in Germany but only in Japan did they use the atomic bomb. While they refuse to admit it, the only reason they could use the atomic bomb on Japan was because of their racial attitude towards Japan. . . . At times it appears to me that the Americans behave more like mad dogs than watch dogs."[28] Also galling, and casting Morita in a bad light, was the fact that while the book was a bestseller in Japan, Morita and Ishihara had no intention of publishing it in English. Ishihara has relented and his part of the book will be published in the U.S., without Morita's contribution.

If these factors weren't enough to stoke Japan-bashing fires and provoke more reasoned concern about Japan's increasing financial stake in the U.S., another event occurred a few weeks later to steel emotions. At the end of October usually conservative Mitsubishi Estate, a key actor in the world's largest industrial grouping, the Mitsubishi group, came through with a shocker. For a mere $846 million Mitsubishi Estate, which has holdings in Tokyo worth $80 billion or more, bought a 51 percent interest in the Rockefeller group. In terms of Japan-U.S. relations the timing could not have been worse. The group, which controls 19 mid-Manhattan buildings including Rockefeller Center, sought out Mitsubishi as a buyer so that the Rockefeller family could diversify its holdings and even though Mitsubishi's stake in the Rockefeller group will most probably be reduced to less than 20 percent by the turn of the century, to many Americans sale of interest in Rockefeller Center was even more troubling than the Columbia Pictures deal. If the films in Columbia Pictures' library can be considered a cultural treasure, their identity with the American public is film by film—*Lawrence of Arabia* or *On the Waterfront*—and not primarily associated with the name Columbia Pictures. Manhattan's Rockefeller Center, on the other hand, looms large as a massive group of buildings soaring from the core of the Big Apple. Home of the Rockettes, it is a cultural icon visited by hundreds of thousands of Americans every year—a physical symbol of America. And then, of course, there is the Rockefeller name—a name connected with all the riches and might of America and here, even they were selling out to the Japanese. For a time it seemed as if everything was lost and people behaved, as Art Buchwald suggested facetiously in a column, as if Mitsubishi would have the temerity to rename Radio City "Radio City Tojo Hall" or have the "Kamikaze Ice Skating Rink at Mitsubishi Center on Fifth Avenue.''[29] Certainly the sale, coupled with Sony's invasion of Hollywood, came as quite a blow.

However, bruised egos usually mend and the furor soon abated, with few bothering to inquire further into Sony's software plans for CBS Records and Columbia Pictures. Also ignored is the fact that, like it or not, Sony is already very much part of the American landscape and culture, selling products Americans will frequently pay a premium for; that its American roots run deep; and that it's done very well by CBS Records while keeping most American management in place. Michael Schulhof, head of Sony's American operations and one of the chief engineers of Sony's headlong plunge into software, said in an interview that two years after the acquisition CBS Records' profitability had doubled and that under Sony it was worth over $4 billion.

''Sony is now a strategically balanced entertainment company,'' Schulhof said in Sony's art and technology-filled offices high above New York's 57th St. ''The balance between hardware and software, between audio and video on a worldwide basis all account for roughly a quarter each of the major components. I'd like to see all of them growing equally.'' He also said he expected there would be a creative interplay between the hard and software parts of the company. ''We recognize that our hardware can't give anybody enjoyment without software and that new markets for software require new hardware.''

If Sony's multibillion-dollar design actually works, it will offer America a new sort of formidable competition, that will be nurtured by Sony on American soil to compete here and around the world. It will also give Sony an even stronger hold on the new, $40-billion a year, high definition television market stretching all the way from the movie studio to the nation's living room. ''We can't guess where the hardware innovations will lead . . . but we will be prepared with the software,'' Morita would later say in discussing his multibillion-dollar software chase. And ready he is.[30]

Sony, in effect, is in the second stage of its *zaibatsu*-like behavior in the U.S. There may be a number of Japanese firms that have been making forays into the U.S., but few have reached the stage of development Sony has in this country. Having joined in the decimation of the U.S. consumer electronics industry and having been at the forefront of Japanese firms setting up manufacturing facilities in the U.S. with its San Diego TV plant, Sony is now branching out and expanding its field of influence. It is highly doubtful that Japanese auto producers, powerful and efficient as they are, would ever be able to do what Japan's consumer electronics firms have been able to pull off—virtually obliterating American-owned firms manufacturing TVs, stereos and the like. Amazingly enough, more than half of Sony's worldwide operations in terms of revenues are now American-based. Ironically, Sony, as a result of these acquisitions and investment in the U.S., is more American than many international, American-based firms.

Unlike Toyota or Nissan or Mitsubishi Motors, Sony didn't arrive in the U.S. with a host of camp followers to complete the vertical integration of its operations. Rather, to a large degree, it set up its own subsidiary operations in the U.S. or bought up companies such as CBS Records and Columbia Pictures to reach its goal. In point of fact, there is no way Sony could have completed its vision of marrying hard- and software with the acquisition of a Japanese record company or film studio. For the sort of global software it needed to complete the puzzle, it had no choice but to go to New York and Hollywood. This is one reason Sony's move to the U.S. looks so different from a Toyota's. In addition, autos are really a mature product that can be enhanced by new technology but are not constantly evolving into previously unimagined forms as Sony's products are.

However, beneath the distinct corporate facades created by a Sony or Toyota there is a common, powerful motivating force that ties such operations together in a similar, *zaibatsu*-like fashion. It is the desire to control, to the exclusion of outside parties—to control one's corporate operations from top to bottom, which is the essence of vertical integration. Of the Columbia Pictures acquisition *Newsweek* accurately pointed out: "the goal was vertical integration—putting together a company that can serve every segment of the entertainment market."[31] The power inherent in such single-minded control is a lesson the boys from Nagoya, the Toyodas and Morita, apparently learned early on in their corporate career. It is a characteristic that lies at the center of the *zaibatsu* way of doing business. For Toyota, the lines of control run through the interlocking minority shareholdings and concurrent business relationships, whereas for Sony outright ownership of most of its 214 group companies[32] has been the preferred mode of control. The CBS Records and Columbia Pictures acquisitions are part and parcel of this sort of control, so it's not surprising that when Morita went after them he bought the whole show. Speaking at the time of the Columbia Pictures acquisition, Morita said: "The strength of my company is we have a policy of producing all key components ourselves. Service industries (which make up more and more of the U.S. economy) do not add value. It's production that adds value. Instead of seeking to buy key components from Japan, American industries should produce those components by themselves."[33]

Now with CBS Records and Columbia Pictures, Sony and Morita have created a unique company that will knock the competition out of their socks if their plan succeeds. Even if it doesn't work completely, Sony has CBS's and Columbia's incredible libraries to churn, reissue and repackage. The closest an American company comes to what Sony has structured is Warner Communications. While Warner will continue to be a formidable competitor to Sony-CBS-Columbia on the entertainment side, it may find itself competitively disadvantaged since it does not have the additional hardware leverage Sony does.

"Software and hardware" says Norio Ohga, Sony's president and CEO, "are two wheels of the same cart."[34] He and Morita may be right and if they are, companies such as Warner's cart may be left in the ditch.

Sony is particularly sensitive about the issue of software, since it feels its technically superior Betamax video recorder lost out to the VHS format because there wasn't enough software produced to play on its machines. It obviously has no intention of being caught short like that again. Commented Sony's Schulhof: "We failed to recognize the importance of prerecorded software. . . . It's not a mistake we plan to repeat."[35]

Over the years the thing that Sony has realized more than most of its competitors is that Americans and the rest of the world—because of changing lifestyles and technological innovations—will take their entertainment in different ways and places. In the era of "Ozzie and Harriet" and "Leave it to Beaver," television sets were large, cumbersome objects taking the place of honor in America's living or family rooms and programming was limited to only a few channels—CBS, ABC, NBC and some local affiliates. Now, thanks largely to Sony and its fierce Japanese competitors, watching TV has become a ubiquitous pastime. Smaller TVs with mini-miniaturized innards first made their way to sit on kitchen counters, to rest on bedside tables and to perch on bathroom stools. In no time at all they could be plugged into the car lighter, taken to the beach or put out on the porch to watch the White Sox or the Yankees. With this ubiquity of the machinery came an ever-broadening array of programming, ranging from cable, to independent broadcasters, to VCRs. Sony, in particular, had found a two-way street to capitalize on where changing populations and new technology can play off each other.

Think of the Walkman invented by Sony, and championed by Morita against a great deal of opposition at Sony. There was no real need for the Walkman and certainly not a readily definable market. But Sony managed to make it seem a necessity, and along the way to creating an overnight success, changed the place where people listen to tapes or FM rock. Crowning every sweaty jogger and young female executive dressed for success with Sony headgear as they made their way down the street took a leap of the imagination that few could envision until it happened. Out of the phenomenal growth of Walkman came increased demand for software, meaning more tapes were used and more radio time listened to. Then the Walkman opened the way for the Discman portable CD player which is helping expand the CD market.

Such is the genius of Sony and Morita that their products have already had a cultural impact on America, having become an integral part of the way Americans live. To be sure, Mitsubishi, Toshiba, Panasonic and JVC have also found their way into American homes and psyches, but not to the degree Sony has. Even before the CBS Records and Columbia Pictures acquisitions, Sony had a unique position in the American cultural landscape. Sony made its name in the U.S. selling high-quality products that played or received what CBS and other entertainment companies sold on the airwaves and in record stores around the world. Barbra Streisand, Pink Floyd and Bruce Springsteen's LPs took a spin on its stereos, and later compact disks played their songs and music on Sony Discmen.

However, when Morita talks about getting the entertainment software for his hardware he really is not talking about a revolutionary idea for the entertainment industry. In some ways he's making a leap of imagination, but in others he's harking back to old ways. Up until the late 1940s movie producers capitalized on a similar idea. Recognizing the power and profits that could be generated from controlling the show all the way from the studio lot to the movie theater and popcorn stand, the studios owned the whole show from production, to distribution, to exhibition in their theaters. Paramount-produced pictures were distributed by Paramount and shown in Paramount-owned theaters across the land, and the same was true for the other major studios. It was vertical integration Hollywood style. In effect, Paramount's splendidly overblown picture palaces were the hardware for films Paramount made on its Hollywood lots. They were the place where one viewed movies, whereas today the so-called movie-going public has a variety of places it can watch movies. Hardware produced by Sony and other Japanese firms are what have changed the viewing locus. By the late 1940s, however, the Justice Department determined that this arrangement was anti-competitive and gave the studios the choice of divesting one of their three operations—production, distribution or exhibition. All the major studios chose to get rid of their hardware—their movie theaters.

There are other parallels from the past. After Thomas Edison invented the motion picture projector, he initially had to produce and distribute movies to make his marvelous machine economically viable. Following a somewhat similar line, the Victor Talking Machine Co. got into the business of selling Victor records to entice people to buy its Victrola record players, while RCA was able to boost the sales of its radios as more and more Americans listened to its NBC radio networks.[36]

As far as Sony is concerned, a chief rationale for purchasing Columbia Pictures was what the studio's software could do for its efforts in the global commercialization of high definition television—a market that is conservatively estimated to be worth $40 billion a year by 2010. There is also the thought that as Sony's and other's prowess in making HDTV equipment grows, there will be a spillover in which HDTV screens and technology will be used in such areas as three-dimensional designing of autos, highly sophisticated computer graphics and medical imaging. As Schulhof said, "bringing 35 millimeter motion picture quality into someone's home is the ultimate goal which we have for hardware and software." However, Schulhof claims that it is not Sony's goal to control the hardware and software market for HDTV, thus locking out a good deal of competition if their system succeeds. He noted that Sony could never produce all the software people will want and that he expected a great deal of competition. But still, if they do succeed in creating the sort of synergy they expect from this hardware-software combination, they and possibly Matsushita will be setting the standard for much of the market. It would be a very enviable and lucrative position to be in. It would also make Sony an even bigger power to be reckoned with in the field of entertainment.

Anyone who has seen HDTV in Tokyo cannot but be impressed with the phenomenal clarity and depth of the images transmitted by HDTV. Even if the first HDTV sets introduced in Japan at the end of 1990 cost about $34,000 each and there was only one hour of HDTV programming a day—not to worry—Japanese electronics manufacturers such as Sony and Matsushita are past masters at soon lowering the price of an expensive consumer product and widening the market.[37] "It is much like the first transistor radio or the first home VCRs," said Sony's manager of HDTV development, Hisafumi Yamada, at the time of the HDTV sets' introduction. "You have to do something at the first stage to get people accustomed to the idea. We think the demand is out there."[38]

But as with any project as massive and potentially rewarding as HDTV, there are bound to be problems along the way. To begin with, the major players in the development of HDTV—Europe, the U.S. and Japan—have not agreed on a common standard for HDTV and basically each needs the other's markets to have its system become really economically viable. Ironically, but not so surprisingly, the U.S. government, which controls access to the largest potential market for HDTV in the world, has done the least towards helping launch a viable system. Initial efforts by Bush administration Commerce secretary Mosbacher to muster government support and funding for HDTV research were ambushed by presidential advisers Michael Boskin and Richard Darman, who carry free market economic portfolios and have repeatedly manifested a marked abhorrence for government involvement in private-sector business. So while the Japanese government has been backing the development of HDTV technologies and a consortium of Japanese firms, including Sony, Matsushita, Toshiba, public TV network NHK and others have spent over $1.4 billion in the area, and while France's Thomson and Holland's Philips have been heavily subsidized by the European Commission in their HDTV efforts, the U.S. is lagging far, far behind in the economic force they've marshaled to support and advance American HDTV.

Still, the race is by no means over and the U.S. may end up as the winner, since its technology could very well carry the day. What the U.S. must do though, is use that lead to re-establish itself as a major factor in the manufacture of the HDTV machines that will use its technology. What's happened is that American scientists apparently have pulled far ahead of the Japanese, who until the beginning of this decade were thought to be the closest to mass commercialization of HDTV. Running quite far behind in second place is the European consortium. Commenting on this dramatic turn of events, FCC chairman Alfred Sikes said, "the conventional wisdom is that we are a poor third in HDTV. It's my view that U.S. companies are on the leading edge."[39]

What General Instruments Corporation, American Telephone & Telegraph Co. in a joint venture with troubled Zenith Electronics Corporation, and MIT have been separately working on is a so-called "digital system" of broadcasting HDTV and much to the surprise of many doubters, they've apparently come up with a far superior mode of transmitting HDTV. The immediate advantage to the digital system of transmission over the so-called "analog method" championed by the Japanese and European groups is twofold: HDTV programming transmitted digitally can be carried over ordinary television frequencies and therefore, it can also be easily received by local broadcasters. By contrast, the analog method transmits HDTV pictures in waves and must use satellites. For local TV stations this is a great drawback, since it is very difficult for them to receive transmissions via this route. In addition, digital transmission, which is the way computers operate and communicate in 1s and 0s, has other major advantages over analog. It easily eliminates double images and static and means that once the technology is developed, a television can become interactive and operate like or as a computer. The FCC has until 1993 to choose a system and the bets are that it will be one of the American-perfected digital systems, especially since the FCC has said that any system it approves must be capable of transmitting programming to local broadcasters. All in all, American technology now apparently has a huge advantage, but American manufacturers and the government must do more to capitalize on this lead and turn it into a real bonanza. Otherwise it will become the sort of fiasco University of Michigan professor of Public Policy Weston Vivian has envisioned: "Nothing says we're going to be the people who manufacture these sets. We could easily be the

94

inventor of algorithms and computer chips that create marvelous opportunities for Japanese monitors.''[40]

Certainly, Japanese manufacturers have the lead in the sort of high resolution television screens compatible with HDTV, but the U.S. does still have one remaining manufacturer of TVs, Zenith Electronics, which rejoined the major leagues in hooking up with AT&T to develop a digital system. This changes the whole picture for Zenith. If Zenith were still operating on its own in the HDTV area its prospects would be slim. Zenith has lost money on its operations for most of a decade and has considered selling off its TV-making business.[41] It would be a pity if this happened—if just as the U.S. and the world is about to enter the new electronics age of HDTV, the last remaining American producer of TVs were to cease manufacturing. Given the stakes involved, a loose consortium of American companies, studios, laboratories and universities should be formed with government backing to vertically integrate the U.S. lead in digital technology with manufacturing. This would be a great way and perfect time for the U.S. to re-enter and gain a dominant position in the consumer electronics industry. It should be a national priority. The Federal Communications Commission won't choose a standard until two years from now and like the Europeans it initially rejected the Japanese standard. However, as might be expected, Japanese HDTV producers have not taken initial rejection of their standard as a permanent no. Japanese producers are also already working on converting to digital. After all, persistence, especially in the face of adversity, is very much part of the *zaibatsu* way of doing business and it is their hope that, as their presence and expertise in HDTV become better known in the U.S., the regulatory climate will become receptive to their endeavors.

Sony, for its part, sees the $3.4-billion Columbia Pictures acquisition as just the ticket to establish the credibility of its HDTV expertise. Commenting on Columbia Pictures' potential in this area, Sony's Michael Schulhof said it would help ''to the extent that maybe we can demonstrate to people the unique advantages of HDTV. Once they see it, they will be unable to return to regular television, much the same way that someone who has a compact disk cannot go back to an LP.'' Specifically, what Sony has in mind is to have Columbia Pictures produce movies on HDTV tape using Sony's HDTV equipment and then making the tape into films that could be shown in movie theaters on Sony's equipment and seen at home on Sony TVs. Along these lines Sony has already provided Columbia Pictures with HDTV production equipment, so as to entice directors into using the format, which is apparently as rich in color and texture as 35-millimeter film and much easier to edit.[42] Creating HDTV film to equal the quality of conventional film currently in use by the studio has been a difficult task, but now Sony appears to have jumped this final hurdle, having produced a film of similar clarity.[43] Thus Columbia Pictures would provide the key to the vertical integration of Sony's HDTV operations by producing hit films on the HDTV format that would make buying Sony's hardware irresistible and vice versa. It would also mean that eventually there would be a larger market for the HDTV cameras, editing machines and special effects machines that Sony is already producing and selling. Sony is very well aware of what a larger market for its HDTV products and the felicities of economies of scale can do for its profits.

The synergy with Columbia Pictures doesn't end with Sony's growing HDTV presence, though if it succeeds to any degree it will be the most important aspect of the acquisition. Recently, Sony has had a runaway success with its lightweight 8-millimeter camera and the tiny 8-millimeter film cassettes that fit in the cameras. Because of their portability and ease of use, Sony's market has grown tremendously from just filming the kids at birthday parties and holiday celebrations. Here again, the idea is that use of this technology can be extended and that one way would be to create an 8-millimeter library of Columbia Pictures films that would be sold or rented in this format and would enlarge the appeal of the mode. In addition, Japan is now ripe for cable TV development.[44] According to Japan's Postal Ministry, about 13 million homes will be wired for cable within the decade, a turn of events that creates an ideal market for Sony's software. Sony could easily set up a cable TV station in Japan and program it with its Hollywood movies and videos made by its CBS Records stars. The Japanese love *Batman* and Michael Jackson doing his "Moon Walk." It's hard to believe there wouldn't be synergy there. Then, too, Sony is betting on the fact that world sales of films and music are expected to grow at 17 percent a year through the end of the decade, compared with a paltry 4 percent for audio and visual products.[45]

Of course, there are risks in the acquisition of Columbia Pictures and CBS Records, and seeking the synergy from marrying hardware and software could backfire. Critics of Sony's massive move into Tin Pan Alley and Tinseltown warn that Sony could be in for culture shock and that the sort of corporate mentality that built Sony into a premier global electronics firm is very different from the sort that succeeds in Hollywood. Much of Sony's success has come from the classic Japanese group structure where individual egos—except perhaps for Morita and his chieftains—count for much less than a general consensus, where job security is a constant and where respect for seniority still holds sway. Hollywood, of course, is the home and nurturing place of the star system, of D. W. Griffith, Samuel Goldwyn and Garbo; the place where the nail that sticks out isn't pounded down but encouraged, where success goes to the biggest ego, where movies are "directed" and not made by consensus. Then, too, outside investors in Hollywood have had a very poor track record, underlining the fact that past success such as Guber Peters' is no guarantee of future hits. Even highly bankable and experienced producers such as David Puttnam and stars such as Dustin Hoffman and Warren Beatty can produce huge flops. Witness Columbia's 1987 film *Ishtar,* which turned out to be one of Hollywood's biggest duds and helped precipitate Puttnam's departure as Columbia's studio head. So if Coca-Cola, one of America's premier companies, couldn't make a go of Columbia and readily sold it for a handsome profit of more than $2 billion, where does Sony get the chutzpah to think it can do any better? There is, of course, the software-hardware synergy that Sony envisions and that Coke didn't have. But Sony has every intention of turning Columbia Pictures around, as evidenced by its hard-won purchase of Guber Peters—a battle with Warner Communications that gave lie to the idea that the Japanese wouldn't stoop to make hostile takeover moves. There may be genius and simplicity to Morita's plan, if it works, but it is a gamble—no question about it—as often the most rational-sounding setups are.

4

Silicon Valley

Japanese investment is used as a vacuum cleaner for acquiring technology and exporting it home. If America intends to win the race based on innovation, it must stop selling its running shoes to the competitors.

—John Stern, Tokyo head of U.S. Electronics Association[1]

Without imminent changes, U.S. and European vendors of information systems hardware risk becoming subordinate research prototyping and distribution arms for the Japanese industry's vertically integrated industrial complexes.

—Charles H. Ferguson, *Harvard Business Review*[2]

For Silicon Valley, its claque and its detractors, the unveiling had all the tension and excitement of an opening night at the opera. There, up on the stage of San Francisco's Symphony Hall, was Steven P. Jobs, the ultimate high-tech entrepreneur—Mr. Silicon Valley incarnate. At 33 he was young, rich, lean and a survivor. Jobs, the brilliant, if sometimes mercurial, founder of Apple Computer Inc., had created the personal computer market almost single-handedly from the late seventies on, first with his user-friendly Apple II and then with his equally brilliant Macintosh computer launched in 1984. Along the way Apple and Jobs would revolutionize the way people around the world use and think about computers, bringing personal computing into the home, schoolroom and office. Moreover, as use of personal computers

spread and became more and more cost effective, the phenomenon would prove a formidable threat even to once-impregnable
mainframe producers IBM and Digital Equipment. By the early
eighties, Apple Computer was as bright and shiny as if it had
been polished by the teacher's pet. The worm, however, was
turning. A year after Apple brought the mouse-driven Macintosh
to market, Jobs had been ousted from his company by none other
than John Sculley, the man he'd personally hired away from
Pepsi to help sell the Macintosh and give Apple's entrepreneurial
operations more structure. Undaunted and in true Silicon Valley
fashion, Jobs bounced right back, forming a new computer company, Next Inc.—its aim: to create the next personal computer
that would revolutionize the industry as Apple had, a goal it has
yet to fully achieve.

So there he was at Symphony Hall, three years after his forced
departure from Apple in 1985, telling the throngs of interested
parties about the genius of the computer housed in Next's elegant
black cube. Originally designed to be sold to universities as
"scholar's work-stations,"[3] Jobs would later target a much larger
market for Next, aiming to establish his new personal computer
line as one of the three major desktop computers used primarily
by businesses. As his ads for Next would make clear, his vision
of Next's future was nothing if not ambitious. "In the 90's we'll
probably see only 10 real breakthroughs in computers. Here are
seven of them,"[4] proclaimed Next's ads, which went on to enu-
merate its unique, pace-setting virtues. Jobs was taking on all
comers competing to decorate the nation's corporate desktops,
and that included mammoth IBM and smaller Apple. In terms of
sophistication and applications, it was also readily apparent that
Next had made a technological mega-leap from the now seemingly slow and crotchety Apple II introduced just a decade before.
But there was also another big difference between the Apple II of
the late seventies and the Next of the nineties—a difference that
tells a lot about where the U.S. computer industry is headed.

The Apple II was state of the art American-style—Next is state
of the art, Zaibatsu America-style. When the Apple II was introduced all its parts, except for its screen, were made in the U.S.[5]
By contrast, at least 60 percent of Next's innards—the parts that
help make the "breakthroughs" of the nineties a reality—were
made by the Japanese. *Res ipsa loquitor*— the facts speak for themselves—and they're devastating. Next is by no means alone in

using a multitude of Japanese high-tech building blocks—many of which are now manufactured at Japanese-owned plants in the U.S.—to create the latest American computer. The sad fact is that many of the parts basic to building a computer are no longer manufactured by American firms, meaning that a Next has no choice but to use Japanese sources. All-important computer components such as floppy-disk drives, printers and dynamic random access memory chips (DRAMs) are now made chiefly by Japan's giant electronics firms, whose market dominance is quickly spreading to many other computer products.

Such a state of affairs is by no means happenstance. It goes hand in hand with Japan's efforts to develop a global computer industry bit by bit and be a world leader in technology, if not *the* world leader. It extends from buying into, or buying out, a host of high-tech companies in Silicon Valley, to bankrolling superstar computer experts at Princeton, MIT and Stanford.[6] It's part and parcel of the Japanese computer industry's phenomenal global growth. By 1992 the Japanese computer industry's share of the world market is projected to have risen to 42 percent from 10 percent in 1980, while the U.S.'s share will have dropped from 82 percent then to 38 percent during the same period. In other words, Japan will have surpassed the U.S. globally in little over a decade, if these projections of the world computer market hold true.[7] Says Intel president Andrew Grove: "Piece by piece they [the Japanese] have staked out the inside and outside of what's a computer. The trend is unmistakable."[8]

What's happening is that Japan's presence in high-tech America is growing in several parallel, *zaibatsu*-like patterns, each reinforcing the other and also America's dependence on Japan. Dependence nurtures a tightening of the web of control. It's happening here in Silicon Valley—a sunny, dusty valley running south from San Francisco to San Jose, as well as embodying the state of mind of and being a metaphor for high-tech America. It's a phenomenon that's spread from Silicon Valley, where the revolutionary microchip was born little more than 20 years ago, across America, to Texas, Illinois, Massachusetts and a number of other states. It's a trend that if it continues—and there is no indication it won't—directly attacks the economic standing of the United States in the coming century. Despite America's historic and up to now pre-eminent position in technology, American leadership in high-tech is losing out to the *zaibatsu* behemoth.

The computer-led electronics revolution, that will be the key factor in economic growth in the twenty-first century, was for the most part created by America and funded by American-led investors. More and more the revolution is being taken over, financed and mass-merchandised by Japanese firms operating here in the *zaibatsu* way. Quite simply, a country can not be a first-rate power in the twenty-first century if it is a second-rate player in this electronic revolution. It is a national problem that in the long run threatens America's economic fabric and security.

In some ways Japan's move into high-tech America is akin to Japanese automakers' creation of Auto Alley. In both cases, the sheer number of related Japanese companies involved is staggering. However, the nature and texture of Silicon Valley are very different from those of Auto Alley and its involvement in the American economy more pervasive and ultimately more important in terms of national economic survival. In Silicon Valley, given the youth and vitality of high-tech America, huge Japanese firms are chasing a moving target as new technology is unleashed at breakneck speed. By contrast, the aging U.S. auto industry is virtually a sitting duck, just ready to be plucked. In Silicon Valley the classic American entrepreneur, a term used infrequently to describe America's auto executives, is confronting the *zaibatsu* monolith and in many cases losing out. In Silicon Valley it's a different time warp, where high-tech development moves with much greater speed. The shelf life for an idea or product is very short and the monetary risk very high. Sony, of course, with its position in consumer electronics and its betting the ranch on HDTV, is an important player in Japan's massive sortie into high-tech America but it's in a different stage of development. As mentioned previously, Sony is already in a second stage of its *zaibatsu*-like development in America. It's not coming *de novo* to Silicon Valley, where it recently acquired Materials Research Corporation, a leading producer of chip-making equipment, for a bargain-basement price of $60 million.[9] Also Sony has always been somewhat of a rebel—a Japanese entrepreneur in high-tech ventures. By contrast, many Japanese firms coming to do business in high-tech America are just off the boat so to speak, a number only just recently having ventured into high-tech investments in Japan. But they've hit the ground running, their wallets bulging with long-term, patient capital to invest.

102

On one level, the Japanese group mentality is running full tilt here, accompanied by all the entangling trappings of the *zaibatsu* way. Huge Japanese electronics firms have arrived in packs to invest billions in Silicon Valley's most innovative firms and in setting up their own production facilities. Both types of investment fit snugly into vertically dependent structures. Lined up in San Jose and San Francisco and ready to loan funds at the lowest of low rates are branches of Japan's largest banks. Moreover, Japanese electronics giants got their first foothold here in a very *zaibatsu*-like way. By inundating the U.S. and world markets with chips sold below cost, they weakened competitors by the mid-1980s[10] and gained market share. Soon they bought into their import-battered American competitors on the cheap. Then, from a lowly position of producing commodity-type products, they relentlessly moved upstream to take over more of the higher-margin, high-tech markets. In broad strokes, Japanese firms' entry into Silicon Valley has been similar to that in other major American industries. However, the actual face-to-face confrontation between high-tech America and high-tech Japan has a distinct character of its own.

On another level, one sees the prototype American entrepreneur-inventor pitted against the group—*zaibatsu* way—in its purest form. Here one sees the raw power inherent in the modern-day, vertical integration of Japan's electronics giants and their horizontal relationships with other groups, the *zaibatsu* way. It's not just Japanese investment in Silicon Valley that's weighing heavily on high-tech America. It is the combined global weight of Japan's nine electronics giants—Hitachi, NEC, Fujitsu, Toshiba, Matsushita, Mitsubishi Electronics, Sony, Sharp and Sanyo—and their lesser competitors, positioning themselves in the U.S. and world markets that can prove so daunting for even the largest and most financially secure American high-tech firms. Only IBM, still the world's largest computer company, has the sort of organically and vertically integrated operation to compete against these companies. Having a Fujitsu or an NEC in fierce competition with a Next or even a much larger Intel is somewhat different from having Toyota or Nissan taking on General Motors or Ford. However, just as GM or Ford, a Next or an Intel is not competing against simply an Hitachi or NEC subsidiary or even the whole Hitachi or NEC operation in the U.S., but against the parallel, global power of the parent. Being canny and creative helps but it's not enough. The situation is far more complex than a David confronting a Goliath—sharp-shooting slingshot in hand.

Silicon Valley, for one, is not Rustbelt America. It doesn't need to be resuscitated. It doesn't need a jump-start. It can create jobs on its own. It can still lay claim to being high technology's birthplace and high technology's future, as Intel likes to say. Its strength has been and continues to be its ability to nurture the hundreds of small start-ups, many of which, like Apple, have turned into very viable operations. It's still a place where Japan has a great deal to learn and knows it. What's always been lacking is capital—long-term, patient capital—and this is truer now than ever. If structure has given strength to Japanese competitors, a lack of structure—a fluidity which encourages creativity—has been one of Silicon Valley's major strengths. These days, however, this very same lack of structure can also leave a small to medium-sized high-tech firm unprotected and undercapitalized when competing with Japan's giant electronics firms. When times got tough, as they do frequently for fledgling firms, they often have no one to turn to for help other than a Japanese firm. Not infrequently these arrangements turn into Faustian bargains. The stark reality is that Silicon Valley is at a distinct disadvantage when doing battle with Japan's much larger electronics firms, especially considering the fast-changing nature of the industry requiring ever-larger amounts of money. Time and technology are in a squeeze as the period between conception and full production becomes shorter and shorter and ever more costly. Just to launch a new generation of chips costs at least a billion dollars, and if one doesn't get to market soon enough, much of the investment in plant and equipment can be lost. But if the investment isn't made, then the technology is lost, as is the next generation. Silicon Valley needs more structured backing—more coming together to compete.

As Charles Ferguson, a former IBM analyst and currently a research associate at MIT, recently wrote in the *Harvard Business Review*:[11]

The Japanese electronics industry is controlled by a small number of enormous, diversified, vertically integrated corporate complexes. Nine companies, with revenues ranging from $9 billion to $60 billion each, dominate the Japanese semiconductor, semiconductor equipment, computer, telecommunications equipment, imaging, office equipment and consumer electronics sectors. Most of these companies also have close relationships with at least one of the six *keiretsu* that control 30 percent of all Japanese assets and whose leadership includes the world's ten largest banks, the world's seven largest trading companies and several of the world's largest insurance companies and securities firms.

Just as important, each major manufacturer leads a corporate complex that includes not only the parent company's divisions but also a network of subsidiaries, parts suppliers, subcontractors and capital equipment suppliers. . . . At the same time, Japanese producers have access to stable capital flows through both their parent companies and their banks. Thus they can absorb short-term losses and engage in comparatively risky, long-term R&D, thereby insulating themselves from the short-term financial pressures that plague U.S. companies.

At the center of this confrontation is control of, or at least the dominant position in the most important industry in the twenty-first century—the computer-microchip-laser-led technological revolution that will continue to change the way people live for many decades to come. Losing out in the steel or auto industries or consumer electronics is bad enough, but losing out in this endeavor is far worse. Without a commanding position in high technology, a country is at the mercy of competing nations and will eventually become a second-class citizen. As a second-class citizen, a nation evolves bit by bit into a kind of technological underclass, with its manufacturers denied the latest in technologically advanced supplies, such as the latest in computer hardware. Eventually, its workers become less skilled and less educated as the high-tech, high-value portion of a product—whether it be a car or a laptop computer—is created abroad or here under foreign, in this case Japanese, ownership.

The sort of diverse, yet frequently interdependent technology developed by an IBM, Next, Intel, or a Cray, or a start-up in Palo Alto, or an MIT laboratory stands to be the driving force of the information age—the brains of the telecommunications, finance and entertainment industries. Moreover, technological innovation is essential to every major industry, from the minicomputers guiding autos and auto production, from machine tools pro-grammed to form fenders to robots welding and painting car chassis, from cameras to CD players and coffee makers. Micro-chips—the wafer-thin heart of the high-tech revolution—may be the rice of the information age but it's a staple that's constantly being refined and redefined.

There is no way one can underestimate the importance of this phenomenon, which has changed the way people think, see, communicate and decide. High-tech America—Silicon Valley—continues to be at the forefront of technical development, but in-creasingly it is losing control of its environment—control of its factors of production. Rather than leading on all fronts, high-tech America is becoming increasingly and disturbingly dependent. Through dependency comes control—leveraged control, or the re-verse—lack of it. What you're seeing is the first stage of control being built in an oblique way. Once that control is established, it burgeons, spreading with rapidity.

Examples of this trend of dependency can be found inside al-most every computer product sold in America, whether it carries the Apple, Hewlett-Packard or Sun Microsystems label. Perhaps one of the most dramatic instances of this trend and one awaited with almost the same anticipation as Jobs's Next was Compaq Computer Corporation's October 1989 introduction of small, notebook-size computers, having the performance capabilities of many desktop computers while weighing from four to seven pounds.[12] Like Apple, Compaq had come from nowhere to grow into a major factor in the American personal and laptop computer market in the 1980s. Much was expected of Compaq and its so-called Compaq LTE, costing from $2,499 to $4,999. Compaq deliv-ered the goods as expected. However, as with Next, much of the little LTE's success could be attributed to the significant Japanese input. Its disk drives and liquid crystal display screens, some of the most innovative parts of the LTE, had been developed by the world's largest watch manufacturer, Japan's Citizen Watch, and in a first for Compaq, which was founded in 1981, it was allowing an outside firm, Citizen, to assemble some of its products. The LTE was being manufactured at Compaq's Houston plant and Citizen's Japan-based facility. Moreover, a look inside the LTE would reveal Compaq employed a number of other parts not manufactured by it, plus ''nonproprietary, industry standard ar-chitectures.''[13]

Next and Compaq may be small in comparison to IBM or Fujitsu but they are two of America's high-tech crown jewels, both of whose very existence is becoming increasingly dependent on Japan in these and other ways. Less than a year after Next's San Francisco debut, Next's ties to Japan grew stronger and more complex. On June 12, 1989, Canon Inc., a maker of photocopiers and cameras and a Next supplier of an advanced optical disk drive, paid $100 million for a 16.7 percent stake in Next, as well as rights to market Next's products in Japan and the rest of Asia. Paying $100 million for 16.7 percent of Next greatly increased the value of Next, inflating Jobs's $12 million investment in Next to an indicated value of $300 million.[14] Again Jobs was on the cutting edge—this time the cutting edge of Japanese investment in America's high technology.

At the time, *BusinessWeek* asked in an article discussing the Next equity sale to Canon: "Is the U.S. selling its high-tech soul to Japan?" The question needed to be asked but apparently few were listening. If Jobs was on the cutting edge of Japan's buying into high-tech America, Jobs was not alone. He had a lot of company who out of necessity were letting Japanese firms take a minority, if important, investment in their firm. Jobs could make a better deal than most start-ups and he did. Jobs had a fantastic record when he started Next and a good deal of patient, institutional backing to get Next going. For most high-tech start-ups the crucial ingredient for success—besides creativity, good management and hard work—has been money, patient capital, which in the past few years has been sorrily lacking in Silicon Valley.

Where was the American capital so desperately needed by Silicon Valley? During much of the 1980s it was out chasing leveraged-buyouts, which offered a much quicker, more assured and higher return than an investment in a start-up, which called for patience and long-term capital. However, the effects of LBOs on venture capital investments didn't stop there. Since almost all LBOs were premised on the idea of financing an acquisition through debt and then paying at least some of it off through selling off parts of the acquired company, expenditures on R&D and investments in new, high-tech ventures were put through another wringer. Obviously, a company newly burdened with debt will be less likely to make a long-term investment in high tech endeavors, and then a company sold off to pay for some of the debt will first concentrate its efforts on standing on its own two feet rather than putting money into research and development or helping finance some fledgling start-up. Commenting on the phenomenon at the time, Jerry Jasinowski, chief economist for the National Association of Manufacturers, said, "R&D has higher risks and longer-term payoffs than most expenditures. It's a highly postponable spending item—a handy target for cost-cutters."[15]

But the fast payback attraction and squeezing-out effect of LBOs is only part of the explanation as to why American capital, so desperately needed by start-ups, began to evaporate in the 1980s. Many institutional investors, who's initially flocked to venture capital investment expecting another Apple Computer to materialize in no time flat, found that the high-tech cornucopia also contained a lot of over-touted lemons and prunes, offering scant fiscal sustenance. With their enthusiasm for start-ups quelled, many institutional investors turned to a quicker payoff offered by essentially less productive investment.

Also underlying the drying up of U.S. venture capital investment is the different nature of much of the American and Japanese capital flowing into Silicon Valley investments. Most of the American capital is institutional, meaning that it is third-party capital, interested principally in return on investment. Other than profit, there is little to gain from such an investment. Japanese capital, by contrast, is corporate-*keiretsu* capital coming from en tities that are in the business of making products and that, because of their *zaibatsu*-like structure, can spread the risk over a number of entities. This is a big difference. It means that a Japanese *keiretsu* investor has more to gain than just return on his investment. If he's a Sony or an NEC investing in a small Silicon Valley firm, he has something to learn which in the long run may be more important than the quantified return on investment. For a Japanese corporate investor there can be a spillover of knowledge which essentially is not available to an institutional investor. It's another reason why Japanese investors in high-tech companies can wait and wait. Then, too, Japanese investors in America's high-tech firms have benefited greatly from the devaluation of the dollar which, while effectively subsidizing America's older, commodity-type industries, has put high-tech firms up for grabs. Japanese investors have also greatly benefited from the relatively low-cost capital available to them.

So for lack of domestic financing many tyro firms have turned to Japan for the all-essential capital infusion, but at a cost. In his deal with Canon, Jobs gave Canon the right to sell Next in Asia— a small concession considering the state of the Asian market—but no rights to Next's technology. Unless Next is as exceptional as its ads claim, selling the black cube in Asia, especially in Japan, will be difficult for Canon, given the Japanese competition and the tight Japanese market. Many American high-tech start-ups that have taken on a Japanese partner in order to stay in operation and continue developing have not been as lucky as Next in hanging on to their particular genius. One would like to think there could be a healthy interchange of technology between American and Japanese firms, but it frequently just doesn't work that way. Giving away technology in such an arrangement has been more the rule of the day. It is the sort of giveaway that has come to haunt America, as products developed with American technology in Japan have flowed back to America to take over markets Americans could have developed themselves with more persistence and patient capital. As mentioned, ubiquitous VCRs and Fax machines are just two examples of American technology becoming commercial bonanzas in Japanese factories.

As Robert Reich and Eric Mankin argued in an article entitled "Joint Ventures with Japan Give Away Our Future" in the *Harvard Business Review,* "On the surface the arrangements seem fair and well balanced, indicative of an evolving international equilibrium. A closer examination, however, shows the deals for what they really are—part of the continuing implicit Japanese strategy to keep the higher paying, higher value-added jobs in Japan and production process skills that underlie competitive success."[16] That Japan would seek to import American, technology acquired either through investment or joint ventures shouldn't come as a surprise. Until recently it didn't have much choice, since its own high-tech efforts often ended in failure, though that's all been changing in the past decade. In the late 1950s Japan realized it had a choice: either develop its own computer industry or remain dependent on foreign, i.e. American, technology. At the time it determined to have a rich and viable computer industry, no matter what. It took time, but with protection from foreign competition, government encouragement and direction and billions in government aid, the Japanese computer industry emerged as a tough, viable competitor in the past decade. However, when it first moved into Silicon Valley, it had to build mostly from scratch, taking what technology it could back to Japan to be pressed into cost-efficient production. Initially, Japanese high-tech firms didn't arrive with the same sort of camp followers as a Toyota or a Honda did, because their industry wasn't as mature. That situation is changing, though, as Japan's technology-based industry matures.

A stunning example of this sort of technology transfer involves Japan's largest manufacturer of agricultural equipment, Kubota Ltd. For close to 100 years of its profitable corporate existence, Kubota had busied itself building excellent rice harvesters, tractors, engines and industrial equipment. Manufacturing agricultural equipment was a good business, but in the early 1980s Kubota's management realized its market in Japan was pretty much saturated and had marginal growth potential. Moreover, when the yen started to ascend after the Plaza Five meeting, it was apparent that exporting such heavy machinery would become more difficult. For a time Kubota tried to ignore the writing on the silo wall, but by 1985 Kubota's management had come to the conclusion that it had best diversify its operations. It was a decision a number of Japan's heavy, one-industry companies were making around the same time. (In a similar vein Nippon Mining Corporation paid $1.1 billion for Gould Inc.)[17] However, few of these companies were as venturesome as Kubota in their diversification moves.[18]

When Kubota decided to diversify and invest in high-tech industries, it set itself a particularly difficult goal—to produce highly sophisticated mini-supercomputer workstations to sell for a hefty $100,000 apiece. It was as if near moribund International Harvester, now Navistar, had decided to branch out from building tractors and trucks into a biotechnology venture. However, Kubota was hardly a hick and it wasn't totally alone when it decided to make its foray into Silicon Valley. If it had been, it would have been an anomaly among Japanese companies. Kubota is a top-ranking member of the huge Fuyo industrial group, which is led by Japan's third-ranking Fuji Bank. It is also a member of the group's exclusive *Fuyo Kai*, or presidential council, which is composed of the presidents of the top 29 companies. Among the Fuyo Kai members, that Kubota's president would meet with frequently, are Canon and the giant electronics firm Hitachi Ltd. All three companies also share many of the same major shareholders, such as Nippon Life, which is the largest owner of Kubota and

Hitachi's shares. Like Kubota, Canon and Hitachi would be making investment forays into the Valley—Canon with Next and Hitachi acquiring an 80 percent, $309-million interest in National Advanced Systems, a partnership with EDS involved in mainframe computers.[19]

Beginning in 1986 Kubota set out in a very sophisticated way to make investments—for the most part minority stakes—in some of Silicon Valley's most promising start-ups. For $32.5 million it got a 38 percent interest in Ardent Computer, a maker of graphics-based mini-supercomputers; for another $6 million an 8 percent stake in Exabyte, a maker of cartridge tape drives; $20 million more bought Kubota 20 percent of MIPS Computer Systems, a leader in reduced-instruction-set computing or RISC; another $15.5 million gave it all of Akashic Memories, a manufacturer of hard disks; and for $750,000 it got a 4.6 percent interest in Synthesis Software, a software vendor for RISC machines. For less than $100 million and in little over two years, Kubota put together a portfolio of some of the hottest new firms in Silicon Valley whose technology it would use to build a mini-supercomputer in Japan. Just three years after it set out to venture into the world of high tech, Kubota shipped its first, highly advanced mini-supercomputer from a new plant north of Tokyo. While Osaka-based Kubota built the mini-supercomputer in Japan, its design is essentially American, since much of the key software, chips and architecture were sourced from the company's U.S. investments.[20] Kubota managing director, Masahiro Yoshida put the relationship very simply: "Everything we know about computers comes from Ardent and MIPS."[21] Since the U.S. remains ahead of Japan in such supercomputer design, Kubota had to transfer American technology to Japan to build its mini-supercomputer but it has every intention of learning from its start-up and eventually manufacturing mini-supercomputers of its own derivative design.

Though Kubota handled this transfer of U.S. technology to Japan deftly and avoided U.S. government objections chiefly because it made minority investments, which frequently go unmonitored or are only reviewed case by case, its initially friendly relationship with its key U.S. investment, Ardent, soon turned extremely bitter. Founded by Allen Michels, one of Silicon Valley's vaunted heroes and once a strong supporter of Japanese backing, Ardent was created to build high-powered, graphic workstations for engineers—the sort of machines Kubota assembles in Japan. For reasons not yet clear, Ardent eventually ran into financial problems and was merged in 1989 with its equally shaky East Coast rival, Stellar Computer, and renamed Stardent Computer Inc. Matters came to a head in July 1990 when Michels, who has since left Stardent, sued Kubota, accusing it of trying to gain control of Stardent's technology by letting it die on the vine for lack of additional capital, while it skimmed off Stardent's key people and technology to a wholly-owned Kubota subsidiary set up in the U.S. to manufacture mini-supercomputers. At the time of the suit Michels said, "they are trying to sweep it all inside and do it at a bargain price. If they want all these things, they ought to buy it and give a fair return to shareholders." Kubota dismisses Michels's charges as "baseless and irrational." Still it is a very difficult situation which is illustrative of how joining in high-tech deals with other investors can backfire, whether with Japanese investors or those from other countries. "They [Japanese investors] wine you and dine you and smile until they get what they want and when they get what they want, they treat you viciously," Michels said.[22]

Michels may, or may not, be correct about Kubota having such diabolical designs on Stardent's technology, but you still can't fault Kubota for showing aggressive imagination in attempting to diversify its operations. One also has to ask why an American firm wasn't in there sparring with Kubota for Ardent's technology. When Kubota's first mini-supercomputer was shipped from its north Tokyo plant, the U.S. Electronics Association's John Stern commented on the event saying, "it's perfectly legal, even admirable. But it's also a little scary."[23] Scary it is—that Kubota can boldly do what it's been doing and that neither the U.S. government nor corporate America seems to care.

While Next, Compaq and Stardent are very different operations, they do have some important similarities. Besides all being premier, American high-tech efforts, what these companies have in common is a dependency—a dependency on Japan. Today, there would be no Next computer or Compaq LTE without Japanese parts and it's a pretty good bet there would be no Stardent without Kubota's money. Of course, Next's suppliers are also dependent on Next to buy their wares, so Next has some leverage, but not to the degree its Japanese suppliers have. They can exist without Next, while the reverse is not true. Like it or not, Next,

Compaq and Stardent are in one way or another beholden to their Japanese suppliers and investors. It is a curious and precarious position to be in, since not infrequently the Japanese firm supplying parts or capital will also be an archrival, with the goal of gaining a greater foothold in high-tech America and gleaning more technology to take back to Japan.

Establishing a dependent relationship is very much in the *zaibatsu* way. Being dependent is part of the ethos. However, there are two general types of dependency in this sort of scheme, with many variations. There is the supportive—give-and-take—dependency which is typical of a group of vertically integrated Japanese companies with historical ties, common goals and cross-shareholdings. Then there is the much less fluid dependency of an outsider. Such a situation is a lot of take and little give, with adversarial undercurrents. The U.S. computer industry is now riddled with the latter sort of dependency on Japanese high-tech products—from supercomputer manufacturer Cray to Digital Equipment, Data General and Wang, on down the line. It extends from commodity-type semiconductors to highly sophisticated laptop screens. IBM alone, because of its size, its largely vertically integrated operations, the vast sums it has to spend on R&D and its constant innovation, has until now been pretty much immune to this sort of relationship, though this is changing as it gets more aggressively into PCs and laptops. It is a dependency that is created bit by bit.

Gaining a controlling position in a product line, a company or an industry by first chipping away at the weak spots is part of the *zaibatsu* strategy. It has a long tradition in Japan that is now spreading globally. It can be seen as a major tactic in Japan's growing presence in computer-related industries and it is an approach that Japan has used in trying to promote growth of its aerospace industry through being a major subcontractor to the world's pre-eminent commercial aircraft producer, Boeing Co. Fujitsu Ltd.'s announcement on July 31, 1990, that it would pay $1.29 billion for an 80 percent interest in ICL P.L.C., Britain's only manufacturer of mainframe computers and Europe's most profitable computer company,[24] is a clear example of this sort of tactic. Commenting on the ICL acquisition, which makes Fujitsu the number two computer company in the world after IBM while pushing DEC into third place,[25] one Tokyo computer analyst astutely observed in the *Financial Times* that "it has been a very typical Japanese strategy. They do not attack head-on but as in the game of Go, they probe patiently at various weak points until ultimately they completely surround their enemy."[26]

It took almost a decade for Fujitsu and ICL to tie the knot as Fujitsu moved inexorably to a dominant position after their initial tryst. The two companies had been working together since the early 1980s, a time when it became apparent ICL would have to develop a new generation of computers in order to remain competitive. Creating a new line of computers is extremely expensive—so expensive that ICL determined it couldn't foot the whole bill that would mount up to billions. Fujitsu came to the rescue. While ICL would build the computers, design the necessary software and assume the costs of marketing the new line, Fujitsu would assume the costly task of developing the essential semiconductors—the heart of the new mainframe. By developing the chips, the circuit boards and the tremendously complex cooling system essential to keeping the system going, Fujitsu saved ICL several billion dollars of development costs, but from then on ICL was beholden to Fujitsu for essential technologies.[27] As *New York Times* Tokyo correspondent David Sanger concludes in an article discussing the deal, "Fujitsu's move may be the purest example of what can happen, gradually and almost without notice, when a company grows dependent on an outsider and a competitor for crucial technologies it can no longer afford to master by itself."[28]

Such a strategy of not making a bold frontal attack but sallying here and there has also typified Japan's approach to the entire computer industry. As described in Silicon Valley, the high-tech community is structured along the lines of an ecological food chain, where the survival of one member along the chain is dependent on a member beneath it. In nature it's a situation where, say, the fox feeds on the rabbit and the rabbit fattens up on grass to be feed for the fox. In Silicon Valley the food chain refers not only to the way one company supplies another with vital parts but also to the technological dependence, say, a chip maker may have on its suppliers—whether it's a supplier of machinery or parts. In other words, the relationship between many a Silicon Valley company and another is seen as defined, yet dynamic and creative—fiercely competitive yet symbiotic. There is technological feedback up and down the food chain—a spillover. A strong and creative computer industry depends on a strong and creative semiconductor industry and a strong semiconductor industry depends on strong and creative machinery producers, etc. Does the arrangement sound familiar? In effect, the food chain is a euphemism for vertical integration, except that until now the majority of Silicon Valley companies didn't have common owners. In another sense a Next or a Compaq or a Stardent is the beluga caviar of the chain, while many lesser-known firms that have been gobbled up are more the meat and potatoes. One needs both.

As might be expected, Japanese firms caught onto the structure right away and have been taking over one link in the food chain after another, so as to have greater control over their environment. Says Sheridan Tatsuno, the founder of NeoConcepts, a marketing firm, and author of *The Technopolis Strategy* and *Created in Japan*, books which detail Japan's unrelenting efforts to establish itself as a front-runner in the high-tech race,[29] "we're losing the whole food chain of supporting technologies." The list is long and growing, as one by one America's home-grown, high-tech building blocks end up in Japanese hands. In effect, what Japan's technically advanced firms have been building in the U.S. is their own vertically integrated group of companies out of these purchases along the food chain and through direct investment. The situation is not without its ironies: as Japan becomes more independent, relying less and less on non-group sources, the U.S. slides more and more into dependency. Independence-dependence are the two sides of this yen-led investment. As a result, the weight and balance of the computer and related high-tech industries are changing—shifting towards Japan.

Japan now dominates the worldwide market for chip-making tools used to manufacture semiconductor chips, and the worldwide DRAM market.[30] A decade or so ago both markets belonged to America. In 1980, nine of the ten top semiconductor equipment companies in the world were American, with Perkin-Elmer leading the pack. Only one Japanese company, Takeda Riken, made the list. By the end of the decade, Tokyo Electron and Nikon ranked in first and second place. Taking the fourth spot on the list was Advantest, the fifth, Canon and the eighth, Hitachi. Four American and one Dutch firm completed the tally.[31] Japanese inroads continue, either through purchase of U.S. firms or investment in the U.S. In August 1989 Sony bought Materials Research Corporation, while Perkin-Elmer, still a leading supplier of chip-making equipment, was almost sold to Mitsubishi group's Nikon except for U.S. government pressure. Materials Research and Anelva, for example, dominate the so-called sputtering equipment market. Such equipment is essential for making chips. While Materials Research is now owned by Sony, Anelva is controlled by NEC.[32] In addition, Canon and Nikon control over 60 percent of lithography equipment production worldwide and have a dominant position in the U.S. in this field. In the case of Sony's Materials Research and Perkin-Elmer, both sought foreign buyers after American companies showed no interest in acquiring them or making additional financing available.[33]

The same sad history has been repeated in the semiconductor industry, where NEC, Toshiba and Hitachi are now the top three producers of semiconductors in the world, with Fujitsu, Mitsubishi and Matsushita taking the fifth, seventh and ninth places, respectively. Motorola, Texas Instruments and Intel fill the fourth, sixth and eighth positions, whereas Philips fills the tenth. Moreover, in emerging technologies Japan dominates flat-panel displays, originally developed in the U.S. and used in laptop computers such as Compaq's (the fastest-growing part of the personal computer market in the U.S.), color flat-panel displays for computers and high definition television, and laser printer mechanisms.[34] In 1988 some $1.8 billion worth of flat-panel displays were sold, whereas by 1996 annual volume is conservatively expected to have risen to $8.5 billion and then grow even faster.[35] It's worth remembering that lightweight, flat-panel screens were invented a quarter of a century ago by RCA scientist George Heilmeier, but that their development was rejected because they were seen as a threat to RCA's existing business. The Japanese, as with so many other inventions spurned in America, latched onto Heilmeier's brilliant idea and, if all goes as expected, they'll soon replace the bulky cathode-ray tubes now animating the world's TVs and computers.

Curiously enough, the *zaibatsu* way of doing business, with its webs of influence and support, is also very well suited to the direction high-tech industries are going. As the use of more and more high-tech products becomes ubiquitous, they are being standardized and taking on the characteristics of commodities. It's the sort of business where economies of scale and access to huge amounts of relatively cheap funds—both attributes of the *zaibatsu* way—can win the day. This has certainly been true for Japan's nine electronics giants—Hitachi, NEC, Fujitsu, Toshiba, Matsushita, Mitsubishi Electronics, Sony, Sharp and Sanyo—who

116

have been able to spread the high costs of their R&D efforts and plant investment over an entire vertically integrated operation. Then, too, an NEC is able to draw on the resources and skills of the number three-ranking Sumitomo *keiretsu*, of which it is a member. Sumitomo group members own about 25 percent of NEC, represent over a quarter trillion dollars in sales and can help obtain investment funds at about half the price an American competitor would pay. The other electronics giants have similar ties to one or another group. Toshiba's ties, for example, are with the Mitsui group, while Sharp is a member of the Sanwa group and has major financial dealings with the Fuyo and DKB groups. Such arrangements mean that when a Fujitsu or an NEC builds a plant in the U.S., the company is of such size that the U.S. plant's production and costs will fit into a global scheme. In addition, it means that if the U.S. economy turns slack, there will be support from home. Also, it's not as if an NEC or an Hitachi has ventured into the U.S. on its own. Rather, as one saw in the auto industry, if one leading Japanese electronics firm decides to invest in a sector of the U.S. his competitors are almost sure to follow suit. Confronting nine Japanese electronics giants running in a pack to invest in the latest U.S. technology is a formidable challenge in itself, but when the *keiretsu* backing in Japan representing perhaps $2 trillion in capital is weighed in, the competition for an American firm is even more daunting.

Silicon Valley is faced with an awesome structural confrontation that is difficult to beat, even if a company is as smart as an Intel or Next. The Japanese are fierce competitors, among themselves and especially with outsiders. As Ferguson points out in his *Harvard Business Review* article:[36]

> Japanese companies also compete with each other—sometimes quite fiercely, particularly in final product markets. But for many reasons—their interlocking investments, their technological dependence on each other, and the strength of government industrial policy—their rivalry is restrained and subordinated to the larger goal of displacing foreign competitors. Thus, the structure of Japanese industry gives rise to technological excellence and to predatory behavior; its extensive interlocking relationships facilitate both technological integration and strategic coordination against foreign rivals. It is a very powerful combination.

117

Of course, one can argue that with its design and software superiority—its sheer creativity, the U.S. has little to fear. It is true that Japan, despite intense efforts and piles of money invested, has had a poor record in innovative design and developing software to run its computers. Part of its problems in these areas can be attributed to the complexity of the Japanese language, which has well over 5,000 characters and 70,000 compounds, and an educational and corporate system that tends to discourage independent creativity. Let's say: Let Japan make the low-margin rice of the electronic age that requires billions of investment and is becoming ever more risky in terms of payback. Let the U.S. be the brains of the information age, doing what it does best, creating at the cutting edge of technology, and it will have higher, proprietary margins. Such a division of labor misses the point. Also such arrogance—the idea that the Japanese are doomed to be copyists—led many in the U.S. to believe that the Japanese could never succeed in the highly creative personal computer market—a belief that has been proven utterly wrong with the fast growth of Japanese-produced laptop computers.

For one, Japanese researchers, many of whom have been trained at MIT, Harvard or Stanford, are becoming much more creative in the areas of design and software. For another, talking about such a division between high-tech brains and brawn is totally unrealistic, since the two are interdependent, playing off each other up and down the high-tech food chain. Manufacturing expertise and engineering prowess can not be viewed separately. As discussed, this interplay is at the heart of the U.S. dependency on Japan, since design can become a captive of hardware, in the sense that it can be limited by it. Eventually the process can control the flow of technology. The utility of a design is in its implementation, and if the ability to implement it is limited, there is a serious economic impediment. As Scott McNealy, president of hot star Sun Microsystems Inc., put it bluntly, "once you control the components you own the industry."[37]

Dependency can have other severe ramifications for the U.S. besides missing out on technological development and being cut out of various stages in the food chain. Think of semiconductors, the brains of virtually every advanced electronic product. Say NEC or Fujitsu develops a new sophisticated microprocessor that gives products ranging from laptops to autos a great competitive advantage in terms cost and performance. And say initial production of the innovative microprocessor is limited. Who do you suppose is going to get the first supplies of the microprocessor?— NEC or Fujitsu's *keiretsu* connections and then their Japanese competitors. American competitors would rank number three on the totem pole. There is evidence that this is already happening in the Japanese-dominated DRAM market, where new Japanese DRAMS are finding their way into Japanese products six months to a year before they're available on the world market. There are also charges that U.S. makers of laptops, medical devices and military equipment are suffering from similar supply holdbacks, while Japanese producers are incorporating the latest technological breakthroughs into their competing products.[38] The implications for American industries dependent on such products—and there are few that aren't—are obvious. They'd be losing out. It is a very insidious situation and companies or industries in such a dependent position would soon be on the decline.

An equally insidious implication of Japan's pre-eminent position in the world semiconductor market is potential to form a cartel. In such a cartel the major nine Japanese chip producers could get together to control production among themselves and set prices. Massive profits from such behavior would be hard to resist and indeed, some claim that's exactly what Japanese producers did during the 1987–89 period, creating severe shortages of DRAMS and profiting greatly from jacked-up markets. Certainly, Japanese companies have never been averse to forming cartels and the Japanese government, in fact, has encouraged them in times of oversupply. Moreover, the group ethos of the nine electronics producers would tend to encourage cartel-like behavior. This behavior can have a devastating affect on industries dependent principally on such suppliers. They are at the mercy of their suppliers.

There are also the strategic, military implications of such dependence. Right-wing politician Shintaro Ishihara gave an extreme example of the potential consequences of this dependency in *The Japan That Can Say No*, "If, for example, Japan sold chips to the Soviet Union and stopped selling them to the U.S., this would upset the entire military balance. Some Americans say that if Japan were thinking of doing that, it would be occupied."[39] Think about it. Think about dependency and if the U.S. wants it. Doesn't this come close to the Trojan Horse former Central Intelligence Agency chief William Casey was referring to, when he was discussing Japanese investment in the U.S.? And think about the fact that a little over a decade ago, Japan, whose computer industry will surpass America's in world markets next year, was thought by many to be incapable of mounting a serious threat to America's hegemony in the most important area of industrial endeavor in the twenty-first century.

5

Boardwalk, Park Place

Lousy, candy houses.

> — Gensiro Kawamoto, Japanese billionaire, appraising
> Hawaii's domestic architecture, after snapping
> up some 170 houses and apartments in a 1987 buying
> spree that cost him at least $85 million[1]

I even have an international ranking: I am the first American
mayor to serve in a city owned by the Japanese.

> —Frank Fasi, mayor of Honolulu, discussing
> the unique qualities he would bring to the
> office of governor if elected[2]

By mid-1988, Hawaiian farmers Ryoei and Nancy Higa were really teed off. For nearly ten years they'd been growing vegetables on their Waianae Coast farm on the west coast of Oahu, when suddenly they were faced with eviction from the 50-acre plot they had leased. Out of the blue, they learned Japanese developer Sanjiro Nakade had designs on their land and 236 surrounding acres, and there was nothing agrarian about them. Nakade, like so many Japanese when confronted with a tract of virtually undeveloped Hawaiian land used for farming or ranching, soon had visions of lush golf courses dancing in his head. To hell with onions and turnips or bovine pursuits.

So up went the Higas' protest banners proclaiming: ''No can eat golf balls''—a perfectly reasonable statement, at least on the surface. After all, tending a vegetable garden seemed more important and more productive to the Higas than having some Japanese tourist tilling their fields with a golf cart and nine iron, though in the long run his leisure pursuits might generate more work. The Higas were not alone in their plight. A number of other Hawaiian farmers and ranchers were vociferously trying to put a halt to Japanese development of their land.[3]

The Higas and their fellow protesters, however, were caught up in a set of circumstances where good sense seems to have frequently gone out the window and where the flood of Japanese money into Hawaii—at first welcomed with outstretched palms—is now viewed with some apprehension as Japan's presence balloons to Sumo wrestler proportions and becomes ever more complex.

What's happened with the Japanese golf course craze, that the Higas and other locals have gotten caught up in, is just one example of the sort of distortions powerful Japanese investments can wreak on a local economy when the interests of the indigenous population are very much at odds with those of the Japanese. It's not just that the Higas and other farmers stood to lose their livelihood to make way for Japanese vacationers, but the fact is that golf, as a preferred recreational pastime, ranks much lower with Hawaiians than the Japanese.[4] The goose that laid the golden egg has also left other trappings along the way and while many Hawaiians have benefited from Japan's massive investment in America's fiftieth state, there are growing doubts and repercussions.

In part, the rush to buy up much of Hawaii's real estate and its related leisure activities is very much in line with the *zaibatsu* strategy and the *zaibatsu* habit of moving in packs, though here the pursuit of profits and pleasure are intermingled. All of Japan's largest industrial groups—Mitsubishi, Mitsui, Sumitomo, Fuyo, DKB, and Sanwa—as well as many other *keiretsu*, have major, direct real estate investments in Japan as a portion of their overall portfolio. Moreover, many of the *keiretsu* are also intimately involved in real estate through group financing of new projects and the activities of group-related construction firms. For the Big Six and the other *keiretsu*, having large real estate holdings is a natural extension of the *zaibatsu* idea of controlling all the variables in business and, given the tremendous cost and scarcity of land in Tokyo, owning real estate becomes another *zaibatsu* hedge against uncertainty. Therefore, it should come as no surprise that there are areas in Tokyo where almost all the turf, the buildings and restaurants are controlled by a Mitsubishi, Mitsui or some other industrial group.

So as *keiretsu* have expanded their industrial base in the United States, their investment in American real estate and financing of construction has also burgeoned. Though purchases such as Mitsubishi Estate's gaining control of Rockefeller Center for nearly $1 billion, or the $610 million Mitsui & Co. paid for New York's Exxon Building or Dai-Ichi Real Estate Co.'s $94-million deal to acquire Tiffany & Co.'s historic headquarters building[5] have given headline status to the growing Japanese presence in the U.S., much of the investment has been less spectacular. This race to acquire American real estate, which abated a little in 1990, dropping to an estimated $10 to $13 billion from a record $14.8 billion in 1989,[6] includes some less-well-known Japanese companies and individual investors as well, many of whom had already made a fortune in Tokyo real estate before staking out claims in Waikiki or Southern California.

But then, Japan's move into Hawaii has taken on spectacular dimensions of its own. Rarely has the competitive pack instinct, a key ingredient in the *zaibatsu* way manifested in varying degrees throughout America, shown its face more clearly than here in Hawaii. Since real estate investment and tourism are not structured with the same hierarchical complexity of a Toyota or Sony's American operations, the latter may offer better examples of *zaibatsu*-like vertical integration, but not of this distinct pattern running with the crowd. Also, as a result of this hyper-group dynamism, Hawaii has become an example of Japan's most extreme and extensive economic penetration into an American state thus far, even surpassing their presence in California.

In the Higas' case they were, first of all, victims of a fluke in Hawaiian law that some claim came as a result of Japanese lobbying and makes it much easier to convert agricultural land into golf courses than into the residential property which Hawaii so desperately needs.[7] Secondly, ever since the Plaza Five economic agreement of 1985, which proved to be the catalyst for the subsequent doubling of the yen's value, Japanese businessmen and tourists have been on a sort of feeding frenzy in Hawaii, frantically buying up luxury goods, from Gucci handbags to Cartier love bracelets, pricey Waikiki condos, downtown Honolulu office buildings, costly land, and hotels and hotels and hotels with

123

seemingly total abandon. When you have Japanese customers lining up on Waikiki's Kalakaua Avenue to get into Tiffany's and there's not even a sale going on, or, when you have real estate speculators such as Gensiro Kawamoto paying millions of dollars for a house and not even bothering to get out of his limo to look at it, the phrase "money is no object" takes on new currency. Golf courses are, of course, very much part of this frenetic scene, with the one proposed for the Higas' vegetable plot being only one of 40 or so planned for Oahu by Japanese developers.[8] To the Japanese salaryman-office worker used to teeing off on a confined Tokyo roof or in one of the city's many multi-story golf ranges, or to the Japanese industrialist who's paid as much as $3.5 million for membership in one of Tokyo's more exclusive clubs, Hawaii—with its fields rolling gently down from volcanic formations to the sea, its balmy, palmy weather and its public golf courses—looks like nirvana and cramped Tokyo seems far, far away.

Like a surfer searching for the perfect wave, the hot pursuit by the Japanese of the world's best golf courses has taken them worldwide, from Australia to California to Connecticut to Scotland, where the game was played as early as 1457. Their passion for golf knows no bounds. For the Japanese businessman relocating in the U.S. or beyond, having a golf course in the environs has almost become an essential perk of the transfer. And as with their purchases of commercial real estate, the Japanese have bought up the real trophy properties—the Rockefeller Centers of the golf world, so to speak. In 1990, controversial and secretive Japanese investor Minoru Isutani's Ben Hogan Properties paid an estimated $1 billion, much of it financed by the Mitsubishi Trust and Banking Co., for the beautiful Pebble Beach properties encompassing 5,300 acres on the Monterey Peninsula.[9] At the time one observer likened the purchase of this piece of Americana to buying Yellowstone National Park.[10] Other Japanese investors have snapped up the renowned La Costa Resort near San Diego and Los Angeles' Riviera Country Club, while Isutani, who has been linked to the Recruit bribery scandal and operates his expanding golf empire through his firm Cosmo World, is also developing the Los Angeles International Country Club in the San Fernando Valley.[11] Even further afield, in Scotland, Japanese-controlled Orient-Express Hotels owns the historic Turnberry Hotel, which was opened on the Ayrshire coast in 1906 as the world's first golf resort hotel.[12] In fact, given Japan's unbridled passion for golf, there are some who claim—facetiously—that the real reason for Japan's economic global expansion is very simple—the search for more golf courses. While this love of golf has spread worldwide, nowhere, other than Japan, has it reached the intensity seen in Hawaii.

When the Japanese find nirvana they don't tend to savor it in solitude or one by one, but flock together to enjoy it en masse. This is what's happening in Hawaii right now. For if the Japanese invasion of Hawaii exemplifies anything, it's a graphic illustration of Japan's group ethos running full speed ahead, which, of course, is a key ingredient in the *zaibatsu* way of doing business. Hawaii may grow pineapple and sugarcane, and operate as a mid-Pacific financial center, but its number one business is still tourism and the Japanese now control Hawaiian tourism from the luxury hotels lining Waikiki's narrow beach, to major shopping centers, to ABC and 7-Eleven convenience stores, to restaurants, to the package tours that deplane from the Japan Air Lines' planes at Honolulu's sprawling International Airport. Precisely how large Japan's stake in Hawaii has grown in recent years cannot be calculated down to the thousandth yen or dollar, since much of the necessary information isn't reported to government agencies. But it is fair to say that Japanese nationals control and influence a major part of the Hawaiian economy—an intelligent estimate would put it close to half,[13] and it's becoming a growing political issue. Moreover, this current influx of Japanese pleasure seekers is not to be confused with Japanese-American citizens who make up 25 percent of Hawaii's 1.1 million residents. Japanese-Americans rank as the largest sector of Hawaii's ethnically diverse population after its whites, who started arriving in the nineteenth century and now comprise 34 percent of the Islands' citizenry. Many of these Japanese-Americans already have dominant roles in the state's politics, its professions and government.[14]

Recently the *Honolulu Star-Bulletin* and Hawaii's KGMB-TV polled residents of the nation's fiftieth state, asking them what they thought of their growing ties with Japan. Close to half of those polled said they believed Hawaii was about to become a colony of Japan only some 30 years after it had become a state. How did they feel about this situation—ambivalent to say the least? While 59 percent of the respondents polled in 1990 said they felt Japanese investment was good for workers and the state's economy, some 67 percent of them blamed the sale of land to the Japanese as the major factor making Hawaii one of the most expensive states in the union to live in. In effect, what the respondents were saying is that they liked Japanese funds flowing into Hawaii, but that they were getting wary and that the flow might be turning into a mixed blessing or no blessing at all. This is a feeling shared by many Hawaiians—that the Japanese situation could be getting close to being out of control or at least out of their control.

———

Given its dulcet climate, in which even the gentle rain is benign, Hawaii is the sort of place where it's hard to get overwrought. Of course, Hawaii has a tough underside—its crime and poverty, its racial problems, its hookers turning warm evening tricks along the Waikiki strip—but they do not set the tone. Volcanic eruptions aside, much of life is laid back and on the surface, with the simple bright patterns of a Hawaiian sport shirt. Still, uneasy, concerned rumblings about Japan's ubiquity have already made their way into the state's airy, open-atrium Capitol building, surrounded by reflecting pools filled from hibiscus-shaped spouts. Abutting the high Victorian Iolani Palace constructed by King David Kalakaua in 1882 when Hawaii was still a monarchy, the roughhewn concrete Capitol building houses 25 state senators and 51 representatives. It was designed by John Carl Warneke in the late sixties and is supposed to be evocative of a volcano rising out of the sea, the Hawaiian islands' genesis. The reverberations in its conic-shaped legislative chambers haven't reached volcanic, Japan-bashing proportions, but they can't be ignored.

Gregory G. Y. Pai, Special Assistant to the Governor for Economic Affairs and formerly chief economist for the First Hawaiian Bank, has been tracking and writing about the Japanese presence in Hawaii for a number of years. An astute observer of the situation, Pai is worried that Hawaii's ever stronger, diverse and more complex ties with Japan have reached a critical point, where increasing conflicts such as the Higas' and other Hawaiians' protests about losing out to Japanese interests are bound to erupt. In his picture-filled Capitol office chronicling his worldwide travels, Pai, a Harvard and MIT-trained economist, discussed some of his concerns in a recent interview. ''I don't want to kill the goose that

laid the golden egg but somehow we must curb the wild horses,''
Pai said, mixing his metaphors. ''What's happening is symptomatic of a global problem which the U.S. created essentially when
it allowed the dollar to weaken in an effort to finance our budget
deficit. The Japanese are only acting like rational investors.
What's happening in Hawaii, though, is we're being ambushed
by this tidal wave of Japanese investment. We can't take a moral
view if it's good or bad. We have to ask how can we manage it
as much as we can to benefit our people and try to control the
negative aspects.''

Pai figures that ''Japanese-induced economic activity'' now accounts for close to half of Hawaii's total economic endeavor,[15] a
really remarkable turn of events since it's taken the Japanese little
more than half a decade to get to this point. During the five-year
period prior to the 1985 Plaza Five Agreement Japanese investment in Hawaii averaged around $160 to $170 million a year, but
then in 1986 it skyrocketed tenfold to $1.7 billion. In 1988, for
example, Pai says that Japanese visiting Hawaii spent $3.7 billion,
resulting in $7.6 billion in total direct and indirect transactions in
the economy. In addition, the Japanese invested $1.6 billion in
Hawaii during the year, meaning that when the indirect effects of
this investment were added in,

> roughly $9.5 billion of economic activity occurred as a result
> of Japanese spending and investment. Given Hawaii's gross
> state product in 1988 of $21.3 billion, Japanese induced eco-
> nomic activity was equivalent in value to 45 percent, or close
> to one-half of Hawaii's total for the year. The result was dra-
> matic in virtually every sector related to tourism, services, re-
> tailing, transportation, agriculture, manufacturing, construc-
> tion and real estate. New business grew rapidly, while
> productivity, employment, and income soared, creating
> Hawaii's greatest period of prosperity since the boom years
> of the 1970s.[16]

According to Pai, Hawaii is faced with a policy of trade-off.
''Clearly there are many short term benefits but our problem is
too much money. And the long term problem created is a loss of
control of resources, a loss of control of land which could be a
tremendous problem,'' Pai said. ''The question is how far can you
go before you go too far and it's complicated by the fact: is it
better to be owned out of Chicago or Tokyo? I tend to think that

we don't want to bar all foreign investment but we need to know more, so that state policy can focus more correctly on it."

Still, from what is known of the situation it is readily apparent that the Japanese pack pursuit of pleasure and luxury purchases has had a tremendous impact on Hawaii and shows no signs of abating. In Waikiki alone, Japanese nationals have bought over 2,000 condominiums worth over half a billion dollars and that's just a fraction of the billions of dollars they've poured into Hawaiian real estate in the past half-decade.[17] However, as Pai pointed out, if the magnitude of Japanese investing has increased enormously in recent years, the nature of this investment has also changed drastically into "a wholesale purchase of assets" of speculative proportions. Traditional modes of investing, such as buying land and building a house, hotel or office on it, create a new asset to add to Hawaii's stock. As a result of this sort of investing, there will also be more jobs—jobs for construction workers as the building is built and service and maintenance jobs once it is completed. However, buying and selling existing houses, condominiums, hotels and office buildings among Japanese nationals, frequently with the same fickle abandon as some women pick up a Louis Vuitton satchel and then switch to a Hermes bag, is another sort of transaction creating considerably less economic benefit to Hawaii or other parts of the United States. When Japanese real estate magnate-speculator Gensiro Kawamoto went on his 1987 buying spree, spending an estimated $85 to $110 million on 170 apartments and houses in three months, much of what he spent went into the Hawaiian economy. Kawamoto, who has the dubious distinction of having bought the most expensive house ever sold in the U.S. when he purchased the Kaiser estate for $43 million, was part of the first wave of post–Plaza Five Agreement, Japanese real estate investors to wash onto Waikiki's shores. This meant that when his white stretch limousine pulled up in front of a Honolulu house and Kawamoto chose to alight from it, the $500,000, $1 or $2 million in cash he offered for the "lousy, candy" house would usually end up in the hands of a native Hawaiian, who, in turn, would spend a portion of Kawamoto's largesse on another place to live on Oahu.[18]

While Kawamoto has apparently hung on to most of what he bought on that first spree and continues to buy—disproving many of his critics who said his buying binge was nothing but pure speculation, this has not been the case with many Japanese.

In effect, what a number of Japanese have created is a hyper-Hawaiian real estate market where only the Japanese, or a Kha-shoggi prior to his financial problems, or Leveraged-Buyout Moguls think nothing of paying $5 or $10 million for what are frequently rather tacky houses with not much land. This is the sort of market where it is not uncommon to hear tales of a house initially sold to a Japanese investor for $500,000, which a year or two later is bought for $5 million by another Japanese who subsequently sells it to a fellow countryman for $8 or $10 million.

The Kahala Avenue area, just a few minutes' drive from Waikiki on the other side of Diamond Head and home of Honolulu's most exclusive Waialae Country Club, site of the Hawaiian Open, is paradise for such Japanese investors with big bucks. All of Hawaii's beauty is there for a price, if you can afford a $10- or $15-million house on the drive around Diamond Head. For a few million less there are a number of pretentious, oversized houses built cheek by jowl within putting distance of Waialae. It is also an area of high frustration for many Japanese, since Waialae, built in 1927 on a then remote part of Oahu used for raising cattle and chickens and now surrounded by multimillion-dollar houses, is extremely hard for anyone, Japanese or not, to get a membership in. Certainly, trying to buy one's way in doesn't work, as a group of Japanese investors discovered. When some Japanese investors offered to buy out Waialae's 1,000 or so members for $1 million each, so they could play the 145-acre course with its century-old trees and open views of the sea, the members, who frequently pass membership on to their children, turned down the offer worth a staggering $1 billion-plus, or about $8 million an acre. Still, despite these problems, Mr. and Mrs. Yasuhi Isobe recently spent $1.2 million for their condominium on Kahala Avenue, Chiyoda American Development Co. paid $9.3 million or just under a million dollars each for ten houses on the street, and Hasegawa Komuten bought a house and six condos there for $6.3 million. In fact, one-third of the 145 houses and apartments that sold for $141 million on Kahala Avenue between January 1987 and April 1988 were bought by Japanese nationals. Moreover, 75 percent of the condominium units that sold around Honolulu for over $1 million during the same 15-month period were bought by natives of Japan.[19]

While multimillion-dollar house and apartment sales represent only a small fraction of Hawaii's housing market—Bank of

Hawaii's chief economist David Ramsour estimates less than 1 percent—such sales have had a much greater impact than this percentage of the market might suggest. Their benefit to Hawaii is scant if any. By the time a house or condominium has attained a million-dollar-plus price tag, it is out of reach for all but a few Hawaiians. Thus sales in this range are for the most part between Japanese nationals trading up market with the rising yen. The result is that these huge sums do not feed back into the Hawaiian economy to help create more jobs and greater investment. For Hawaii such sales are sterile, since the funds involved bounce from one Japanese-controlled bank account to the next.

What remains though in Hawaii is the inflationary impact of these sales. Kahala and Waikiki homeowners who've chosen not to profit from skyrocketing prices have seen their real estate tax bills shoot higher and higher as tax assessors have reassessed the values of their properties in light of recent sales. Living next to the Isobes of Kahala or the new owner of the Kaiser estate, Gensiro Kawamoto, or other Japanese multimillionaires can be expensive in ways not initially anticipated, forcing some landowners to sell out because of the burdensome new taxes. In addition, million-dollar sales at the top end of the real estate market have had a ripple effect on the rest of Hawaii's housing market, as sellers at every level raise their expectations of what they can get for their house or apartment. Economist Ramsour disputes this view, saying the Japanese have been used as scapegoats when the real cause of Hawaii's incredibly high housing costs is its archaic regulations that have made Hawaii not unlike Japan, in that only 4 to 5 percent of the land is used for housing. It is true that Hawaii's restrictive land policies have caused prices to rise but it doesn't mean, as Ramsour contends, that the impact of the Japanese herd mentality hasn't filtered through the rest of Hawaii's real estate market. When the high end escalates, middle-price-range properties are usually bid up. No one holds back. This is human nature and it's a pattern that has been seen around the country, from Boston to New York to Los Angeles, as residential property prices escalated. However, in an economic downturn such as the current one, it is usually the middle-level properties whose prices plummet first, with the high end of the market being the last sector to feel the pinch. Obviously, another impact of inflationary pressures on housing is that owning any form of housing becomes accessible to fewer and fewer people. In Hawaii's case a

house with an average price of $345,000[20] is out of reach of an
ever-greater percentage of the economy, since the employment
trend there is towards lower-paying service jobs which are part
and parcel of the boom in tourism.

Spectacular as the sale of $10-, $20- or $30-million-dollar houses
may be, they are only part—the speculative part at that—and in
fact a small part of the Japanese search for pleasure in the Hawaiian Islands. It is a search that has made the islands increasingly
dependent on Japanese tourism to survive and prosper. Speaking
to the Honolulu Japanese Chamber of Commerce in November
1989, economist Pai pointed out: "The general effect that foreign
investment has had in increasing Hawaii's overdependency on
tourism, has had the effect of perpetuating Hawaii's long-term
drift toward a low-wage service economy. The overall loss of control over Hawaii's assets, particularly in terms of the visitor industry and commercial and business assets, has also generated widespread concern." Certainly, the tourists and investors who've
shuttled back and forth from Japan to Hawaii in droves are the
leaders of this trend. Still, as important and pervasive as their
presence is, it takes a little time and digging to see how important
they've become to a community they bombed at Pearl Harbor
only half a century ago.

Walk along Waikiki's Kalakaua Avenue, which runs towards
Diamond Head and the hyper-expensive Kahala area, and one
is at the epicenter of Japanese entrenchment in Hawaii. Yet the
Japanese presence is not at first that apparent. One is not over-
whelmed by how Japanese the place has become, even though
Hawaii has long been the number one destination resort for Japanese holiday seekers, with some 1.4 million or about 17 percent
of the 8.5 million annual Japanese vacationers heading for Waikiki
and other island spots.[21] Sure there are plenty of groups of Japanese flowing amoeba-like in and out of Tiffany's and Alfred Dun-
hill, adding to their burden of glitzy shopping bags with each pit
stop or stopping to rest from their heavy day of shopping and
dine at Furusato Sushi. But they're only part of the scene. The
names of the shops are Hawaiian, American and European—
many of the same names you'd see lining New York's Madison
Avenue or Chicago's Michigan Avenue or Beverly Hills' Rodeo
Drive. Waikiki and much of Hawaii are still very much American
in appearance, with their mixture of tourists in country-club
plaids and florid linen jackets, their beefy midwesterners in poly-

131

ester shorts and black shoes and the aging, dropout surfers who've ridden the crests and hollows of too many drug trips. But appearances are deceptive, because almost every hotel along the strip is Japanese-owned and almost all the luxury stores that line the street draw their life-blood from Japanese tourists.

About midway down Kalakaua Avenue, opposite the 1,230-room Hyatt Regency Waikiki built for $100 million in 1976 and sold in 1987 to the Japanese firm Azabu USA Corporation for $300 million, is the main access to Waikiki beach. As world-renowned beaches go it's not unlike many of the thousands of tourists who clog its shores—it's beyond its prime. It's long and wide enough to support a couple of hotels such as the old Royal Hawaiian and the Halekulani with grace, but not the number of Japanese-owned hotels and condominiums that now crowd its narrow shores and nearby streets cheek to cheek. It's crowded enough to make any Tokyoite feel at home. Beneath dusty palms and the Prince Kuhio Seiko Clock given by tour leader JAL PAK are plain park benches hyphenating the approach to the heavily foot-pocked sand and the beautiful sea beyond. It's a middle-aged American place where light blue and yellow polyester lives and thrives, stretches its pores, suns itself, slouches on the benches and rests before being loudly hustled to join a "real" Hawaiian outrigger trip being launched at the far end of the beach. These tourists flown in from the Mid- and Far West are not Hawaii's big-time spenders, though. They buy the 89-cent rattan beach pads, the six-packs of Bud and five-pound cans of Macadamia nuts—plain or chocolate—at the Japanese-owned ABC stores seemingly on every corner of Waikiki. Toting their Sony video cameras, they're seen shopping at the older, budget-priced Outrigger strip shops buying souvenir T-shirts at TEES and Tops. For the most part these are not the people who flock to Ferragamo to buy a $350-pair of shoes, a $500-tote bag at Hunting World, a $1,000-pocketbook from Hermes, a lacquer and gold pen from S.T. Dupont Paris, or a $1,500-Giorgio Armani men's suit. The Japanese, who are by and large more expensively dressed than their American counterparts as they make their way along Kalakaua Avenue, do in droves.

On average, Japanese tourists spend five times more a day than their American counterparts. Economist Pai figures that on any given day during 1988 a Japanese national on holiday in Hawaii forked out about $530, whereas an American tourist from the mainland spent a comparatively paltry $117 during the same 24-hour period. Doing Hawaii on $500-plus a day takes stamina of a sort and it can add up to a lot of money for the shops lining Kala-kaua Avenue. For a tour group of, say, 50 Japanese salarymen and their wives, such spending translates into more than $50,000 a day or $350,000 a week. So while the Japanese represented only a quarter of the tourists visiting Hawaii in 1988, the $3.7 billion they spent added up to nearly half of all visitor spending during the year. In addition, while tourist traffic from the mainland U.S. grew a meager 1 percent, the number of travelers from the Far East, mainly Japan, rose 17 percent.

Shopping along Kalakaua Avenue may be a heady vacation pastime for many Japanese visiting Hawaii, but the yen doesn't stop there. The majority of the largest and most expensive hotels along Waikiki and on the other islands are all Japanese-owned. According to a Kenneth Leventhal & Co. study of hotel ownership in Hawaii, Japanese interests now own 92 percent of the deluxe-class rooms which cost upwards of $300 a night for a decent, ocean-view double, 57 percent of the state's luxury rooms and 54 percent of the first-class rooms. Along Waikiki, of the 43 major hotels owned by foreigners, 35 belong to Japanese investors and these are the best hotels there. Halekulani Corporation, a subsidiary of Mitsui Real Estate, owner of the Exxon Building in New York, owns the venerable and revamped 456-room Halekulani begun in 1907. It also owns the somewhat less classy Waikiki Parc which overlooks the Halekulani's rooftops. Down the beach from the Halekulani is Hawaii's most famous hotel, the still luxurious Royal Hawaiian, the ''Pink Palace of the Pacific'' to some. Built in 1927 by the Matson Navigation Companies for $4 million, the Royal Hawaiian was the destination resort for the rich and famous who sailed there from America to Hawaii on Matson Line's *Lurline.* Here Douglas Fairbanks and Mary Pickford spent vacations and Nelson Rockefeller and Henry Ford II brought their brides on their respective honeymoons. Just behind the hotel, a short walk through its lush garden, is the Royal Hawaiian Shopping Center, home to many of Kalakaua Avenue's most expensive shops. Now the Pink Palace is owned by Kokuusai Kogyo, which also owns the Sheraton Waikiki and Sheraton Maui.[22]

Japanese investors have pursued the same pleasure principle on Hawaii's other islands, where, as on Oahu, they have not just bought prime hotel properties but also have done handsome, expensive renovations where necessary. On the big island of Hawaii, all ten foreign-owned hotels are owned by Japanese, including the huge 1,234-room Hyatt Regency Waikoloa bought by K. G. Corporation in 1988 for $360 million and the 310-room Westin Mauna Kea Hotel purchased by Seibu Railway Co. in the same year for $315 million. Over on Kauai and Maui the story is the same. Six of the eight foreign-owned hotels on Kauai are in Japanese hands, while eighteen out of twenty on Maui are also Japanese.[23] These are hotels with familiar North American luxury chain names such as the Four Seasons, Grand Hyatt, Intercontinental, Marriott, Sheraton and Ritz Carlton.

Moreover, Japanese investment in Hawaii spreads much further into the nooks and crannies of the islands than just hotels, resorts, houses and apartments. There are literally hundreds of Japanese-owned firms that have set up offices or joint ventures in Hawaii to offer a myriad of services and products, from Meitus Advertising's joint venture Advertising Works, to Blue Hawaii Travel, to renovator Boss Corporation USA, to Foremost Dairies, to First Insurance Co., to Hawaiian Dredging and Construction, to Island Homes Real Estate, to International In-Flight Catering Co., to Love's Bakery, to the Maharaja Night Club, to freight forwarder Nippon Express Hawaii, to Nomura Securities International, to Sony Hawaii Co., to the Sanwa and Sumitomo Banks, to costume renter Watabe Costume Service.[24]

Then there are the major Japanese investments in Honolulu office buildings, restaurants, golf courses and clubs, land under development and massive chunks of undeveloped land. Drive from Waikiki to downtown Honolulu and one passes the Japanese-controlled Ala Mona Center, which for a time was the world's largest shopping center and is still impressive with its 150 stores and restaurants. It's one of the 27 shopping centers and department stores owned by Japanese interests. Then downtown there's the Amfac Center sold to the Mitsui group for $141.5 million in 1988, just one of the 29 office buildings acquired by Japanese in the past few years. There are also 75 Japanese-owned restaurants with such diverse monikers as Cock's Roost, Hawaiian Hut, Kelly's Pastry Shop, Señor Popo's, Pearl City Tavern, Spencecliff Bake Shop, and three Tony Romas.[25]

And biggest of all is the $3-billion Ko Olina resort being developed on a rather remote part of Oahu's west coast not far from the Higas' vegetable plot. About a 45-minute drive from downtown Honolulu, Ko Olina, which means fulfillment of joy, is a joint venture of TSA International Ltd., a Japanese development company; Kumagai Gumi Co., the huge Japanese construction company; and Hawaiian real estate developer, Horita Corporation. With more than a bit of hyperbole, Ko Olina bills itself as "the world's most perfect resort"—a claim that could only be taken literally by vacationers who would describe Waikiki in similar terms. Certainly, the approach along Farrington Highway to Ko Olina is unprepossessing. Leaving over-developed Honolulu behind, one is soon driving through a rough, scruffy landscape populated with an occasional run-down house or shack-farm and locals known for inhospitable, sometimes criminal treatment of tourists—details left out of Ko Olina's glossy, lyrical sales literature. So, too, is the fact that not far to the left of Ko Olina's 642-acre plot stands the sprawling Campbell Estates' industrial complex.

Such details don't deter Horita Corporation chairman Herbert Horita from waxing mystical about his first glimpse of Ko Olina: "When I first saw it, it was as if the land spoke to me. I could feel the spirituality of the place. It was like all the men and women who had been here before me were telling me this was 'the place,' that this magnificent Hawaiian land was ready to be used again to achieve greatness. It is the most profound experience I've ever had in my business life."[26]

Certainly, the scene changes dramatically upon entering Ko Olina. A couple of hundred million dollars and three years' work have transformed Ko Olina's land, which it bought from Campbell Estates in 1987, into a lush, manicured site where by the year 2000 a whole slew of apartment buildings and hotels will have risen. However, to put first things first in true Japanese fashion, an 18-hole golf course designed by golf course architect Ted Robinson was already in place on a recent visit. Passing the golf course one arrives at a hipped-roof visitor center with a black stone memorial to the left of its entrance dedicated to Kumagai Gumi's deceased chairman, Mr. Jinichi Makita. It was Makita "whose vision brought credibility to the development of West Beach and whose support brought reality to this fulfillment of joy"—not to mention all Kumagai Gumi's money. Beyond, four smallish, crescent-shaped lagoons blasted from the coral shore will make up for a lack of a natural beach. There's still a lot of work to be done during the decade for Ko Olina "to achieve greatness." Eventually this spiritual place will have 4,000 hotel rooms, managed by Lowes, Four Seasons, JAL and others, 5,200 condominium apartments, a 400- to 450-slip marina, a shopping mall fronting the marina and train rides around the resort on the nineteenth-century Oahu Sugar Company railway.

So you may ask what's so bad about all this—Ko Olina and the rest. Construction is booming and unemployment is low. The Japanese have brought money and up to a point helped create jobs. The surface of Hawaii hasn't changed that much and Hawaii is mostly surface anyway. This is the best of all possible worlds—right? Unfortunately, it's just not that simple. For Hawaii, the planeloads of Japanese tourists and investors crowding into the islands represent a loss of control on a number of levels—a state of affairs that's bound to create more conflicts.

Think of the old adage: "Money talks." Japanese money talks in many ways—some as splashy and gauche as a white stretch limo and some as subtle and powerful as an Edo-period bronze. The Japanese are past masters at political lobbying, having perfected political gift giving to an intricately balanced art where giving tit-for-tat can be a highly complex affair. However, in Hawaii's case, so much Japanese money has flowed into the islands in the past half decade that it doesn't even have to open its mouth to speak to make a point, its presence already bulks so large. Japanese money doesn't have to launch a concerted lobbying effort to have its wishes known. At this juncture the Japanese don't have to do anything. If you're in a dinghy with a 400-pound Sumo wrestler, you're considerate and mindful of his wants even if he's not troublesome at all. It's in your best interest to keep him in a congenial mood, while you row.

This dependent relationship, however, goes further. First there are the tourists from Japan. Over the long run it is in Hawaii's best interest to diversify its economy, whereas it's becoming ever more dependent on the vagaries of tourism, particularly Japanese tourism, as more and more tourists flock to Hawaii and its agricultural enterprises cut back their operations. Such a dependence on a service economy began in the 1950s, when taking care of the military stationed in Hawaii displaced agricultural endeavors such as raising pineapple and sugarcane as the state's number one provider of paying jobs. Then beginning in the 1970s, tourism replaced the military as the island state's biggest spender and that's how it's been for the ensuing years—a trend that is expected to continue into the next century. Most jobs in tourist and related service industries—cleaning rooms at the Hyatt Regency or waiting on customers at Gucci—are relatively low-paying. Moreover, unlike manufacturing a Sony Walkman or a Nissan Infiniti, such jobs add little value to Hawaii's economy and are in many cases interchangeable between one employee and another. Even more troublesome is the fact that the business of taking care of tourists is historically volatile, subject to violent ups and downs and over-building. There are heady times when booking a holiday room is virtually impossible but there are also mean times, forgotten in the euphoria and hyperbole of over-building, when rooms remain vacant for weeks on end and rates are brutally discounted. Miami has learned this lesson time and again, that flocks of tourists don't come with the regularity of swallows making their annual flight to Capistrano. So too with Waikiki.

Then, with Japanese nationals accounting for about half of Hawaii's economic activity, a downturn in Japan's economy or a severe drop in the Japanese real estate or stock market could be very traumatic for the fiftieth state's economy, not to mention the entire U.S. economy. It should not be forgotten that much of the Hawaiian real estate purchased by Japanese nationals has been financed by funds borrowed against Tokyo real estate. If a Japanese bank calls in or asks for more collateral for a loan, one of the first things that would be sold to raise cash would be Hawaiian real estate. It's also a pretty sure bet that the Japanese will depart or cut back in the same manner they came—en masse. A trickle will turn into a flood in short order. Any large-scale Japanese withdrawal—painful as it will be—will create lower house prices. However, cheaper housing won't necessarily be such a great bonanza for Hawaiians, since unemployment will be high as a result of the plunge in tourist traffic. It's nice to have cheaper housing if you've got the money to pay for it.

If there's a loss of control through this dependence on Japan, there's also growing concern that Hawaii and Japan's interests diverge on a number of points. The Higas' plight is a case in point where they're being run over by Japan's stampede for golf land. Their protest banner—"No can eat golf balls"—is right on the mark. In effect, the Higas are being asked to decamp in order to accommodate a pastime that ranks very low on most Hawaiians' leisure-pleasure scale. When 2,333 Oahu residents were polled during a ten-day period in November 1988 as to their leisure preferences, golf as a recreation hardly scored a hole in one. Asked to rank the importance of various city park and recreation services on a scale of 100, municipal golf courses came in with the lowest ranking of any pastime with an abysmal 57 percent, followed by tennis courts with a 74 percent level. At the top of the heap were beach parks, the zoo and children's play equipment, with respective scores of 95, 92 and 90 percent. In terms of usage, golf courses scored even worse with Oahu's residents, with only 24 percent of those questioned saying they played golf at the municipal courses. Again beach parks, zoos and quiet parks were way up there in terms of recreational usage.[27]

If golf courses rank at the bottom in terms of Oahu residents' preference and usage, Oahu still cannot be faulted for providing anything less than the national average of 18-hole golf courses for its population. The National Golf Foundation, a lobbying group for the golf industry, says an acceptable yardstick for a large metropolitan area such as Honolulu and its environs is one 18-holer per 50,000 of population. The City and County of Honolulu golf courses handily meet this standard at present, even when daily visitors are included. Meeting this standard for an increased population by the year 2010 means that an additional five courses will have to be created. Adding five new courses to Hawaii's recreational facilities early on in the next decade may sound somewhat ambitious, given Oahu residents' general lack of interest in golf and the cost—from $16 to $20 million, with land costing $15,000 an acre and a $1.5-million clubhouse, but it's in the minor leagues in comparison to what Japanese investors have on the boards.

Just how frenzied the Japanese golf stampede has become is readily apparent from a report prepared in August 1989 for Honolulu mayor Frank Fasi's office by the Department of Land Utilization, which said it had "received an avalanche of permit requests and inquiries for permits for golf courses." At the time over 40 new 18-hole courses were under way or proposed, at a total cost of close to $1 billion. If they were all built, they would use up 7,500 acres and 30 million gallons of scarce water a day. Seven thousand five hundred acres may not be a lot of land in Texas or Alaska but in Hawaii, as in Japan, it's a great deal since there is an artificial shortage in both places. In some ways it's ironic that the Japanese would lead the rush for Hawaiian land since Hawaii's land problems bear a striking resemblance to problems the Japanese left at home. As in Japan, a paltry 4 percent of

Hawaii's land[28] is zoned for residential use, with the remaining 96 percent held by the huge land trusts, such as Bishop and Campbell estates created in the nineteenth century, the government and farmers. Also as in Japan, protecting Hawaiian agricultural land is a politically sensitive subject, though the constituents are different in the two countries.

To put the importance of 7,500 Oahu acres in perspective, all one has to do is realize that during the 20 years prior to 1984 less than 10,000 acres of Oahu land were rezoned from agricultural to urban use. In the 1963–84 period, private developers had asked that 30,654 acres of agricultural land be rezoned so that they could develop it for housing and other uses. What they encountered was a bureaucratic bottleneck and a great deal of opposition to taking the land out of agricultural use, even though Hawaiian agriculture was on the decline.[29] Approval of a typical subdivision from initial application takes about six years, whereas it took Herbert Horita over a decade of tough negotiating to get his $3-billion plans for Ko Olina accepted by the planning commission. Moreover, the way to approval is paved with costly and time-consuming studies, including environmental impact statements and archeological studies, with the admirable goal of preserving Oahu's distinct beauty and character. It would be nice to say that Japanese real estate development had the effect of making Oahu a better place to live but this is not the case, especially for average Hawaiian wage earners, who have seen their real earnings decline in purchasing power, whether they're buying a house or food imported from the mainland.

A lack of buildable land and new affordable housing has been translated into incredibly costly housing, a situation that has been further aggravated by the influx of Japanese investors.[30] While an average single-family house can be bought for $96,200 on the mainland, a similar house costs almost four times as much in and around Honolulu, with a median price of $345,000. What you're talking about here is a very modest house—nothing fancy for $345,000. The housing at Ko Olina, for example, will be considerably more expensive. Still such a house is obviously out of reach for the average Hawaiian with a per capita income of $17,000, whereas for many a vacationing Tokyoite $345,000 is little more than mad money. The fear is that, given such costly housing, Hawaiians, especially the young, will be forced off the islands in search of affordable housing.

With such prices, it's no wonder the Higas, who tilled their coastal vegetable plot not far from the site where Ko Olina is rising, were upset. Obviously settling in Ko Olina would be out of the question. What was particularly galling to the Higas and other farmers was the fact that the Japanese were benefiting from a loophole in Hawaiian law making conversion of farm land into golf courses much easier than for residential use. When so-called Chapter 205, which delineates the permissible use of Hawaii's agricultural land, was amended in 1985, it allowed golf courses to be developed on marginal agricultural lands. What it also did was speed up the process for obtaining a special permit from the Land Use Commission to build a golf course.[31] Not only were the Higas faced with losing their livelihood to Japanese in pursuit of sport and pleasure, but they knew finding a new place to work and live, given the cost of housing on Oahu, would be next to impossible. They also knew "No can eat golf balls." Japan's pleasure was their pain.

6

Wall Street

The U.S. bungled its economic management and sank itself.
. . . If Japan didn't help out with its debts, the American
economy would collapse. Therefore, it is more fitting for Japan to receive a certificate of gratitude from the U.S.

—Hajime Karatsu, Tokai University professor
and former Matsushita Electric executive[1]

We have to live within our means. . . . Then we won't be so
dependent on Japanese money. It's one thing to get hooked
on a Sony Walkman, or on a Toyota. But when you get
hooked on their money, you're hooked.

—Lee Iacocca[2]

Forty-nine stories below the pristine World Trade Center
tower, battered arks of American commerce—rusted oil tank-
ers, barges ferrying rail cars, and garbage scows—float slowly out
of New York Harbor on an early December day, leaving Manhattan's tip to the port and to the starboard the Statue of Liberty and
Rikers Island. For some time now one of the Port of New York's
biggest imports has been Japanese money and moneymen emi-
grating here in hot pursuit of U.S. investments, whereas ironically one of the Port's largest exports has been the refuse of a
consumer society—the tons and tons of garbage shipped from its
decaying piers that no one wants to take in, except at a price.
Here in the Dai-Ichi Kangyo Bank's sprawling, lower Manhat-

tan office, Takasuke Kaneko, an affable senior vice president and general manager, is discussing how Dai-Ichi Kangyo, the world's largest bank, has just recently bailed out Manufacturers Hanover, the seventh-largest bank in America. As part of the arrangement revealed two months earlier, Dai-Ichi Kangyo also acquired a controlling, 60 percent interest in Manufacturers Hanover's jewel, CIT Financial, in a $1.4-billion deal that marked a number of firsts on Wall Street[3]—a place where Japanese banks rushing to expand their operations have had a good deal more firsts to cheer about than Japanese securities firms who've embarked on a similar expansionary path.

Ever since Dai-Ichi Kangyo and Manufacturers Hanover first disclosed their intentions in September 1989, Japanese investors have been on a roll, creating an ever more complicated web of economic dependency between America and Japan—a web that has included Sony's acquisition of Columbia Pictures, a second Tokyo-triggered plunge in New York Stock Exchange prices and Mitsubishi Estate's stunning purchase of controlling interest in Rockefeller Center, all in the intervening two-month period. Unlike Tokyo, where foreign investors are, for the most part, given short shrift and frozen out of any meaningful investments by the *keiretsu* system of interlocking shareholdings, America has been a wide-open, eat-as-much-as-you-can buffet for dollar-rich Japanese investors, catered to by a host of Wall Street investment bankers, brokers, mergers and acquisitions specialists and their ilk.

For if Japan is woefully poor in traditional commodities such as oil, lumber and iron ore, it has one commodity in abundance—money, the cement of the *zaibatsu* way which has laid the foundation for Japanese investors' easy move into the United States. Commenting on Japan's rich position in the world economy, Citicorp chairman John Reed once remarked, "I view Japan to capital as I view Saudi Arabia to oil."[4] And as Japan's investment in the U.S. has broadened and become more sophisticated, so too have the financial services offered by its giant banks and security firms. They're learning how to dress up, shape and form this basic commodity—money—so that their clients can make better use of it and they can make greater profits and gain greater market share, the latter being a key ingredient of the *zaibatsu* way as practiced by a Toyota, Sony or NEC.

However, for those Japanese financial institutions, such as Dai-

Ichi Kangyo who set up operations here in America years before the current boom in Japanese investment, their initial lure was to take care of their *keiretsu* companies and other Japanese firms, frequently helping facilitate the flow of exports to the U.S. and assisting in setting up American distribution channels. Remember, at the top of the six largest industrial groupings in Japan sits a mega-bank, such as Dai-Ichi Kangyo whose ties to group member companies are threaded with interlocking equity interests and loans. After all, a *keiretsu* without its bank is like a family without a nurturing, demanding mother, or a pyramid without its peak—an unnatural state of affairs. Then there is a synergistic relationship between a bank and its industrial client that is vital to economic growth. As a company's operations expand aided by bank borrowings, the bank also grows as a result of this business. In addition, in a *keiretsu* the economic effect of a bank-borrowed yen or dollar is multiplied as it passes through various companies within the *keiretsu*, bouncing back and forth from company to bank to company to bank, etc. Also, by borrowing from a Japanese bank in the U.S. rather than directly in Japan, a company avoids the currency exchange risk inherent in bringing funds directly from Japan, while also maintaining its group ties in a new environment.

So initially when a Japanese firm decided to buy a company or build a plant in the U.S., more often than not a Japanese banker would be there ready with advice and financing, but nothing too sophisticated. However, when the tidal wave of Japanese investment funds began flowing into the U.S. around the mid-1980s, Japanese bankers and securities firms naturally moved to expand their operations on Wall Street so as to gain some of the rich rewards flowing from deals generated by this investment. As Japanese financiers rapidly saw, loaning money to help finance a $1-billion acquisition can be far less profitable than being the idea-man, the catalyst for the merger. Moreover, the payoff from the latter endeavor is almost immediate. They also saw that branching out into America's vast financial markets, which fund the world's largest and most varied economy, could prove to be very profitable, while also providing more varied services for its customers. Along the way their business grew far beyond catering to the needs of their fellow countrymen. "At first in the 1960s and 1970s Japanese banks just followed the industrial companies who were their customers in Japan. But about 1980, they began to approach U.S. corporations and by the mid-1980s they saw opportunities in the middle markets,"[5] Takanori Mizuno, director of the Japanese-sponsored Institute for Financial Affairs, said at the time the Dai-Ichi–Manufacturers deal was initiated. Dai-Ichi Kangyo's investment in CIT is an apt example of such efforts to have a more diverse line of services.

Moreover, the union between Manufacturers Hanover and Dai-Ichi Kangyo is an example of Zaibatsu America working in full force on both micro- and macroeconomic levels. It got its collective impetus as a result of both the burgeoning of Japanese financial institutions around the world and the concurrent huge Japanese capital flows that flooded into the U.S. after the 1985 Plaza Five devaluation of the dollar. It also underlines the strong ties that bind the U.S. and Japanese economies on both the micro and macro levels in very significant ways. Symptomatic of these trends, Japanese banks' share of international lending skyrocketed from 20 to 38 percent in the 1983–88 period, spurred on by the rising value of the yen in the latter half of this period and the fact that Japan became the world's largest exporter of capital in the 1980s, with an annual outflow of about $80 billion a year.[6] Moreover, according to the Bank for International Settlements' tally, Japanese banks saw their foreign assets grow at a 31 percent compound rate during this same period. All of this growth has come as Japan's huge banks and securities firms have rushed to expand their global operations offshore Japan, in London, New York and beyond, seeking new markets and also the rich benefits inherent in the economies of scale. This expansion has also occurred as America's giant international banks, who led global banking in the 1960s and 70s, are seeing their role eclipsed by Japanese and European banks and are pulling back dramatically from their foreign operations.[7] Manufacturers Hanover is just such a bank, who's had to cut back because of problem loans and heightened competition in its international markets.

In the U.S. such global growth has meant that Japanese banks now control an estimated 15 to 20 percent of America's banking assets, with a much higher proportion in areas such as leveraged-buyouts where their participation has averaged about 40 percent.[8] In California, America's most populous state, Japanese-owned banks already control about 25 percent of the market and their share is growing.[9] Moreover, at the end of 1988 Japanese banks had more than $300-billion worth of assets in the U.S.[10] Dai-Ichi

144

Kangyo, for example, already has $30 billion in assets in the U.S. which places it among the 20 largest banks in America. Even larger are Bank of Tokyo with $44 billion in U.S. assets, Mitsubishi Bank with $33 billion and Fuji Bank Ltd. with $31 billion. Ranking just behind Dai-Ichi Kangyo in terms of U.S. assets are Sanwa Bank, Industrial Bank of Japan and Sumitomo Bank, each of which has more than $20 billion in U.S. assets.[11] As this lending has grown, they have gone upmarket and gotten more return for their money. Dai-Ichi Kangyo's tie-up with Manufacturers Hanover fits right into this pattern of asset growth in the U.S. So despite some initial and recent setbacks, the great majority of these firms are here with every intention of staying and growing.

For Dai-Ichi Kangyo—an establishment that likes to be known around Japan as the bank with a heart and has a stylized heart running rampant at its Tokyo headquarters, decorating elevator doors, clocks and executives' lapel buttons—the arrangement with Manufacturers Hanover marked the biggest investment by a Japanese bank in an American financial firm.[12] It was also the most far-reaching agreement to be negotiated between two financial giants, in that it bound Manufacturers Hanover, hard pressed because of troubled loans to less developed countries, and Dai-Ichi Kangyo into a continuing working arrangement.

So what does this marriage of convenience mean for Manufacturers Hanover, other than a much-needed infusion of capital? For one, Manufacturers Hanover will be more greatly influenced by the global growth of Japanese financial institutions and the explosion in the outflow of Japanese funds into the U.S.—two factors which operate sometimes in tandem and at other times in a symbiotic way. It also means ceding some control to Dai-Ichi—more than either will initially admit. According to the $1.4-billion deal, which Manufacturers initiated with the help of Goldman Sachs, Dai-Ichi Kangyo paid $1.28 billion for its 60 percent interest in CIT and an additional $120 million for a 4.9 percent share of Manufacturers that it has agreed not to increase for ten years.[13]

Dai-Ichi's Kaneko said that Dai-Ichi wanted CIT's know-how in order to meet the needs of its clients—Japanese and other—that fell in the middle market, but that it really only made the investment in Manufacturers because of the bank's insistence. He said it would have taken Dai-Ichi ten to fifteen years to develop the position CIT has. Though the margins the $10 billion in assets CIT offers are particularly attractive, there's nothing fancy about the way they do business, helping to finance the business of America's medium-sized companies through its 50-some offices around the country. Manufacturers Hanover's interest rate spread—the difference between what it pays for its money and what it gets from lending it—averages around 2.4 percent, whereas at CIT it's more than double that—more than 5 percent.[14]

"We cannot wait 10 to 15 years. We needed the position now. So our quickest way is to acquire CIT," Kaneko said. A good many other Japanese banks have taken a similar approach in order to get into the middle market and develop another niche as they branch out in the U.S. In fact, Dai-Ichi Kangyo's investment in CIT can also be seen as a classic *zaibatsu* case of moving with the pack, albeit in Dai-Ichi Kangyo's case at a somewhat tortoise-like pace.

Back in 1983 Fuji Bank paid $425 million for Walter E. Heller International Corporation, a troubled finance company into which Fuji poured another $1 billion and is only now beginning to see some turnaround.[15] Then in 1985, Sanwa Bank bought beleaguered Continental Illinois Corporation's leasing unit which had about $500 million in assets. A few months before the Dai-Ichi–Manufacturers deal came to fruition, Security Pacific Bank sold 5 percent of its consumer and commercial finance operations to Mitsui Bank for $100 million, giving it an option to acquire an additional 5 percent. Around the same time Japan's largest leasing firm, Orix International, paid $190 million for First Interstate Bancorp's leasing operations.[16]

Though Dai-Ichi Kangyo's purchase is large and sets a new precedent, it is just a drop in the proverbial bucket in terms of the tens of billions of dollars that have inundated Wall Street since the mid-1980s as Japanese banks and securities firms have recycled some of Japan's vast trading profits and savings into U.S. government securities, direct investments, stocks, real estate, bonds and loans to U.S. and Japanese companies. However, it should also be remembered that besides arriving with trunk loads of money to set up business here and help ease the way for their *keiretsu* group customers, Japanese financial institutions had another huge plus on their side: access to competitively less expensive funds that they could lend at low, low rates.[17] Though this advantage has lessened recently as Japanese interest rates have come more in line with those prevailing in the U.S., the impact of this state of affairs has been very far-reaching, giving Japanese banks and their client firms enormous competitive clout.

Northwestern University economist B. Douglas Bernheim and John B. Shoven of Stanford calculate that during the 1980s the United States was burdened with the highest capital costs of any of the world's industrialized economies, with American firms having to pay nearly twice as much in after-tax terms for the capital they use than their Japanese counterparts. In Japan the weighted average of debt and equity costs after taxes hovered around 2 ¾ percent during the period, whereas in America similar costs were about 5½ percent.[18] Though a higher American rate of inflation partially explains the marked difference in capital costs, the real culprit is America's abysmal rate of savings. As a percent of gross domestic product, the Japanese save nearly twice as much as Americans, having a 26 percent rate of savings in 1989 as compared to 15 percent in the U.S.[19] Though there was a slight increase in Americans' rate of saving in the late 1980s, it had been steadily declining during the decade. The implications of a higher propensity to save are simple enough: there's more money around to lend and therefore it will be lent out at cheaper rates. It's a simple matter of supply and demand.[20]

Then Japanese banks have other advantages working for them. They can sell equity in Japan at price-earnings multiples that run six to ten times higher than those of their American counterparts. This also reduces the cost of capital they lend out and invest.[21] In addition, when they have to raise additional capital as they recently did to meet International Monetary Fund capital requirements, they have a ready market for their shares—their *keiretsu* member companies will readily buy up additional shares. Moreover, their top credit ratings mean that they can borrow money in the U.S. to lend or finance their expansion here at a lower cost than most of their American competitors. When Sumitomo Bank, the world's third-largest with assets of $407 billion, recently raised $500 million in ten-year subordinated notes, it arranged to pay only 9.55 percent a year for the money. By contrast a Chase Manhattan or Chemical Bank would pay over 11 percent for similar long-term funds borrowed at the same time.[22]

Having access to cheaper money is a tremendous advantage. Its benefit to Japanese firms and financial institutions setting up business in the U.S. cannot be underestimated. Financing a plant or an acquisition in the U.S. at half what an American competitor has to pay gives a company great leverage. It also means the company can spend more on plant and equipment, as many Japanese have, and still remain competitive. The capital differential can have other devastating implications for American firms. With the cost of capital being a prime consideration, if not the number one preoccupation of many American firms, the top jobs at many American companies have fallen to accountants and corporate finance types trained to squeeze the last dime out of an investment. By contrast, many of Japan's most successful companies, benefiting from freer access to relatively cheap capital, are managed by generalists or engineers whose first interest is in making better products and gaining market share. High-cost capital also helps explain the short-term orientation of many American firms. It is frequently a matter of necessity. It is estimated that, given the high cost of capital in the U.S., an American company investing $100 million in a new plant has to demand that the operation break even and start paying for itself within 5.7 years. Because of the lower cost of capital, a Japanese firm making a similar $100 million investment can wait up to 10 years or longer for the operation to start making money.[23] Cheap money explains in part Japanese stick-to-itiveness and long-term orientation. It also gives new meaning to the phrase, "Time is money," in that money also buys time.

Think of what money is. It's one of the world's basic commodities—it's the glue of commerce and the fertilizer of prosperity. It can reverse poverty. It gives power but in itself it's neutral, faceless. It's just some fleeting numbers on a currency trader's video screen. It slips through people's fingers like water. It's a bit like water, but not a force of nature. It's hoarded and saved. It's like a flawless diamond, no color, just facets, beauty in the eye of the beholder. It takes on personality when it's used for something— to save, to lend, to buy, to give, to bully, to belittle. The difference between a dollar or a yen lies partly in what's printed on the face of the paper, maybe the grain of the paper, how the bill is cut. But it's also what it represents and what people believe it represents.

Curiously enough, Japan's huge securities firms—the Big Four Nomura, Nikko, Daiwa and Yamaichi—haven't been nearly as successful at making a significant splash on Wall Street as their banking brethren. This is not for want of spending billions of dollars and countless hours in an effort to gain a major, major place on Wall Street as part of their push to become global marketeers.[24] They have yet to reach the sort of global Wall Street presence envisioned by Nomura chairman Setsuya Tabuchi, where by "the year 2000 Nomura's headquarters will not be in Tokyo but on a satellite orbiting the Earth, uplinking and downlinking information and electronic transactions instantaneously across the globalized axis of the London, New York, and Tokyo markets."[25]

Certainly, Japanese securities firms already have very important operations here, but as yet they haven't massed into the sort of financial juggernaut many feared they would in the mid-1980s. All four, who rank among the top ten securities firms in the world, faced staff cutbacks and losses in their New York operations during 1988 and early 1989.[26] In part these problems were attributable to overexpansion in the post–Plaza Five Agreement period, the lingering effects of the 1987 crash which never totally disappeared and tended in the late 1980s to curtail the flow of new Japanese funds into U.S. equities, and the general malaise that had been creeping into Wall Street and other world securities markets. Then the 1990, 40 percent plunge in the Tokyo stock market and heightened competition there further exacerbated matters for Japanese securities firms. It should also be remembered that if these Japanese securities firms were having trouble making a buck on Wall Street in the late 1980s, so too were their American counterparts. But these factors are only part of the reason why major Japanese securities firms have found Wall Street tough going.

The real money that's been made on Wall Street in the past decade has been in fancying up, dressing up money in fantastic new guises such as LBOs. This is what much of the securities business is about—creating so-called new investment vehicles, new products, new ways of making money out of money, new options, futures and swaps. Sometimes it looks like the Emperor's new clothes and sometimes it is. It's what's called having ideas. Japanese securities firms initially were short on ideas when they set up business here. They've faced and have yet to lick certain knowledge and cultural barriers, though they're fighting hard to overcome them.

Though the Japanese securities firms have honed highly developed trading skills and portfolio techniques in Tokyo, upon entering American markets full force they've had to learn a whole new host of stock market skills that reflect a revolutionary understanding of how assets and markets work. They're moving up the learning curve but at times it's been difficult, particularly while both the New York and Tokyo Stock Exchanges went into a 1990 nervous breakdown. But they're hardly giving up. Rather they're voraciously studying and acquiring the techniques of high-tech, post-modern finance as fast as they can. They're not only endowing chairs at America's most prestigious business and law schools—Nomura already has Nomura professorships at Wharton, MIT, NYU and Harvard Law, but they're investing heavily in high-tech portfolio management firms and high-tech equipment so as to eventually be operating in the sort of world Nomura's Tabuchi envisioned.

Such setbacks, though, don't mean that Japanese securities firms won't persist and aren't expanding on Wall Street. Remember, the first Toyotas sold over here were flops, and look at where they are now. When Japanese firms have been faced with a paucity of ideas in other areas such as high-tech they've bought them, acquired them through joint ventures, or eventually assimilated them through hard study. That's what they're doing in Wall Street and the payoff, as they realize, will be some time in coming. The pack has arrived on Wall Street, it just hasn't taken form yet. But wait.

Nomura has a $100 million, 20 percent stake in merger specialist Wasserstein, Perella & Co. and a joint venture with high-tech money manager Rosenberg Institutional Equity Management. Also seeking to tap Wall Street's brains is Nikko which paid $100 million for 20 percent of former Commerce secretary Peter Peterson's Blackstone Group, the catalyst in the Sony-CBS Records and Columbia Pictures deals, and has a half share of Wells Fargo Investment Advisors.[27] Other securities firms have been following suit, as also have major Japanese banks and insurance companies.

Sumitomo Bank invested $500 million in premier investment banker Goldman Sachs, but has yet to get any substantial rewards out of its 12.5 percent interest because of banking restrictions. Nippon Life's $508-million stake in troubled Shearson Lehman has been a disappointment, as has the $300 million Yasuda Mutual Life has placed in Paine Webber's coffers. More successful has been the Big Four securities firms' move into the elite group of primary dealers in U.S. government securities, a natural area for them since Japan has become one of the most important purchasers of U.S. debt floated to feed America's bloated budget deficit. Moreover, Japanese banks—the Industrial Bank of Japan, Long-Term Credit Bank of Japan and Sanwa Bank—that have gained entry into this area through investment in primary dealers, have also been doing well. But this again is not much of an ideas business, though a great deal can be made and lost in the endeavor.

The cultural differences that Japanese securities firms confronted when they decided to enter Wall Street full force were particularly hard to surmount. When they arrived en masse setting up large offices all over Lower Manhattan, they were fat and self-satisfied, with a different mind-set. Since stocks are still bought and sold under a system of fixed commissions in Japan, much of the money these firms made came from clerking stocks rather than fighting for commission business. This meant that these firms came to America largely with a clerk's mentality, horrified by the six- and seven-figure salaries some Wall Street dealers with ideas or hustle were making. They've had to adapt and at times this has been painful but they're doing it. Wall Street of the 1980s was the wild west of finance—a place where confrontation rather than consensus ruled the day, where the ruthless aggressiveness of an Ivan Boesky or Michael Milken was heralded as genius and revered by many underlings until they were indicted on criminal charges, and where the big money was made in arbitraging the shares of a prospective takeover, leveraged-buyout fees and the repackaging of LBOs. This was all part of fancying up money. Though Japanese firms and banks provided much of the funds for these activities, they were for the most part excluded from the more profitable aspects of these deals.

Japanese banks, for their part, have done better here than Japanese securities firms because they haven't had to dress their money up that much and also there are just more places for a bank to do business once it's gotten its feet on the ground. Most banking is still pretty basic, much of the profit being based on the spread between what funds cost and what they're lent at. It's a function that can branch out into a number of areas.

What's also happened thus far is that Japanese banks have been more successful at bringing the *zaibatsu* way of doing business to the U.S. than Japanese securities firms. The banks have come into the U.S. market and gained market share in the same manner as the Japanese makers of autos, computer chips and steel—gliding in on the wings of cheap exports, in the banks' case cheap money. Now that they've established themselves and have an important place in the market they're moving upscale, just as the auto and chip producers have, into the higher-margin areas. This is what Dai-Ichi Kangyo's buying a controlling interest in CIT is about, moving into more profitable niches. Other areas of Japanese banks' niche building are municipal finance and LBOs where the collapse of the proposed UAL buyout was the latest example of just how volatile ties with Japan can turn out to be.

One of the most spectacular areas of growth for Japanese banks has been in municipal bond financing. In 1983, Japanese banks did virtually no business in this letter-of-credit market, where a bank guarantees a municipality's bonds. Today they are the biggest issuers of these guarantees, accounting for over 50 percent of the market for municipal bond offerings a year.[28] They have grown to their pre-eminent position in this area because their high credit rating allows them to charge less for the service than the majority of competing American banks.

As far as LBOs are concerned, Japanese banks who eagerly bought up as much as 40 percent of the larger deals in better times have been on the retreat since the fall of 1989. At the time it was estimated Japanese investors had $20 billion in LBO loans and another $35 billion in LBO loan commitments outstanding, placing them just behind America in terms of exposure. Japanese banks had been pulling back from LBOs since the summer of 1989, but after the $6.75-billion buyout of UAL Inc. collapsed because Japanese banks demurred partially at the behest of the Ministry of Finance, there was no question as to what their position was. It had a very dramatic effect. On a Friday afternoon in October, an hour before trading closed on the New York Stock Exchange, investors learned the UAL deal had fallen through because Japanese banks had not put up their expected share. In one hour the Dow Jones plunged 190.58 points, the biggest drop since the 508-point October 19 crash, also triggered in Tokyo.[29]

Scary! News travels fast in the computer-driven information age which the Japanese are striving to dominate.

Take heart. A month and a half after the 190-point plunge, the gold-trumpeted angels and soaring, stories-high Christmas tree had been lit uptown at Mitsubishi-controlled Rockefeller Center, and American consumers are still shopping with abandon while Kaneko talks quietly about Dai-Ichi Kangyo's expansion in America as the morning sun fills his World Trade Center office.

7

Welcome to Japan, Home of the Zaibatsu Way

Where America Plays Trivial Pursuit

It is much harder to nullify the results of an economic conquest than those of a military conquest.

—Takahashi Korekiyo, Japanese prime minister 1921–22[1]

Using group power, they can engage in cutthroat competition.

—Iwao Nakatani, Osaka University professor,
on Japan's industrial groupings[2]

Other than the Imperial Palace and Gardens a few blocks away, this flat, nondescript plot of land now known as Marunouchi is one of the most expensive pieces of real estate in Tokyo, and for that matter in the world. It is also a wellspring of the irrepressible *zaibatsu* way, an area where forming and sticking together in groups pervades all walks of life, from the gaggles of dark-suited office workers dashing to and from lunch straight up through the hierarchy of Marunouchi headquartered corporations. Here, corporate neighbors incestuously possess parts of one another through intricate cross-shareholdings; here, having gone to the right university and having the right connections can mean more than having the right answer; here, paternalistic marriages are still arranged by corporations; here, outsiders are given little room.

This, the center of Tokyo's business district, is quintessential corporate Japan. It's here that vast Japanese fortunes have been made and now reside. From here and the neighboring Otemachi section, the taut, sinewy arms of corporate Japan flex, stretch and pull in their dollar, pound and franc profits—profits that have been flowing in so rapidly that there aren't enough people or ideas to handle them. Here some of the world's largest banks and brokerage houses—Mitsubishi, Fuji and Industrial Bank of Japan, Daiwa and Nomura Securities—take and invest the savings of Japan's thrifty populace in stocks, bonds, real estate and U.S. Treasury bills.

Nearby is the Marunouchi's support system. A short walk or cab ride away are Japan's Parliament, the Diet, and its powerful ministries—MITI and the Ministry of Finance, prime architects of the Japanese economic miracle and major factors in Japan's global web of influence. Just around the corner in the Otemachi is the Keidanren, Japan's most prestigious and powerful business-lobbying group, whose members give hundreds of millions of dollars a year to political parties, chiefly the ruling Liberal Democratic Party. A few blocks away is the geisha-stocked, neon-glitzed Ginza for an evening's entertainment.

And it is from here and the surrounding Tokyo *keiretsu*-megapolis that the *zaibatsu* way has been fashioned and exported to create unique, economic strongholds in key sectors of the U.S. economy. Japan's growing stake in Auto Alley, Wall Street, Silicon Valley and Hollywood didn't come out of a vacuum, but has developed as an extension of Japan's economy and culture. It is not by chance that a Toyota settling in Georgetown or a Mitsubishi Semiconductors setting up a plant in North Carolina will show some striking similarities in the vertical, *zaibatsu* way their businesses burgeon. Dissimilar as building a car or fabricating a chip may be, the common thread, learned here in the group from kindergarten on, is the *zaibatsu* way of group behavior. To understand both what's happening in America and the *zaibatsu* monolith many American businesses confront in Japan, one must look to the origin, culture, social structure and evolution of the *zaibatsu* way in the context of Japan's changing economy.

From here in Japan we'll see how the Mitsubishi group has grown into the world's largest industrial entity, spreading its net throughout the world; how MITI continues to help orchestrate Japan's stunning progression into the twenty-first century, the electronics-driven information age which is giving shape to Japan's high-tech presence in the U.S.: how, save for some outstanding exceptions, America's presence in Japan is still largely limited to the less important, surface sectors of the economy; how Texas raider T. Boone Pickens has tried to shatter the *zaibatsu* monolith presented to outsiders but with little success; and how U.S. negotiators in Tokyo naively believe they can significantly change the *zaibatsu* way through their talks on the Structural Impediments Initiative (SII) which are partially aimed at opening up the *keiretsu*. This is where Japan's presence in the U.S. is coming from and what Americans are up against when they try to set up business in Japan. Paradoxically, while the *zaibatsu* way of doing business is internally dynamic, competitive and ever-changing, the face that it presents to outsiders is of the enigmatic, *zaibatsu* monolith.

For starters let's look at the Marunouchi where the Mitsubishi group was born. If Tokyo has a piece of real estate that comes close to New York's Rockefeller Center, it's the Marunouchi. The two, however, could hardly be further apart in appearance and spirit though some of the 1950s' and 60s' style lobbies in the Marunouchi attempt a poor imitation of Rockefeller Center's elan. Also, except for the scarcity of land in Tokyo, there is no rational justification for the fact that a square foot of Marunouchi land or office space costs ten times more than a comparable spot in New York, Paris, or London. Looked at objectively in terms of ambiance, one would expect the reverse to be true.

There's nothing glamorous about the Marunouchi—no vaulting dreams. Money wears a drab color of black and grey in the Marunouchi. It is money counted out on grey steel, formica-topped desks—money toted up on hand-operated adding machines and abacuses. It is not funny money or money for fun. It's not money to be spent on luxury—buying real luxury is a relatively new experience for egalitarian-claiming, post–World War II Japan. It is money for saving for a rainy day. Rich as it is, the Marunouchi doesn't wear the face of Mammon—a face of voluptuous greed. It's a blank face with little enjoyment or fantasy.

At Rockefeller Center the statue of Atlas shrugs his mighty frame and the buildings soar on mid-Depression dreams of romance and glitz. Lobbies of black marble and gilt ring with the high-energy trot of New Yorkers and visitors making their way. Money is a green thrill, seemingly abundant and uncounted, a shot of adrenalin. Here Fred Astaire, in top hat and tails, dances the Rainbow Room evenings away with Ginger Rogers high above Manhattan. Rockefeller Center is New York, America at its best—lost America.

The Marunouchi is different. You can't imagine anyone dancing or even dreaming in these squat, flat-roofed, grey buildings. These are feet-on-the-ground, bourgeois, no-nonsense buildings that were seemingly cut out of the same 1950s' pre-cast concrete mold. Solid, somber, and boring—they march along the Marunouchi streets in rigid order. Ironically, one of the shabbiest of all is where Mitsubishi Estate, owner of over half of the Rockefeller group, is housed.

As in the rest of Tokyo, a more modern, dynamic, worldly style of building is cropping up at the fringes of the Marunouchi, but it has yet to change the Marunouchi's stolid, humorless atmosphere. Mitsubishi Estate does have a grand $45-billion dollar plan to raze the whole area and replace it with super skyscrapers. But it will be years in coming.

If the Marunouchi is a microcosm of corporate Japan today, there can be no doubt whose territory this is. Other companies may operate and prosper in the Marunouchi, but Mitsubishi is the dominant force here and has been for over a century. This is Mitsubishiville, home of the world's largest group of related companies—offspring of the prewar Mitsubishi *zaibatsu* that have combined revenues of close to half a trillion dollars. The Mitsubishi seal—the three-pronged star forming an equilateral triangle— is ubiquitous.

The Mitsubishi group is the largest of the six pre-eminent industrial groupings, or so-called *keiretsu*, that include the Mitsui, Sumitomo, Fuyo, Sanwa and Dai-Ichi groups. According to a report issued by the Fair Trade Commission of Japan in August of 1989, these six groups occupy an incredibly powerful position in Japan's economy.[3] Interestingly enough, their position now of controlling nearly a third of Japan's economy is similar to their pre–World War II status—a rank that was briefly undermined when the occupation sought to break up the *zaibatsu* after the war. Together, these six *keiretsu* control an incredible 27 percent of Japan's assets and 25 percent of its sales, which is pretty much how it was in 1939. Moreover, these figures significantly understate these *keiretsu*'s web of influence in the economy since the FTC's calculations include only the 193 companies most closely associated with these *keiretsu*. In Mitsubishi's case, for example, the FTC figures are based on 29 companies that are members of Mitsubishi's most elite inner circle through large cross-shareholdings, shared directors and related business dealings. Not taken into account are the hundreds or possibly thousands of companies that are part of the Mitsubishi group in varying degrees.

"When one observes the fact that a powerful corporation of each group exists in each industrial sector, it is impossible to ignore their great influence," the FTC report concludes.[4]

The Mitsubishi empire, or *zaibatsu* as it was soon to become known, was founded at the beginning of the 1868 Meiji restoration by Yataro Iwasaki, a rough, tough young man who came from a samurai family that served the powerful Tosa feudal clan of Osaka. Even Mitsubishi's recent official history notes that Yataro Iwasaki has been described by some biographers as a "monster" or a "mettlesome adventurer" and adds that Tokyo University professor Takao Tsuchiya said "in the long history of Japan it would be difficult to find someone as terribly aggressive as Yataro Iwasaki." However, such criticism is dismissed by Mitsubishi, which claims his aggressiveness and business can be "summarized as an expression of patriotic sentiment deeply rooted in the character of a samurai."[5]

Before 20-year-old Yataro left home to make his fortune in Tokyo, he climbed the mountain behind the Iwasaki home one last time and left this message carved in the staircase of the "Star" Shinto shrine sitting atop Mount Moyken: "Business nationwide is awaiting my skills. If I fail to become a great success, I swear that I will never return to climb this mountain."

It is this proud, uncompromising samurai past that the Mitsubishi seal harkens back to. A combination of family crests—the *sangaibishi* or three-tiered water chestnut leaves of the Iwasaki family and the *mitsugashiwa* or three oak leaves of the Yamauchi family, lords of the Tosa group—the seal can be seen everywhere in the Marunouchi decorating sewer covers, the entrances of buildings and the thousands of calling cards exchanged daily in the course of business.

And no wonder since Mitsubishi Estate, the member of the Mitsubishi group that recently bought a controlling interest in Rockefeller Center, owns much of the land and 24 prime office buildings in the Marunouchi. In turn, Mitsubishi Estate's largest shareholders are Mitsubishi group companies—Mitsubishi Trust, Meiji Mutual Life, Mitsubishi Bank and Tokyo Marine—which also make their corporate headquarters in the Marunouchi in Mitsubishi Estate-owned buildings. This, however, is just a fraction of the Mitsubishi web of interlocking shareholdings which spread invisibly throughout the Marunouchi.

Like Mitsubishi, the Marunouchi has a noble past—a past in sharp contrast with its current look. As with so much in Japan, there is a continuity that survives earthquakes, war and political upheaval. Now the domain of the lords of commerce and industry, a little more than a century ago the Marunouchi was the preserve of feudal lords. During the Tokughawa Shogunate which lasted almost three centuries, the *daimyo* or feudal lords built their regal palaces here. Eventually the site was called the Marunouchi because each of the mansions had a name that ended in "maru." Thus Marunouchi can be translated rather roughly as the daimyo mansions. When the daimyo order ended with the beginning of the more open and egalitarian Meiji restoration, some of the samurai went into business to form huge industrial combines and the area became government property. After the noble daimyo estates were razed, the site was turned into an army drilling ground and barracks until it was purchased by Mitsubishi's second president, Yataro's younger and equally autocratic brother, Yanosuke Iwasaki.

In 1890, a hard-pressed Imperial Diet put the Marunouchi up for sale, asking the leading *zaibatsu* families—Mitsui, Mitsubishi, Okura, Shibusawa—to bid on the property. Eventually, Yanosuke Iwasaki bought some 135,000 *tsubos* or about 108 acres of the Marunouchi for the then princely sum of ¥ 1.5 million or about five times the going rate for comparable property in central Tokyo. While some of his competitors thought he was a fool to pay such a price, Yanosuke had a plan for the property, though all he would say when asked about the purchase was, "Who knows? Maybe I'll plant bamboo and keep tigers there." He also knew that the purchase strengthened Mitsubishi's already strong ties with the government.

Although *Mitsubishi-ga-Hara* or Mitsubishi Field as it was known for a time lay fallow, Yanosuke had plans to develop it into a modern business community, having learned from his adviser

Heigoro Soda that the duke of Westminster had become immensely rich because he owned land in downtown London. Perhaps for this reason, when Yanosuke decided to develop the Marunouchi and build paved roads, he chose a pseudo-British style for the three- and four-story redbrick buildings erected along the straight avenues with names such as First London. As a business district the Marunouchi didn't begin to blossom until 1914, when the redbrick Tokyo Station was built right in its center. Its preeminent position as the business center of Tokyo became undisputed, after the devastating 1923 earthquake and ensuing fires leveled most of the wooden office buildings in central Tokyo while leaving the brick and stone buildings of the Marunouchi intact. Hundreds of companies took temporary refuge there and have stayed on.

Today, Yanosuke's laughable investment in Mitsubishi field is estimated to be worth between $80 to $100 billion and control of it is just part of the wide economic swath the Mitsubishi group cuts in Japan and the world.

While there are a number of major differences between the pre–World War II Mitsubishi *zaibatsu* and the current Mitsubishi group, there has been a continuity of action and purpose that extends from the late nineteenth century to today. If there weren't such continued shared purpose, the group would not exist today with major members owning an average of over 25 percent of each other's shares. Moreover, if Mitsubishi's history bears a close relation to the history of modern Japan, it and the other major industrial groupings have also served as role models for much of modern Japan's corporate behavior. It is a way of doing business that has influenced such diverse companies as Toyota, NEC and Sony.

The *zaibatsu* way of doing business—forming and sticking together in vertically and horizontally integrated industrial groups—is a very strong tradition in Japan, with equally resilient social and cultural underpinnings. What has changed somewhat is the corporate structure it now inhabits. And this in turn has modified the *zaibatsu* way somewhat. In a dynamic relation such as this, form follows function and function form. But a leopard doesn't change his spots. A liter of Romanee Conti tastes pretty much the same, whether it's poured from a round or square decanter. It's a question of degree.

Certainly, today's *keiretsu* are not ruled in the autocratic way

Yanosuke ran the Mitsubishi *zaibatsu* at the turn of the century. Nor is their corporate structure based on a pyramid of power with the owning *zaibatsu* family sitting at the top. There is a hierarchy, but consensus, frequently a form of hidden intimidation rules the day. At times, the structure is more apparent than at others, but visible or not the group ethos rules the day.

The totality of Japan's culture and consciousness pervades every part of life. Here in Japan one derives much of one's identity from the institution—the school, the town, the corporation or the club one belongs to. Given the pervasiveness of the group ethos, it's not surprising that there is no word in Japanese for leadership.[6] Within the group, whether it is familial, social or corporate, there is generally a common structure where "members are tied vertically into a delicately graded order,"[7] while outside the group competition with other like groups is fierce. Key to the structure of this relationship is how people of higher and lower status interact in a so-called *oyabu-kobun*, or, literally, parent-child or patron-client, landlord-tenant links of dependency.[8] John David Morley aptly describes some aspects of this relationship in his novel *Pictures from the Water Trade*,[9] when he discusses how a baby is carried on a mother's back or *onbu*, as this form of carrying infants is called:

> It sometimes seemed . . . that the self-insufficient Japanese remained suspended onbu-style throughout the course of their lives, always bearing and being borne by others, equally indulged and imposed upon, as ambiguous in terms of their mutual dependence as the entire Japanese archipelago itself, sprung on a buoyant volcanic cushion between the Pacific Ocean and the Sea of Japan.

As can be imagined, the dynamics of such dependent relationships within a group are never-ending, always changing and, when harnessed as within a corporate group, extremely powerful. The other side of the coin, the ugly negative side of the group, is not to belong, and within and outside Japan non-group members are frequently viewed with suspicion and derision.[10] In its extreme such a group mentality translates into the sort of mono-race, racist attitudes that until recently allowed routine finger-printing of Japan's ethnic Korean minority, who number nearly 700,000 and have lived in Japan for decades but can not become full citizens unless they submit to an official investigation and adopt Japanese names.[11] Or there's the way the some three million Burakumin—the so-called "hamlet people" or former outcasts descended from butchers, leatherworkers and gravediggers—continue to be discriminated against.[12] Or there's the sort of apparently commonly held view of the United States' racial diversity expressed by then Prime Minister Yasuhiro Nakasone, who in 1986 when commenting on the Americans' skills said, "On the average the United States is lower because of a considerable number of blacks, Puerto Ricans and Mexicans."[13] Unfortunately, such behavior is also part of the group ethos.

It's a warm, Sunday afternoon in January and Tokyo's Omote Sando, with its low-lying, 1920s' Dojunkai Aoyama apartments and shade trees, has almost the feel of a provincial town in the South of France. For one used to the unsmiling, thin-lipped hustle of the Marunouchi or the loud, neon hype of the Roppongi shopping, restaurant and nightclub area, Omote Sando Street comes as a pleasant and unexpected surprise. The broad street with its flower-filled planters is closed for the day and crowds of young and old Japanese move in a relaxed, meandering way not seen in most of Tokyo. The dress is for the most part expensive casual and the look rich, in keeping with the shops that line the street such as Hanae Mori and New York's Paul Stuart. Perhaps because of the harmonious relation between open space and the neighborhood's relatively low buildings, there is also an unaccustomed feeling of luxury. Tokyo may be on its way to becoming one of the richest cities in the world, if not *the* richest, but except in places such as the Omote Sando, its wealth is not on display to any degree. In the past, wealth went into objects that were frequently hidden away—antique lacquer, screens, porcelain, or paintings put on display during different seasons—but not so much into obvious luxury. The Japanese have always excelled at making beautifully honed, artistically intricate and subtle objects—expensive and rare but not extravagant, not wasteful. The country still clings to the myth that it is egalitarian, with the rich and less rich living right next to each other. Neither the consumer nor conspicuous consumption has, until recently, been given much court. One had to go abroad to get name-brand luxury. That's changed.

Turning right onto the Meiji Dori, a major shopping street

where Mercedes, BMWs, Porsches and cars of lesser lineage jam the way, the mood changes as the pace quickens. It's more youthful and less luxurious, verging on Tokyo frenetic. Further down Meiji Dori at the corner of Takeshita Street, groups of youths cruise by the Cafe Royal at the base of the Palais France. Many have come from shopping Takeshita Street, a sort of narrow, Kings Road–Greenwich Village bazaar lined with small shops where fashions for young Tokyoites are frequently born and hung out on the street to be inspected and tried on. At first one is struck by the refreshing individualistic look of young passersby, until one notices the group influence—every fifth youth wearing a similar new leather jacket or sheepskin flap hat or grey sweatshirt with Georgetown University writ large, or the gaggles of young girls dressed to Kewpie doll sweetness, or the day-off punks all having been rinsed with the same hair dye. Moreover, they cruise the Meiji Dori and Takeshita Street wearing a certain self-conscious air—as if they've spent half a day putting themselves together to look casual. Curiously enough, a number of the newly designed, narrow five- and six-story buildings lining the Meiji Dori make a similar statement in architectural terms.

Different though the Omote Sando, the Meiji Dori and Takeshita may be in style and ambiance, they do have more in common than proximity. The common thread is a pervasive Japanese love of things American—at times somewhat ersatz American, but still American. It's strung through Takeshita Street with its Cafe Donky, Chicago, Do! Family, Wild Cat, Last Scene, along the Meiji Dori with Nautica, Lee Jeans, Eddie Bauer and Beams, a sort of Japanese L.L. Bean where one can buy $300 moccasins and Armani suits upstairs in a rustic environment and on down the Omote Sando, with Paul Stuart, the Key West Club and Foot Jogger. In the environs are Brooks Brothers, McDonald's, and something called Kiddyland. The fact is the Japanese may have a distinct and often closed society, but a fascination with American products and culture from Coke to Kentucky Fried Chicken to Schick Razors to Amway cleaning products, to Polaroid cameras, to Levi-Strauss jeans to Michael Jackson, has also been stitched into the Japanese consciousness. If Captain Perry of the Black Ships, the man who opened Japan to the world in 1854, were to come back and stroll around Omote Sando, he might conclude that Japan had really given the world and in particular the United

States access to its markets as a result of his efforts a century before.

Unfortunately, such a conclusion would be fallacious. What you see here is just what it is, the surface and not the center of the Japanese economy—like the label sewn on a new Paul Stuart jacket, or the Kentucky Fried Chicken box thrown in the trash after Colonel Sanders' fare has been consumed or the costumes young Japanese self-consciously don on their day off.

What is particularly impressive is that a buttoned-down Brooks Brothers or a more free-wheeling Kentucky Fried Chicken have been able to succeed in one of the most tight-knit sectors of the Japanese economy—Japan's retail trade. To penetrate the market has been a hard-fought battle. Not even the Japanese dispute the fact that Japan's retail sector is in many ways hopelessly antiquated, fragmented and inefficient—one of the major reasons Japanese consumers pay dearly for their daily rice and the rest of their household needs. However, with Japan's 1.3 million small shopowners competing against the nation's farmers for the title of being the Liberal Democrat Party's biggest supporter,[14] they have the political clout to conduct their business pretty much as they want to.

Japanese retailers' powerful position has been somewhat weakened as a result of agreements reached by the U.S. and Japan in April 1990 in the so-called Structural Impediments Initiative talks—rather unsatisfactory efforts to open Japan's economy to U.S. investment and create more of an equilibrium between the two countries' economies. As part of the SII agreement, which both President Bush and Prime Minister Kaifu pushed for, Japan agreed to open up its retail sector through changing some legal impediments to expansion. In particular, Japan said it would modify a law that required neighborhood approval for any new store larger than 600 square yards. In theory, this modification should work in favor of foreign retailers, especially those used to selling their wares on a large scale as many American firms are. In fact, though, it may very well not turn out that way.

Japan's larger retailers also see the modifications as an opportunity and they could very easily squeeze out their eager American competitors. Despite continuing resistance at the community level, the number of large Japanese retailers planning to open large-scale stores doubled in 1990 to 1,600. Such plans haven't deterred mass retailer Toys "R" Us, which intends to open 100 stores in Japan in the 1990–94 period, but the threat of heightened Japanese competition which is already plugged into the country's Byzantine, wholesale distribution system could dampen some American retailers' hopes of entering the market. McDonald's, 7-Eleven and Kentucky Fried Chicken have battled successfully in the Japanese market but they really never had competition of a similar, fast-food, convenience-store ilk. Japan's ubiquitous noodle shops and sushi counters are fast in serving up their soup and *sashimi* but they're different sorts of operations from a McDonald's or Kentucky Fried Chicken. The Japanese have grown up with the former and are just getting used to the latter.

Such market niches are just the sort the Japanese like to point to, encourage and take as examples of the great progress American firms are making—examples of what American firms can do if they try hard rather than saying the Japanese market is impossible to penetrate. These are indeed rich, visible niches but they are just small potatoes in terms of the Japanese economy, hardly penetrating the country's core.

The point is that what Americans can achieve in the retail sector is just skimming the surface of the Japanese economy. It's all very nice but in the whole scheme of things it doesn't add up to much. It's the frosting without the cake. They're never going to get enough business to make that much of a difference in either America's trade deficit with Japan or America's skewed investment relation vis-à-vis Japan. The plain fact is you have to sell a lot of soft-shouldered, three-button Brooks Brothers suits or Nautica jackets to counterbalance the effect of exporting one $40,000 Toyota Lexus or Nissan Infiniti, and those exports, especially of Lexus, are burgeoning as Americans trade in their BMWs or Mercedes for their Japanese counterparts. Moreover, much of the merchandise carrying American labels is actually made in Japan.

In terms of investment, American retailers' growing presence in Japan, while heartening, does little to counterbalance the diverse character Japanese investment is taking in the U.S. Despite market-opening efforts urged upon the Japanese by American negotiators, there is still very little symmetry between America's holdings in Japan and Japan's growing possessions in the U.S. Of course, America's spending more than it's been making tips the investment balance heavily towards Japan's buying in America. As part of the current imbalanced Japan-U.S. trade equation,

164

Japan has more to invest in the U.S. than vice versa. But that's only part of the lack of symmetry. As previously discussed, Japan's investment in the U.S. is targeted at the vital parts of the economy—autos, high technology, steel, finance and entertainment. Moreover, this investment is structured in the distinct *zaibatsu* way, adding further to its formidable challenge. Retailing, important as it is to the economy—and it's more important in the U.S. than in Japan because the American consumer frequently leads the economy while his Japanese counterpart has had a less important role—is not in the same class as autos, high technology, steel and finance.

American firms have had major successes in some of these areas. IBM, Texas Instruments and Motorola, to name just a few American companies, have all made impressive places for themselves in Japan's high-tech infrastructure. In addition, Du Pont, Exxon, and General Electric have significant positions in the country's industrial base. In the case of the latter three companies, their way has been eased through with the Big Six industrial groupings. Du Pont has strong ties and joint ventures with companies in the Mitsubishi and Mitsui groups. Exxon, for its part, has joint ventures with companies in the Mitsui and DKB groups and a 25 percent interest in Toa Nenroyo Kogyo, which is a member of the Fuyo group's presidential council. GE's main partners are Mitsui, Sumitomo and DKB, when it's not running its own subsidiaries in Japan. These American firms, however, are more the exception than the norm and, aggressive and innovative as most of them are, they are not playing the sort of role Japanese firms are in the U.S.[15]

Why is this the case? There are a number of explanations other than the fact that many American firms lacked the desire or the gumption to carve out a niche for themselves in Japan. It should be remembered that not so long ago—even in the 1960s—Japan was regarded as a developing country, an image Japan hung onto as long as it believably could. In addition, during the time of Japan's economic resurgence, many American firms, turned off by the immense difficulty and heavy restrictions involved in investing there, were directing the bulk of their energies and investment capital in the opposite direction—towards establishing a position in Europe and the emerging European community. This was the "American Challenge" chronicled by French author Servan-Schreiber in his best-selling book, *Le Défi américain*. While

165

the challenge never reached takeover proportions, Japanese bureaucrats studied the phenomenon and ironically took precautions so that what was happening in Europe wouldn't transpire in Japan. They needn't have worried.

All this meant that Japan could protect industries targeted for growth—steel and autos for example—and hardly anyone would object until low-priced Japanese steel or auto exports began inundating their home markets—frequently taking market share with under-priced, dumped products. By this time these protected industries would be so well established in Japan's economic fabric that it would be pointless for a foreign firm to try and establish a significant position in the industry in question. Though such protection eventually greatly buttressed Japan's mercantilistic success—a success initially based largely on converting raw materials into finished goods to be sold on world markets—it made good sense to have a strong Japan in the Far East, especially along geopolitical lines.

So the restrictions against entering Japan's market, either through exports or investments, were tolerated and stayed in place much longer than they realistically should have. For the bold firm seeking to set up business in Japan, the usual route would have to be a joint venture with a Japanese firm that would frequently require the sharing of technology. By now, most of these investment restrictions have been lifted, as well as the vast majority of direct and indirect tariffs. Japan presumably would now have a hard time restricting the import of popular American skis with the excuse that Japanese snow is different, or American beef on the grounds that the Japanese have a different digestive tract and can't stomach the stuff. They can stomach a T-Bone steak in New York but not in Tokyo?

But that doesn't mean a foreign firm seeking to invest, and expand and dominate a high-tech market in Japan will find an easy road. There's the example of America-invented semiconductors, that continue to have a meager percentage of the Japanese market despite many hard-negotiated agreements for a more open market. Or that a Motorola wouldn't have outrageous obstacles put in its way—by the Japanese government in concert with Japanese firms—so as to protect the Japanese telecommunications industry and try and prevent Motorola, a pioneer and leader in the field, from setting up a cellular phone system in Japan. Why do impediments to making serious investments in Japan still exist?

166

In a word, because the *zaibatsu* way of doing business is how Japanese firms operate with a vengeance at home, with government encouragement. The *zaibatsu* way is how Japan lives economically. It has been engrained in the nation's economic character for well over a century and it's not going to change. Why should it? There is little reason to believe the Japanese are going to alter their ways despite the SII efforts to tackle what they call the *keiretsu* business practices. American trade negotiators, after decades of hassling with their Japanese counterparts, have finally realized—at least to a degree—that applying their standards of economic behavior doesn't define the reasons for Japan's economic success or why American firms have such a difficult time getting started in Japan. Going along as Americans have, expecting the Japanese to be free traders and free marketeers is not just being naive. It's being stupid. America has had plenty of time to learn that Japan operates by its own economic standards and that it has to recognize this if it is to get on with its own business successfully. With American markets wide-open, enticing Japanese investment, the lack of reciprocity is alarming and patently absurd.

Look at what happened in the construction industry. American construction firms, such as Bechtel, are truly international companies, building huge projects around the world. Construction is a business Americans are good at and their expertise and efficiency are called upon from the Middle East to South America to Europe but not Japan. The country may have a great, efficient rail system—the Bullet Train is a marvel even after a quarter of a century's use—but when it comes to constructing roads and airports Japan hardly ranks in the top tier.

A couple of trips through Japan's principal airport, Narita, would make one think the Japanese knew next to nothing about constructing convenient, traveler-useful terminals. After a long, outrageously expensive journey to Narita, a traveler arrives in one of the most ill-equipped, overcrowded major airports in the world—better suited to a third world country. It's similar to Tokyo's highway system, which is totally inadequate to handle the city's current level of traffic.

Yet when it came to awarding contracts for the $8-billion Kansai airport being built outside Osaka in the Inland Sea, not one American bid was initially accepted. And while parts of the landfill sink into the Inland Sea, American firms continue to be denied any significant access to the project.[16] A little more than two years after American firms, by agreement with the Japanese government, were supposed to have greater access to this huge project, they were again shut out for no apparent reason except that they weren't Japanese.

AEG Transportation Systems Inc., a joint venture of AEG Aktiengesellschaft and Westinghouse Electric Corporation, has been building people movers—the wide rubber bands that move passengers along the interminably long distances from the so-called "jetway" where people "deplane" to their baggage—for two decades. So having built 11 of these around the world, the AEG joint venture thought they stood a good chance of winning the Kansai airport contract. Expertise, however, doesn't win the day in Japan, at least if it isn't Japanese. A joint venture of Sumitomo and Niigata Engineering, neither of which has ever built an airport people mover, won with a bid that was 40 percent less than the experienced AEG venture offered. The bid was like many in Japan where a Japanese company is willing to take a huge loss on a project so as to learn and also get its foot in the door and close out foreign competition.[17] It's been seen a number of times when a foreign company is seeking entry into Japan.

As Congressman Jack Brooks, chairman of the House Judiciary Subcommittee on Economic and Commercial Law, testified in May 1990 at Hearings on Foreign Corporations' Anticompetitive Practices:

> In its simplest terms, a *keiretsu* is a business cartel composed of a dominant Japanese manufacturer and its major suppliers. Each company in the *keiretsu* owns a piece in each of the other members. For all practical purposes, these companies act as one company with the dominant parent company calling most of the shots . . . [a bit of an exaggeration]
>
> We have seen this practice before in dealing with Japan. The form may be slightly different and the name changed, but essentially it is the same collusive system designed to block the U.S. corporations from entering the Japanese market while at the same time targeting U.S. industries for Japanese domination.
>
> In the construction industry the *keiretsu* [formed an arrangement that] was called "Dango." Through this system, Japanese construction firms, prior to the award of a large public works project, would get together at the local "Tea" house

and divide up the contract. Later the Japanese government would have a showcase "Competition" and American companies of course would be allowed to submit bids. However, for some reason they never seemed to win a contract. In fact, U.S. construction firms over the last twenty years have made almost no sales in the Japanese market, which is roughly three quarters the size of America's market. In the meantime Japanese firms increased their sales in the U.S. market from $50 million in 1981 to $3 billion in 1987 and it is still growing . . .

The *keiretsu* and other forms of collusive business practices in Japan have little, if anything, to do with making products faster, better, and cheaper. [This is debatable as seen at Toyota.] In my view, its sole purpose is to ensure that the Japanese economy continues to be controlled by a few rich and powerful industrialists who are using the system to target U.S. industries for extinction.

———

They lunch on simple fare, they know about power. Some curry, some tea will do when they meet each second Friday of the month on the top floor of the Mitsubishi Building in the center of the Marunouchi. They've met ever since it was legally allowed in the 1950s, and before that they met in the neighboring tea and geisha houses and clubs, and before that, before the war, their predecessors met in the Marunouchi. Power is what they are about, these faceless men who control 5 percent or more of Japan's gross national product, the heads of the 29 companies that form the *Kinyo-Kai*, Mitsubishi's presidential council. This is the world's largest corporate enterprise, employing hundreds of thousands of workers around the world in thousands of subsidiary, group operations. In the U.S. alone the company *Guide to Mitsubishi Companies in the U.S.* runs 124 pages, listing hundreds of operations across America ranging from manufacturing cars, to making silicon chips, to banking to real estate. As with Mitsui and Sumitomo, the two other groups whose roots go back to the prewar *zaibatsu*, the companies these men represent are mainly from the pre–World War II Mitsubishi *zaibatsu*.[18]

These men, however, are different from the Iwasakis, who had total power over their group—the Iwasakis who ruled at the top of the hierarchy and knew everything—the proud, samurai-descended Iwasakis who came from Osaka. These men get their life, their identity from the group but the group seemingly has a life of its own. It's a lonely life but the ego is still there—beaten down like the proverbial Japanese nail that sticks out, but ready to pop up. Having been trained from early childhood how to re-act—the right reaction counts. Truth, as in many parts of Japan, is relative, relative to whom you're talking to, relative to whom you want to please. Truth here is relative to Mitsubishi. You say no when you know yes and yes when you know no. These men are part of the ultimate power group in Japan. What does power get you? Power. You share in power, sleep in power, shower in power. But it's the group's power. It's a powerful group to be a member of. Discovery comes, then it's lost. That's part of the fun and fear of the group—being on top and bottom at the same time. Even if you've been educated at Tokyo or Keio University, stud-ied at Harvard, Oxford, MIT or Stanford, and return, the lure is still there. There are groups and groups. This is the top of the corporate groups—the biggest and the one where the web is drawn tightest. It has a siren call in Japan. It's the ultimate *keire-tsu*, a term that is ultimately open to many definitions because of its complexity.

Naohiro Amaya, former MITI vice-minister, who having de-scended from heaven, as they say in Japan, is now head of the Dentsu Institute for Human Studies, likened the structure of a *keiretsu* to a polymer, a chemical compound consisting of a num-ber of structural units bonded together at various points. A thoughtful, charming, and at times outspoken man, who is widely credited with having the force of vision in the late 1960s that greatly helped Japan become the economic heavyweight it currently is, Amaya said American corporations were more like monomers, the simple molecules that may become structural units of a polymer. Discussing *keiretsu* and the Japanese economy in his spacious Tokyo office recently, Amaya said:

> The problem of the *keiretsu* is that this *keiretsu* bond is intan-gible. It's not institutionalized. There is no contract—no formal institution. However, a *keiretsu* is the mentality of mutual trust, so that an outsider can not measure how strong this relationship is. It depends. There are strong *keiretsu* and there are weak *keiretsu*. It varies like people—the dynamics.
> There's also the efficiency, because communication is much smoother in a *keiretsu*—the communication of information is

much quicker than with outside people. Therefore, when company disputes take place within a company it's easier to get a solution . . . this is one reason the Japanese are reluctant to get close to the Americans because of the litigation. In a *keiretsu*, they seldom use a lawyer. It's more efficient, with these long-standing business relations. Of course, every member of the group has the freedom to get out of a *keiretsu*. However, being a member of the group is more profitable. . . .

It's a sort of mutual insurance. It brings members of the *keiretsu* stability, efficiency, and less fuss in doing business. That's the bright side of the *keiretsu*. The dark side is big companies could impose on weaker companies . . .

What the Japanese have created, in conjunction with their developmental state, is a unique, indigenous form of capitalism that reflects and is cut out of the woof and warp of Japanese society. In fact, Japan expert Chalmers Johnson, author of *MITI and the Japanese Miracle* and a professor at the University of California, claims that the *keiretsu* is Japan's "most important contribution to modern capitalism" and that the challenge it poses "is one of the main intellectual challenges of our time."[19] And as Amaya noted, this form of capitalism has been nurtured in a free market economy that is distinct from America's or for that matter, Europe's. Amaya claims Japan "invented industrial policy" so that it could emerge from the nineteenth century as an economic power and not be like India.

"I don't think the American [free market] model is the universal model and superior to others . . . ," Amaya said. "There are degrees of freedom. As compared to the model of the Soviet Union, we can say Japan's economy is much freer. If you compare it to the U.S., the American economy is much the freest."

So what do the gnomes of Mitsubishiville do when they lunch once a month at the *Kinyo-Kai?* What is their presidential council's agenda? Or for that matter, what do the heads of the other major industrial groupings—Sumitomo, Mitsui, Fuyo, Dai-Ichi Kangyo and Sanwa—discuss at their own similar monthly meetings? This actually is an important question, since an honest answer would give valuable insight into the group dynamics of Mitsubishi, how the chosen 29 reach a decision, and how this unique form of capitalism operates. However, if you believe what Mitsubishi says,

171

it's really quite amazing that the lunches have been going on for nearly four decades since the war and for decades before the war, given the purported blandness of the intellectual fare proffered there. Certainly the lure couldn't be the food.

Asked about the goings-on at the *Kinyo-Kai*, Masao Takemoto, a spokesman for Mitsubishi Corporation in Tokyo, took the party line, saying the presidential council members get together to discuss "social contributions, world trade fairs and how to divide the companies' charitable contributions." The heads of Mitsubishi's 29 major companies, who never discuss the meetings with outsiders, must have a lot of time on their hands and a high tolerance for boredom, since their efforts in the areas of charity and community works have hardly been outstanding. For example, the Mitsubishi Foundation gives away about $2 million a year, a paltry sum in terms of a company Mitsubishi's size but really grandiose in a country not known for its eleemosynary efforts. Charity begins at home is a phrase that should have wide currency in and around Tokyo, though companies like Mitsubishi are reluctantly learning that it's politic to give substantial amounts to American institutions to ease the way to social acceptance. Even Dodwell, whose meticulously factual, *Industrial Groupings in Japan* gives a wonderfully detailed analysis of corporate Japan, takes the Big Six *keiretsu*'s description of what happens at their respective presidential council meetings with a grain of salt.

Commenting on the custom, the authoritative Dodwell says:

> The presidential councils meet regularly every month . . . to exchange views on the general economic and financial situation, promising business, the state of R & D, maintenance of intra-group trademarks and company names and labor problems, as well as to make decisions on joint investment in new industries, on the allocation among members of political contributions, conducting of public relations activities for the entire group, rehabilitation of financially troubled group companies, key personnel appointments, etc . . .
>
> The members of the presidential council, however, do not want the council to be identified as a "policy-making body" for the whole group. They claim that the presidential council should not be associated with the image of the holding company of the pre-war *zaibatsu*. According to them, the council is only a meeting to be held regularly for fostering friendship

among the presidents of the group; every member is independent and no one is bound by the decisions or recommendations made by the council. The reader is left to judge the credibility of this statement as the discussions carried on by the councils have never been disclosed.[20]

How this tight group of 29 Mitsubishi companies—a group where one company owns an average of over 25 percent of others in the group and the cross-ties grow yearly—is harnessed into action, if indeed it is, is a matter of debate. But the fact is that when they do join to act, the effect can be quite stunning in terms of energy, speed and focus. According to one theory, the center of corporate group control was lost with the dissolution of *zaibatsu* after World War II and no longer exists. A number of Mitsubishi pretty much say this when they discuss Mitsubishi's operations. In a very strict, literal, linear sense this may be true. But this is focusing on the letter of the corporate law rather than the spirit— the subtle reality of how the will of the group is communicated into action, into long-term risk taking and into group rescue efforts when necessary. A more logical explanation is that control— albeit a peculiar, often indirect sort of control—resides in and around Yohei Mimura, chairman of Mitsubishi Corporation, and the *Kinyo-Kai*, the combined positions making him head of the Mitsubishi group. The latter case helps explain the group dynamism inherent and visible in Mitsubishi's operations.

In its pure form, either scenario is scary. Having the world's largest corporate enterprise bumbling along helter-skelter this way and that is a disturbing enough idea but then, having the opposite—group members jointly focused on a fierce, global pursuit of market domination—is almost more troubling. The truth probably lies somewhere in between which is really a very Japanese solution—balancing seemingly contradictory elements to create a reality of their own. The balance, though is tilted heavily towards the latter scenario—leaning towards control. The other implies chaos, which the Japanese abhor and avoid at any cost.

Taking the company line and becoming quite adamant on the subject is Takayasu Miyakawa, a director of Mitsubishi Research Institute Inc., which is located in the Mitsubishi-owned Time Life Building. "Actually Mitsubishi is completely different from before the war. Then the *zaibatsu* holding company made strategic decisions about the Mitsubishi companies," Miyakawa said in de-

173

scribing how the companies operate. "After World War II those Mitsubishi companies became independent even though there were interlocking shareholdings. . . . There is no decision-making institution which controls or governs the companies."

Other Mitsubishi executives, when asked, would like one to think group companies act totally independent of each other, even though this often is clearly not the case in Japan or abroad; even though they frequently enter new global markets in tandem, with a Mitsubishi company being supported by a bunch of Mitsubishi suppliers, Mitsubishi bankers and the Mitsubishi trading company; even though they get together to fund their own space satellite so that information from their companies around the globe can be shared; and even though they join together to bail out companies such as Akai Electric Co. that get in financial trouble or rescue those that are about to be taken over by someone outside the group. In the Mitsubishi world what they call a chance meeting—the fact that Mitsubishi Estate happened to be helped by Mitsubishi Bank and Mitsubishi Trust in its acquisition of a 51 percent interest in Rockefeller Center—looks more like a convergence of corporate planning or at least corporate togetherness.

When Mitsubishi hands out a fat packet describing who they are, included in the materials is a recent article from the Swiss business monthly magazine *BILANZ* that graphically illustrates the circular form of the Mitsubishi group. The article concludes: "Mitsubishi is everywhere. It is as if the 100 largest Swiss concerns including heavyweights like Nestlé, Schindler, Sulzer, Buhr-le, Ascom, Ciba-Geigy, Alusuisse and Electrowatt were to band together. Combined they make the same turnover as the 29 members of the *Kinyo-Kai*."[21] Think about it. As depicted in *BILANZ*, in the center circle and the surrounding concentric circle are the chosen 29 companies—most chosen before the war—while the second, enclosing circle comprises a recently created group, the public affairs committee of 11 companies. This second tier is Mitsubishi's castle wall or moat, the face it wishes to present to the outside world. The companies forming it, Mitsubishi Office Machinery, Mitsubishi Atomic Power and Precision, are very important to the group's well-being but not central to it—not the core.

What's at the center? Mitsubishi Bank, the world's third-largest bank, Mitsubishi Heavy Industries, which built the legendary

Second World War Zero fighter plane, and Mitsubishi Corporation, the world-renowned trading company that carries on the old *zaibatsu* tradition of being the group's salesman, promoter, and in foreign lands, nanny—these three companies forming the three facets of the Mitsubishi diamond seal. These are three heavy-weight companies that had the force of character to arise from the war more powerful than ever, yet if you believe the Mitsubishi group story, have lacked the will to join forces in competing in the world. The group companies, according to this line, operate in the sort of power vacuum that Karel van Wolferen describes in his fascinating book *The Enigma of Japanese Power.* Japan's political process, as discussed in his book, appears as a machine lurching along propelled by various factions but with a frightening lack of central control or purpose.

''Power in Japan is thus diffused over a number of semi-self-contained, semi-mutually dependent bodies which are neither responsible to an electorate nor, ultimately, subservient to one another,'' van Wolferen writes.

> While all these bodies share aspects of government, it is impossible to find one among them that gives the others their mandate. No one has final responsibility for national policy or can decide national questions in emergencies. Japan here differs from societies, such as that of the United States, where power is fragmented among numerous councils, agencies, boards, courts and the like. In the latter there still is a line of command; there are ways of getting through to a center, of having that center make and implement policies. Japan is different again from West European societies, even those with very strong interest groups that diminish the power of the center. At European cabinet meetings, initiatives are taken and decisions are ultimately made. In Japan the various ''governing'' bodies remain themselves ungoverned.[22]

Such a description rings truer when dealing with Japanese politics than in depicting the country's economic endeavors. Having Mitsubishi and the five other industrial giants existing essentially ungoverned but with similar dynamics suggests a pack of yapping hounds let loose to chase down a fox or a rabbit. Certainly, when similar companies from two or more of the major *keiretsu* target a market for market dominance there is an animal dynamism and they do move with the speed, vigor and brutality of a pack. But there is also some control, some direction—at least some sense of perspective once the scent is caught, some checks to balance the situation.

A group such as Mitsubishi can't be defined solely in circular terms such as depicted in *BILANZ* or in the horizontal and vertical terms as described by Dodwell. Like any living organism it's a combination of interdependent factors forming different patterns. However, what distinguishes a Mitsubishi and the other giant groupings is the vertical integration of their group companies and the way they hang together on a horizontal frame. It's a very powerful combination. Look at a chart of the holdings and cross-holdings. At the top, the head, there's the Mitsubishi triumvirate—Mitsubishi Corporation, Mitsubishi Bank and Mitsubishi Heavy Industries. From the head, the arms stretch out with samurai strength horizontally, from which hang the other 26 jewels of the Mitsubishi empire and other major Mitsubishi firms. Each group tumbles down with its appendages in parallel, vertical integration, penetrating separate sectors of Japan's and the world's economy. In banking there's also Mitsubishi Trust and Banking; in insurance there are Meiji Mutual Life, Tokyo Marine and Diamond Credit; in chemicals there are five major firms; then there's the ubiquitous Mitsubishi Oil with its three-pronged star, Mitsubishi Metal, Mitsubishi Electric, and Rockefeller Center's new 51 percent owner Mitsubishi Estate; and of course there's Nikon, Asahi Glass and the Mitsubishi shipping firm, Nippon Yusen.

These are a few of the major, billion-dollar firms and commercial endeavors that are part of the Mitsubishi group. Simple? This is just the crème de la crème of the thousand or so of Mitsubishi's vertically related companies. Moreover, being fierce competitors and strong supporters of the *zaibatsu* mode of doing business, the other five major Japanese *keiretsu*—Mitsui, Sumitomo, Fuyo, DKB and Sanwa—are hung in similar horizontal and vertical ways. This may sound complicated enough. But then there are the cross-shareholdings and cross-business dealings between group companies—the buying and selling between companies which don't show up in these delineations. And then there are the expectations, the unspoken obligations, the dependencies, the school ties, the family ties, all of which are part of the second-Friday-a-month cheap curry and tea lunches.

If the *Kinyo-Kai* lunches are never-never land for most of Mitsubishi's hundreds of thousands of workers, in their exclusivity—

in their somewhat childish, little-boys-club exclusivity—they are very telling. What do they tell—a lot? For one thing, foreigners— foreigners seeking to sell or invest in Japan—can complain about the closed nature of the Japanese economy but not get to the sub- stance of how they are shut out. Such complaints are part of the current SII negotiations, though it doesn't yet appear that the American negotiators have much of a clue as to the scope, influ- ence and deep-rootedness of the *zaibatsu* way of doing business. To expect the Japanese to change such fundamental ways of oper- ating in any significant manner is naive to say the least. The plain fact is, Japanese society is going to have to change a great deal before this changes.

Moreover, Americans or Europeans aren't the only ones being shut out. The reverse of being a member of a group is being an outsider and in Japan the idea of foreignness and being a foreigner isn't limited to national borders. A Mitsubishi man or company is foreign to a Mitsui man or company, while an IBM man is more foreign to both of them. In and around Tokyo there are countless examples of this exclusionary corporate togetherness. There are restaurants, tea and geisha houses that are Mitsubishi, or Mitsui or one of the other large *keiretsu*'s territory. Mitsubishi men would not be caught in a Mitsui house or vice versa.[23] If one has lunch at the Mitsubishi Bank, Meiji Mutual Life or Asahi Glass cafeteria, supplies of beer are plentiful and they're all Kirin, another major Mitsubishi company.

This sticking together in tightly competitive groups can also have lethal effects on outside competitors or outsiders trying to become part of the group. It would not be unfair to say that many a group's goal is to cut the competition off at the knees, especially when they're in pursuit of gaining market share—a constant goal that ranks far higher with Japanese firms than their American counterparts who are more concerned with the tangible and im- mediate rewards of profits. Competition in Japan is fierce and it is this sort of competition that Japanese firms are establishing in the U.S.

The kind of inefficiency that Americans ascribe to such arrange- ments—the American assumption being that vertical integration will make suppliers secure, sloppy and indolent—is kept in check by the intensely competitive environment within and outside each group. It is also kept together by force of personality and training. If one has been brought up from the age of four or five to believe that one's identity is as part of a group, then, unless one is an exception, one has the right group responses. Even Japan's geography has contributed to this sort of group behavior. Japan is hardly a country where Horace Greeley could have said "Go west young man, go west" with any sincerity. When a Japanese developer advertises houses in Yokohama as a way of getting away from "the Tokyo *keiretsu*," it's really a kind of joke, because the crowding together in Yokohama is not that different from nearby Tokyo. There are very few "wests" in Japan—very few places for the individual to be independent and alone. So far as the competitive nature of the Japanese is concerned, it's a trait that extends from the largest *keiretsu* to the individual shopkeeper, though on a one-to-one basis it becomes less efficient.

Walk around the Ueno-downtown Tokyo district on any day or early evening and one would have to believe that Japan, like equally chauvinistic France, is a nation of shopkeepers. Rows of competing fishmongers, sweet stalls, vegetable and meat stands line the neighboring streets, spreading out in all directions from Ueno Station. It may now be an inefficient way of selling to Japan's highly selective shoppers, but it's colorful and certainly competitive. The Japanese may not consume at the same rate as their American counterparts, but it would be wrong to believe they're not heavy-duty consumers. They're seen shopping all the time.

As William Dizer, chairman of ARCO Chemical Asia Pacific Ltd., a subsidiary of ARCO Chemical, noted during a recent interview, "You've got to be just as competitive as Mitsubishi or Mitsui." An astute observer of the Japanese who's been working with them for close to 40 years, Dizer said his company had done very well in Asia and that when it was involved in a joint venture with Sumitomo it found being part of the Sumitomo *keiretsu* very helpful in gaining business, since old school ties and established relationships are so important in Japan.

"The concept of the *keiretsu* is so foreign to the way we do business—you know you'll get the business. It adds a certain degree of stability and they know they can get better prices," Dizer said in the midst of packing up for retirement. "I would say in Japanese industry there is a very high degree of *keiretsu*. It's something that moves from raw materials to finished goods. You find it burgeoning in all aspects of business. As a company develops, it develops vertically. It's usual that as a company grows its ties become institutionalized.''

So here you have Yataro Iwasaki's proud samurai dream—the Mitsubishi group—in full flower existing as Japan's number one industrial group and the number one industrial conglomeration in the world. And now abandoning a somewhat slower gait, it's aggressively branching out around the globe, in the rest of the Far East, in Europe and the U.S. On a global scale, after a number of secret talks in Hong Kong, Tokyo and Stuttgart, in 1990 it formed an alliance with Germany's Daimler-Benz in what the *New York Times* called ''one of the largest industrial link-ups in history.'' The connection between Mitsubishi and Daimler-Benz was symbolized by the fact that both have the diamond corporate seal—Mitsubishi's diamond is fat and Daimler's prongs thin—but the ties ran deeper. These two industrial groups were the major forces that supplied the Axis powers during World War II. Mitsubishi remains ever-proud of the fact it led production of the Zero figher plane and the Musashi battleship. Memories harking back to World War II are indeed scary, but they miss the point— both Mitsubishi and Daimler-Benz are currently doing just fine economically and as they are presently constituted they present a formidable financial force. It's more fruitful to look at the future of this incredible grouping rather than its past. History may repeat itself but usually it adds a new twist.[24]

This controversial arrangement between Mitsubishi and Daimler-Benz came about after a number of Japanese companies began directing much of their new foreign investment to the European Community of 1992 and Mitsubishi became increasingly frustrated with some of its American partners.[25] There had also been a great deal of friction between Japan and the U.S. concerning whether America was or would be giving away technology in its commercial and military joint aircraft ventures with Mitsubishi. The fear is that as Mitsubishi is contracted to do more Boeing work, it will move up the learning curve and acquire more technology. As has been seen in the area of high tech, Japan is extremely facile at learning how to build various integral, high value-added parts of a machine—a computer or a chip-stamping machine for example—and using them as building blocks to take over larger parts of the high-tech industry. It's the old story of once they've got their foot in the door, what are you going to do.

Exactly what shape this alliance will take has yet to be seen, but the prospect of Mitsubishi and Daimler-Benz joining forces on a number of planned commercial fronts—ranging from auto production, to semiconductors, to aerospace—offers a formidable threat in the European Community, in world markets and in the U.S.

As might be expected, many of Mitsubishi's group's hundreds of investments in the U.S. amounting to many billions of dollars are arrayed in the *zaibatsu* way, fitting comfortably in vertical integration. The major Mitsubishi players are already firmly established in the U.S., ready to help out and lead the way for the latest camp followers. The $846-million purchase of a 51 percent interest in Rockefeller Center Properties by normally staid Mitsubishi Estate—a move, though they deny it, orchestrated by Mitsubishi International Corporation and Mitsubishi Bank and Mitsubishi Trust & Banking—was their most public and dramatic move, but other investments will probably have a longer-term effect on the U.S. economy.

A recent *BusinessWeek* article entitled "Hands across America: The Rise of Mitsubishi"[26] detailed some of Mitsubishi's successful forays into the U.S. and it's really quite remarkable. Certainly Mitsubishi group companies helped pave the way. Takeshi Yano, head of Mitsubishi Bank North America, which has $40 billion in U.S. assets and does 10 percent of its business with group companies, in the article said of their efforts to help out Mitsubishi companies venturing into the U.S., "If they need financing overseas, it's very natural for them to come to Mitsubishi Bank."

For one there's Mitsubishi Motors Corporation, which saw its car sales rise by 35 percent in 1990, continued to gain market share in depressed 1991, and has certainly been made to feel at home by its group suppliers. According to a University of Michigan study, Mitsubishi's Bloomington, Illinois, joint venture with Chrysler—Diamond-Star Motors—buys air conditioners from Mitsubishi Heavy Industries' California facility; glass from the group's Asahi Glass in Ohio; starters and cruise controls from Mitsubishi Electric's facility in Cincinnati; springs from Ontario's Mitsubishi Steel; processed steel from Mitsubishi International in nearby Joliet; discs and drum brakes from affiliated Ambrake Corporation; ball bearings from United Globe Nippon in Chicago Heights and NSK Corporation in Clarinda, Iowa; steering columns from Nastech Manufacturing in Bennington, Vermont;

lighting equipment from Battle Creek's I. I. Stanley; and antennas from Mitsubishi-related Harada Industry. The engines and transmissions, however, come from Mitsubishi in Japan. American workers in Bloomington put it all together.[27]

And then there's the example of Mitsubishi Semiconductor, a subsidiary of Mitsubishi Electric. When Mitsubishi Semiconductor began to set up operations in North Carolina, it

> . . . asked the *keiretsu*'s trading partner to handle purchasing and warehousing. Also lending a hand were group member Nippon Yusen, a shipping company and Mitsubishi Bank, which provided some start-up capital. ''When we came to the U.S. we asked other Mitsubishi companies to support us,'' says Mitsubishi Semiconductor president Tadaaki Mizoguchi, whose plant nestles among the North Carolina pines. ''If we had to develop everything from scratch or ask other [outside] companies we are not familiar with, it would be more difficult.''[28]

The finished $200-million-dollar semiconductor- and wafer-fabricating plant is a model of vertical integration and control of the food chain. The fabricated wafers that Mitsubishi Semiconductor fashions at the North Carolina plant come from Mitsubishi in Japan and are then processed into their final form on Mitsubishi Electric machinery there. Besides giving Mitsubishi Semiconductor control of production from beginning to end, it is estimated that operating in this style means that an astounding 90 percent of the value of each chip comes from the group. In effect, the North Carolina plant is a refinement on the proverbial ''screwdriver'' plant, since chips are actually worked on there rather than just having workers put finished parts together. Mitsubishi Electric's new Braselton, Georgia, big-screen television plant is more of the ''screwdriver'' ilk, where all the major, value-added, high-tech parts come from Mitsubishi-controlled sources abroad. Its large picture tubes come from Mitsubishi Electric's Kyoto facility, while the TV's chassis is supplied by a Mitsubishi Electric subsidiary in Singapore.

The Mitsubishi group connection can work wonders in other ways, though Mitsubishi executives usually insist that the convergence of two, three, or more group companies to facilitate each other is pure coincidence and that group companies operate independently of each other with no assurance that group assistance is in the offing. So when Mitsubishi Corporation recently beat out GE Plastics to buy Pittsburgh-based Aristech Chemical Corporation for $877 million, Mitsubishi Bank and Mitsubishi Trust materialized out of the blue to underwrite the buy-out. Then, a few months following the Aristech acquisition, another amazing coincidence occurred. Mitsubishi Kasei, Mitsubishi Gas Chemical, Mitsubishi Rayon and Mitsubishi Petrochemical, four companies with combined sales of $11 billion, each bought 4.48 percent interests in Aristech. Will the coincidences never end in this well-ordered world?[29]

Minoru Makihara, the St. Paul's School- and Harvard-educated Mitsubishi man, who was president of Mitsubishi International Corporation when interviewed and has moved on to chairman, subscribes to this episodic, chance-filled view of the Mitsubishi world. Makihara's office is a huge, swanky corner office on the twenty-second floor of Continental Bank's Madison Avenue building, not far from Rockefeller Center. Some nineteenth-century paintings decorate the walls, while the Mitsui-Mitsubishi golf trophy rests on a shelf. Makihara, a slick-looking 61-year-old, works from both sides of a desk placed in the corner of the room, a sort of control center. As head of Mitsubishi International he's been a chief shepherd along with the Mitsubishi Bank for Mitsubishi group companies making forays into the U.S. Three-quarters of an hour late for the interview, this day, however, Makihara is principally concerned about moving a Japanese school from Queens to Greenwich where there have already been protests by local residents claiming that the presence of a Japanese school will further aggravate traffic congestion in one of corporate America's prime suburbs.

According to Makihara, it may appear as if Mitsubishi Motors parts suppliers followed it to the U.S. as part of an overall plan, but that just was not the case. There was no plan, Makihara said. They just came along to conduct business with Mitsubishi and other companies—to be "helpful." Makihara said what worried him particularly was that Americans think "there is a concerted effort to shut out other sources" of supply by Mitsubishi and other Japanese firms. He said this is not the case. A self-described advocate of free trade, Makihara said the Japanese auto parts suppliers' rush to enter the American market had "nothing to do with the *keiretsu*" setup.

Along similar lines Makihara said he had no knowledge of Mitsubishi Estate's plans to acquire its controlling interest in the Rockefeller Center group until just before the announcement a few days before the interview. He said that if Mitsubishi Estate had consulted his firm, they "would have made a better deal." So if you take Makihara at his word, things just happen helter-skelter with happy coincidence in the Mitsubishi world—sort of like a Dickens plot.

———

Remember, this is the same Mitsubishi, which until it was disbanded after the end of the war—very much against the will of the last Iwasaki to head it, Koyata Iwasaki—employed about one million workers. While the Sumitomo, Mitsui and Yasuda *zaibatsu* agreed to be voluntarily broken up at the "suggestion" of Allied Forces in October 1945, Koyata Iwasaki resisted for some time, reasoning that "Mitsubishi has in no way performed in bad faith, nor has it done anything wrong to the nation or society. We have simply fulfilled the obligations that naturally had to be fulfilled by the citizens of this country."

Apparently, disheartened by the prospect of Mitsubishi being ripped asunder, the samurai-proud Koyata Iwasaki died on December 2, 1945, at the age of 67, after having written his final poem:

Autumn, a season of great variety,
A diseased goose, motionless,
Lies still on the frosty ground.

So where's the sick bird? It looks more like a phoenix.

8

MITI City

I fear that we Americans are in for a rude shock. We may have been the leading innovators in the past, but this situation is rapidly changing. . . . Indeed, we are seeing a fundamental shift from "Japan Inc." as we knew it in the 1950s and 1960s to the "Japan Tech" of the 1990s—a transition from imitation to innovation, from copying to creativity.

—Sheridan Tatsuno, *The Technopolis Strategy*[1]

In technology, except for aerospace, Japan will win.

—Akihiro Okumura, Keio University
professor and MITI adviser[2]

Toshio Shimada is an open and relaxed Japanese computer scientist in his mid-forties, who's working at the cutting edge of technology—trying to make so-called "parallel computing" work so that supercomputers can do their stuff with even greater speed, skill and grace. In many ways he's far removed from the mercantile hustle of the Marunouchi. Sporting a floppy grey sweater and sandals, Shimada would look right at home in any research center or university around the world—whether thinking and tinkering here at Japan's Tsukuba Science City or at MIT where he studied in the early 1980s and would like to return sometime. Still, Shimada and Japanese computer scientists like him are somewhat of an anomaly—in fact, some might call the term Japanese computer scientist an oxymoron. A mere decade

185

ago, no one would have thought Shimada and his brethren would be working and competing along the high-tech boundaries of parallel computing. That perception, though, is changing very rapidly as the Ministry of International Trade and Industry and Japan's giant electronic *keiretsu*—NEC, Fujitsu, Toshiba and the like—continue to join forces here, in the rest of Japan, and around the world to propel Japan's scientific development with the speed of a Bullet Train leaving ancient Kyoto for Tokyo or beyond.

Computing in massively parallel ways—marshaling a Lilliputian force of hundreds of processors to tackle an enormous problem[3] is yet another area targeted for conquest by MITI and a familiar group of Japanese computer companies that frequently work in concert with MITI. Though Americans, who invented and perfected this technology are still far ahead of the Japanese—by most accounts 128 months to two years in the lead, MITI and its corporate cohorts are determined to be number one in this highly important endeavor. And they'll persist in their pursuit despite some embarrassing failures such as their fifth-generation computers which if they worked would translate languages and understand speech. Such a joining together of corporate Japan and MITI here at Tsukuba City and in close to 30 smaller sites around Japan is all part and parcel of the *zaibatsu* way to success. The road to becoming the world technology leader in the twenty-first century may have been tough for the Japanese, especially since they were coming from way behind, but they're closer than ever to their goal. As a two-part editorial in the *New York Times* said in May 1990:

> After MITI's decades of careful tending, the Japanese computer industry has grown into a colossus. It now possesses commanding strengths in memory chips, chip-making equipment, flat panel displays, laser printer engines and optical disks. By 1992, projections show, its share of the world market will have reached 42 percent, up from 10 percent in 1980. The U.S. computer industry's share by contrast will drop from 82 percent in 1980 to 38 percent in 1992.
>
> Japan may have stumbled in its highly publicized effort to produce a Fifth Generation computer that can talk to people, but its Government fostered computer industry puts U.S. companies under ever-greater pressure. Japan is now mounting a challenge to U.S. supremacy in a promising technology, massive parallel processing.[4]

The point is that MITI, whose force recently has been somewhat underrated, is very much alive and well and frequently still calling the shots in its synergistic relationship with Japanese industry—in this case Japan's high-tech *keiretsu* establishment. The NECs and Fujitsus that flock to Japanese science centers such as Tsukuba to create dazzling high-tech breakthroughs are not an odd aggregation of loosely related companies chasing after new technology at the behest of MITI. They are a group of fiercely competitive but closely related and similarly *keiretsu*-structured companies that run together in a pack—here or in the U.S. By and large, they are the same companies that MITI suckled and protected until they'd grown large enough to take on the world. They are the same companies encountered in the U.S. hustling for number one spot in semiconductor or laptop sales. They are also the same companies who've frequently made it so difficult for U.S. companies to penetrate the Japanese high-tech market in any meaningful way.

Though MITI's role of coordinating, launching and trying to hedge the risks of high-tech innovation has changed as Japan has turned into an economic and technological powerhouse, its guiding hand is still very much in evidence—from fostering and financing new technology to writing legislation that will be passed in the Parliament for its support. The impact of MITI's unique coupling with Japanese industry continues and can not be underestimated. Massive as this impact has been in the United States, it is just the beginning, just as Japan's takeover of VCRs, Fax machines and copiers is just the hors d'oeuvres. Beyond the grazing, there's still a full meal to feast upon and MITI is there helping to stir the pot. So don't write off MITI's high-tech endeavors as little more than being at the cutting edge of a Kobe steak. Less than two years ago a *BusinessWeek* article called MITI "the Sugar Daddy to end all Sugar Daddies." It's still true.[5]

Currently, the special force of MITI's marrying its money and ideas with corporate Japan can be seen in areas ranging from developing tiny micro robotics, to helping so-called "fuzzy logic" become an economic reality, to making vast strides in superconductors, to promoting HDTV in a big, big way. And frequently, as in the past, the high-tech ideas MITI and its corporate followers run with are American in origin—great ideas that Americans have created but then done little or nothing to develop further or convert into commercially viable products.

A few examples of MITI's hand at work:

• There's *fuzzy logic*, yet another American invention, that the Japanese are bound to make billions out of—perhaps $2 to $3 billion a year.[6] Invented in the mid-1960s by University of California computer science professor Lotfi Zadeh and largely ignored in the U.S. until the Japanese came along, fuzzy logic is a revolutionary technology that allows computers to deal with the world in a more realistic, refined way.

Before fuzzy logic was conceived of by Zadeh, computers could only operate in a precise, either-or world, where everything was either black or white, where there was the right or wrong answer but nothing in between. Of course, as Zadeh realized, most reality lies somewhere in between and what his fuzzy logic does is make it possible for computers to work in shades of grey.

Potential applications of fuzzy logic are estimated to be in the hundreds and perhaps even the thousands (which is a pretty fuzzy statement but true). Concrete examples of what fuzzy logic can do in the commercial world are already coming to market. Fuzzy, belying its name, allows cameras to focus more quickly, air conditioners to operate more fuel-efficiently and the new "palm top" computers to recognize and respond to handwriting. And these are just a few of the applications.

So if fuzzy was scoffed at in the U.S., how did it get off the ground? In 1988, MITI set aside $70 million dollars to establish and fund for five years the Laboratory for International Fuzzy Engineering Research and soon it was joined by 46 Japanese companies contributing their time and money to fuzzy pursuits which are obviously already clearly bearing fruit.

There is one American company making fuzzy logic chips to help computers run in their fuzzy way—Togai InfraLogic Corporation, which was founded by Masaki Togai in 1987 after he left AT&T Bell Laboratories where he co-developed the world's first fuzzy microprocessor. Guess who funded Togai's start-up—Canon and other Japanese companies; and guess who's buying 95 percent of his output—Japanese firms.

• Then there's the area of *microrobots*—motors, sensors and other devices so small they barely span the breadth of a human hair.[7] When and if their potential is fully realized, they'll be able to deliver medicine in the human body, or discover defects in nuclear reactors or help construct advanced microchips.

188

It's a new, new technology but in some ways its story has a very familiar plot and actors. Again, micromachines were initially developed at Bell Labs and leading research centers such as MIT and the University of California at Berkeley. U.S. spending on micromachine research, though, is relatively modest with the National Science Foundation coming through with less than $2 million a year and industry a couple more million.

Enter another familiar face, Sugar Daddy MITI and the stakes are upped tremendously. MITI is launching a $167-million, 10-year project to develop microrobots that will fund research at five national labs, university research teams, and private-sector labs. Hitachi, Nippon Steel, Nikon, Toshiba, NTT and NEC reportedly will also be involved in the project.

Says George Hazelrigg, head of NSF funding of U.S. micromachines research: "We still have the top laboratories and we're doing cutting-edge research. But we're always worried that someone will go zooming by."

Guess who?

• Then, of course, there are the hundreds of millions of dollars MITI and Japanese private enterprise have invested in supercomputing—the area in which scientist Shimada is delving into potential parallel ways of computing. Shimada is a senior research scientist specializing in computer architecture at MITI's Electrotechnical Laboratory, Japan's largest research facility with a $70-million annual budget to spend on its staff of nearly 600 scientists working in Tsukuba City. One of Shimada's heroes is MIT professor J. B. Dennis, who in 1974 suggested a special model for parallel dataflow that has apparently been an inspiration to him. Shimada calls him "a great scholar" with great respect. The speed and efficiency inherent in massively parallel processing has been likened to 52 people searching a deck of cards—it can be done in an instant.[8] However, until recent breakthroughs in programming, its future has been discounted because getting such a system to work has been massively complicated.[9] "The world," said George Lindamood, a researcher at the Gartner Group who tracks progress in supercomputing, "is moving to massively parallel computers more quickly than I would have thought even recently."[10]

For someone who's spent a number of days in the Tokyo *keiretsu* trying to get honest, direct responses to simple questions, meeting Shimada is a delight, even if the 36-mile trip to Japan's high-tech capital—Tsukuba City—has been low-tech Japan at its worst. Japan may be in high gear at Tsukuba City to lead world technology in the twenty-first century. However, its outmoded, clogged road system is in low gear, forcing buses ferrying visitors to and from Tokyo to grind along frequently at 10 to 15 miles an hour for hours and hours. Japan, low-or-non-tech, is what the Japanese have to live with, even such talented people as Shimada. Here scientists working on some of the world's most difficult problems live in the sort of housing that in most developed countries other than Japan would only be built as low-cost, subsidized buildings for a Chicago's Cabrini Green or Robert Taylor Homes. They look like instant slums, but in Japan their poured-concrete walls, prison-like windows and running balconies don't nurture such graffiti-rich rot. It's the sort of schizoid existence that the Japanese seem to handle so well—the balancing of two atypical experiences, the beautiful and the ugly hand in hand, or the coin-clinking Pachinko pinball parlors next to Shinto shrines. It comes partially from growing up in tight spaces where privacy is more a mental feat than an architectural feature. It's the ability to accommodate two parallel realities, making a new truth out of combining the two.

On this cold, drizzly winter day, Shimada has a problem. The blue-and-white-striped, supercomputer Sigma-1—the machine he's so proud of that stands a couple of feet high in a room across from his office—is out of sorts. He wants to show it off but a faulty disk won't let him. The Sigma-1 won't work, the terminal screens are blank grey and he's sure the fault lies in an American disk.

"At first I said it's one of those American disks but it's a Fujitsu," Shimada said laughingly. It's the sort of thing that happens frequently with computers that are stretched to the limit. But what Shimada says is also quite telling on at least two counts. It's natural that he'd assume the faulty disk was American since, as we've seen, so many of the technological building blocks—the brains and the hardware that Japan has used to get into the world of high-tech—are of American origin. Of course, every day as Japan develops more highly sophisticated technology that can stand on its own, this dependency diminishes. Moreover, if Japan's entry into this never-never world of high tech has not always been easy, they'll persevere. The Japanese have the determination and wherewithal to stick with it for decades and decades and decades. Tsukuba City is a case in point.

Tsukuba City, which began to take shape in the 1970s when the government chose to consolidate all its research laboratories here, is on its own a huge $5.5-billion effort to take Japan into the twenty-first century in high-tech style. It is, also, only part of Japan's so-called "Technopolis" strategy, which is weaving its way throughout the country. According to MITI the word *Technopolis*— a term first coined by MITI in 1980—means a high-technology industrial complex. Curiously enough, its actual design has a good deal to do with the concept and layout of Japan's feudal castle-towns. "The basic idea behind the Technopolis Project," MITI says, "is to realize rural serenity in the city and urban activity in the country. The Technopolis Plan is a new strategy for the development of relatively backward regions, aiming at the creation of attractive towns in which industry, academia and residential space are closely interrelated. . . . The Technopolis Project gives us an advance view of the 21st century."[11]

The reality—the advance view of the twenty-first century at Tsukuba, the "City of Brains"—is, however, complex, sterile, and at times confusing—neither country nor city. As Sheridan Tatsuno said in *The Technopolis Strategy*, his excellent book describing Japan's high-tech efforts: "On the surface, Tsukuba does not seem special; it lacks the color, excitement, and variety that Tokyo has to offer. Yet the peacefulness is only a mask. The real drama lies out of sight, hidden behind the walls of the faceless research institutes that line its boulevards; for deep within these temples are the research projects that will dramatically transform Japan within the next ten years."

Plunked down on flat farmland splaying out from the foot of Mount Tsukuba, this over-planned city has a daytime population of 150,000[12] working, for the most part, in its central research area covering 44 square miles. Some of Electrotechnical Laboratory's esteemed neighbors are the Ministry of Education's High Energy Physics Laboratory, the Tsukuba Space Center and Nippon Telegraph and Telephone's Telecommunications Development Center. The whole high-tech complex, in which corporate and government research facilities are interlaced and the line between research and commercialization often nonexistent, actually encompasses 110 square miles including the towns of Kukizaki, Sakura, Toyosato and Tsuchiura City located on the shores of Lake Kasumigaura—Japan's second-largest lake.

Tsukuba's initial launching in the 1970s was far from propitious. "Tsukuba was new and unpopular . . . scientists howled. Tsukuba offered . . . a dearth of shops and an overabundance of ennui."[13] Given Japan's self-acknowledged need to become more creative in scientific endeavors—to shed its copyist ways, it was almost as if it couldn't even create a place in which to create. The "City of Brains" appeared to many to have been mindlessly conceived.

But after a clumsy start Tsukuba appears to have gained momentum and more respect. Scientist Shimada, the father of two, says it's "halfway city, halfway town," and that after working in Tokyo for 20 years he likes having the countryside around. "It's a good place to study," Shimada said. What really gave the place a boost was the Tsukuba Exposition of 1985, a sort of coming-out party for Japanese technology that cost $850 million to put on and attracted 20 million visitors. Though Americans also displayed their high-tech wares, the Tsukuba fair was a sort of love-in for Japanese technology.

There were big, big-screen televisions and robots of all sorts, that proved to be particularly popular attractions. They also displayed Japan's undisputed skill in this area. MITI's Mechanical Engineering Laboratory, known as MEL, showed "a crab-like robot that can climb stairs and a spider-legged robot that clambers up walls with its rubber suction cups. However, Professor Ichiro Kato of Waseda University stole the show with his dancing robot, called WABOT I, that can flex its hips and walk sideways and organ-playing WABOT II, which has a computer-controlled TV camera 'head' that hears requests, then plays the tune from sheet music with its mechanical fingers and legs."[14] And then there was the Fanuc Man, the crowning glory of Japan's robotics, a 16-foot-tall, ambidextrous robot, weighing 25 tons, that had the samurai strength to lift 500-pound barbells and a calligrapher's dexterity to assemble a small replica of himself—the perfect man from an island state.[15]

Though Tsukuba's biggest fans in 1985 were the kids who were awestruck by the high-tech, high jinks of Fanuc Man, WABOT and their multi-geared brethren, its impact wasn't limited to the juvenile members of its audience. Tsukuba 1985 also gave Japan and its bureaucrats at MITI a good deal of brawny, Fanuc Man confidence that has carried over into other parts of the Techno-polis strategy. That's the curious thing about world's fairs which Tsukuba 1985, in a sense, was—for all their hype they tend to galvanize an optimism and forward thinking that brings disparate issues together dynamically. Such positive thinking lives on after the actual event as more than a memory. Robert Moses' bitterly fought 1964 World's Fair was somewhat of an exception, but then there are the inspiring examples of Chicago's 1893 Columbian Exposition, New York's 1939 World's Fair and the 1958 World's Fair in Brussels. The 1965 Olympic Games staged in Japan prompted the country to improve its infrastructure, build new hotels and create the Bullet Train, which 25 years later is still a fast, fantastic, on-time transportation system. It should be remembered that the Japanese, true to the *zaibatsu* way, are particularly adept at tying forces together to focus on one objective and this is precisely what they're doing in the world of technology.

Tsukuba City, vast as it is, is just part of the Technopolis strategy's grand design. Strung across Japan are 26 areas that have been chosen as Technopolis sites and, despite the difficulty of setbacks at intermingling universities, research and industry, work is progressing—albeit at different rates. In the Toyama Technopolis area, for example, which encompasses the two mother cities of Toyama and Tokaoka, four towns and a population of 568,291, local residents are working on biotechnology and developing new materials, while in the Hamamatsu area, with its three cities and two towns, residents are involved with photo technology, electronics and communications. Then there is Kansai Science City, which has been conceived on a totally different scale.

Currently under construction in proximity to three of Japan's largest cities—Osaka, Kyoto and Nara—and the new Kansai airport, is Kansai Science City which is expected to be completed during the first decade of the twenty-first century.[16] Government-MITI cum industry-backed Kansai Science City will cost more than $30 billion just to get the basic structure in place and it is expected that 380,000 people will live there when it is in full operation. Such a huge, expensive effort may sound like throwing money at a problem, with little assurance that the Kansai high-tech efforts will succeed. However, first indications are that it is working well. Its costly ion engineering center, which is investigating how atoms ''behave when in a coating on a semiconductor chip or on ceramic,'' is reportedly off to a good and productive start.[17] The center was so expensive that no single company wished to pay for it. Instead, MITI set it up and then leased it to 65 companies large and small, though mainly the large. Michael Current, a speaker at an ion center seminar held in Osaka in March 1990 and a senior scientist at California semiconductor production specialist, Applied Materials, said of the center, "It's intended to be a really vibrant place and I'm sure they will achieve that. I really don't think they'll mess it up."[18]

Interestingly enough, Kansai is being built on the remains of Heijo Palace, one of Japan's oldest cultural centers. This follows a pattern in the Technopolis strategy—a pattern of continuity that one finds so frequently in modern Japan. As Sheridan Tatsuno pointed out in his book:

> Japan's technopolises are more deeply influenced by traditions and customs that go back hundreds of years. Indeed, the Technopolis Concept can be viewed as a modern version of castle building because of the central government's major role. Like the Tokugawa shoguns who oversaw the construction of castle towns in the sixteenth century, MITI originated the Technopolis Concept and selected the prefectures that would build the technopolises. And just as Japan's feudal castles spawned new castle towns, the universities and research institutes in these technopolises are expected to generate a contingent of talented workers and new start-up business.[19]

As early as the 1950s—long before the Technopolis strategy took shape, Japan realized that to grow as it wanted to and use its highly educated work force best, it would have to have its own home-grown computer industry. This was long before anyone, including the Japanese, realized how important computers would be to the economic life and fabric of a country. So with MITI's patient nurturing of the efforts of NEC, Hitachi and Fujitsu in this area and its closing the doors to almost all foreign entries, MITI and its corporate alter egos forged ahead. While outsiders other than IBM were for the most part kept out of the Japanese market, the fledgling Japanese computer companies became the great acquisitors of foreign computer technology—chiefly American computer technology at low prices. The results of this joining together in the *zaibatsu* way have been stunning.

Despite these massive strides, Japan still has major hurdles to

194

overcome in high-tech areas. One of the biggest problems Japan continues to face is wrenching its rigidly trained scientists out of their group mold so that they can be more adventurous and creative. However, by readily admitting the existence of this problem and trying to do something about it, the Japanese appear to have won some ground.

Koichiro Tamura, director of the Information Science Division at the Electrotechnical Laboratory, said in an interview at Tsukuba in January 1990 that this problem with creativity has meant that the Japanese have been much more adept at building computers—the hardware—than in creating the programs—the software. Tamura, a less relaxed man than Shimada, who spent 18 months at Berkeley as a student and has recently been trying to recruit American scientists to work at Tsukuba, said it may take a few generations to change the way research is conducted in Japan where the individual is not as strong as the group.

"Well, you may know that the level of hardware in Japan is very comparable to that in the United States but the software is just so-so," Tamura said. "We are not good at original research. I think it's an historical problem because for a long time we had to catch up. For many years we had a model to follow. Also to pass a college entrance exam you don't have time to be creative."

Comments such as Tamura's are heard frequently in Japan today. At times they're made candidly, voicing strong criticism of Japan's strict educational system, while at other times they're meant chiefly to lull competition into complacency. Though there's a good deal of evidence to back up such feelings of creative inadequacy, dwelling on such qualms masks Japan's highly impressive strides in high-tech endeavors.

Japan may still not have the vast array of computer software that supercomputer leader and founder Cray Research Inc. can offer, but NEC, Fujitsu and Hitachi are making machines that are already faster—and in some cases much faster—than Cray's.[20] Moreover, these companies have two other big advantages over their U.S. competitors—the many pluses of vertical integration and almost fanatical backing from MITI in the supercomputer area. NEC, Fujitsu and their ilk are producing all-important processors which are often speedier than those used by Cray. Moreover, Cray is becoming increasingly dependent on Japanese processors. Discussing the advantage of vertical integration, Akihiro Iwaya, a senior program manager who plans NEC's supercomputer strategy,[21] said, "We have our own chip divisions. They can custom-make the high-speed chips we need. Cray can't. They have to buy them from Japan." The implications of such an ar-rangement for Cray or another American firm are devastating, as Stephen Cohen, director of the Berkeley Roundtable on the International Economy recently noted. Asked Cohen, "How do you make a better computer than Hitachi and market it sooner if you are dependent on Hitachi for computer chips? The answer is: No way."[22]

It should also be remembered that, added to the advantages of vertical integration, an NEC or a Fujitsu draws vast benefits from Japan's peculiar hybrid, industrial state capitalism that is fre-quently both MITI-led and driven. Japan's efforts to be a force in HDTV, aerospace, robotics and bio-technology are also greatly enhanced by this unique combination as Japan moves into the twenty-first-century information age. Moreover, more conven-tional economic endeavors such as making autos, forging steel, refining chemicals and building ships owe a good deal of their prosperity to MITI's efforts on their behalf. This special combina-tion of government and industry joining together to perform a targeted task has not limited its magic to the high-tech area. High-tech is just the latest economic endeavor to be blessed with strong government backing. It's a pattern of behavior that has been exer-cised in highly successful ways since the Meiji restoration.

For example, from the time Japanese steel exports to the U.S. first started taking hold on the American market, Japanese pro-ducers were playing from a stacked deck. In the beginning they benefited from cheap labor, cheap money, new, more efficient equipment and an undervalued yen. Added to this was the role the government played through the beneficial offices of MITI. Ja-pan's steel-producers prospered in a closed, controlled market, with a mercantilistic thrust towards the world. MITI also encour-aged heavy financial leverage in the beginning, coupled with low-cost loans from the government and private banks. Japanese steel companies were encouraged and coddled by MITI to become the most efficient in the world. MITI had made the establishment of a world-class steel industry a number one priority for Japan.

MITI and Japan also realized that manufacturing steel on a global scale was essential if Japan were to take a major posi-tion in the post–World War II industrial economy. Making steel also fit perfectly into Japan's mercantilistic design since raw-material-short Japan could import iron ore, coking coal, etc. from abroad and forge it into steel—steel which over time could be converted to higher-value steel products and eventually Nissans and Toyotas.

More recently, when the Japanese steel industry began to see its profit margins squeezed by competition from low-cost steel producers in the newly industrialized countries (NICs) and the effects of the appreciating yen, MITI again stepped in to rationalize the industry. Realizing that Japan's steel products would have to cut back or flounder, MITI helped them restructure their industry in an extremely elegant manner. With MITI's aid, workers faced with layoff were shunted to other industries, while the companies themselves formed a cartel. Each firm was assigned a certain level of production to cut back. By working together, the companies achieved their goals with much less pain than had been expected. Such MITI-inspired government rescue efforts have also been seen in the shipbuilding and chemical industries.

It's 6:30 at night and the bus returning from Tsukuba is already two hours late, snailing its way into Tokyo past a Roger Brown-like cityscape. It's a bit like Sartre's *No Exit*. An appointment is being missed and nothing can be done about it—nothing. The other passengers—all male—doze or do as they do on most forms of transportation, read their pornographic comic books, filled with bound women. The driver, in his blue uniform, blue hat with black visor and white gloves gripping the steering wheel, is a paradigm of Japanese patience.

MITI, where are you when I need you?

9

Slim Pickens

The Japanese market will open up. We're just seeing the beginning.

—T. Boone Pickens re his 1989 raid
on Koito Manufacturing Ltd.[1]

Ours is not the rugged and brutal capitalism of the eighteenth
and nineteenth century.

—Kazuo Nukazawa, head of Japan's biggest business lobbying
group, the *Keidanren*, at the time of Pickens's raid[2]

Down on the trading floor, where rubbing an eyelash can
mean buy Matsushita and four fingers raised an order for
Hitachi's shares, pandemonium reigns. It's reigned for months
and months going on a year now—a churning, teeming sea of
black, shiny heads, white shirts, arms outstretched Laocoon-like,
some blue and tan jackets, palms up signaling a sale, palms
turned in for a buy. The group is at a swirling, frenzied pitch. No
Japanese patience or politesse here. No room to bow. One might
get knocked over and trampled—just rush, push, shove, grimace,
wince and sell, sell and sell on the Tokyo Stock Exchange. There
is seemingly no structure. This is deceptive. When push comes
to shove, the *zaibatsu* way is very much in play. It is here that
much of the postwar growth of the *zaibatsu* way was created
through a protective web of interlocking shareholdings, financed
with low, low-cost funds and nurtured carefully to be spread

199

around the world by its high-energy practitioners—Sony, Toyota, NEC and countless other Japanese firms.

Since the beginning of the year Japanese share prices have been caught in a deadly undertow. On December 29, 1989, the Tokyo Exchange's Nikkei index reached an all-time high of 38,915 having become the world's largest stock exchange in terms of trading volume, with many stocks selling for as much as 120 times earnings, multiples almost never achieved on the New York or London Stock Exchanges. Then the tide turned. Twelve months later, at the end of 1990, Japanese investors who'd made undreamed-of fortunes in the prior decade faced a stock market that had shed just under 40 percent of its weight thrashing about for its life. The melee continues, though in early 1991 the market did begin to recover.

There are many mega-yen investors who caught the rising speculative tide in 1989, and to their regret, stayed in too long and got carried out to sea. But there are few more exceptional than Texas oilman and corporate raider T. Boone Pickens—Boone-San as he has gotten to be known. His is a cautionary tale and an apt reminder of how futile America's SII efforts to open up Japan's markets will be. Reciprocity, opening markets as they are in the U.S., is not in the *zaibatsu* deck of cards.

Though Pickens came to Tokyo on a speculative sortie, his is not so much a story of financial loss, so far as one can tell, as one of a foreigner facing the *zaibatsu* way head on, openly attacking it and getting nowhere, fast or slow. The confrontation, which tells a lot about what American companies are up against in taking on a Japanese *keiretsu*, reached its nadir in mid-1990, well over a year after Boone-San had plunged into the Tokyo market. By then Pickens, who was in a progressively compromised position, had become Koito Manufacturing Ltd.'s largest shareholder, with no say in the Toyota group company's management and little hope of ever getting any. Boone-San, who likes to cast himself as a knight in shining armor, also turned out to be something much less—more like a tarnished sham. But his battle and what he confronted were very real and his pickings slim.

The whole Boone-San affair came to a real head on June 28, 1990, when Pickens, his wife and an entourage of 30 or so American Koito shareholders, whose airfare Pickens had picked up, arrived at Koito's annual shareholders' meeting in Tokyo seeking to assert Pickens's rights. The Texas raider continued to seek several seats on Koito's board of directors and a say in how the company was run. Pickens, no slouch at hustling publicity for his causes, had seen his Koito campaign widely covered in the Japanese, American and European press. Moreover, before the meeting Pickens sent out saccharine videotapes to Koito shareholders showing him on horseback in Texas asking for board representation and increased dividend payments.[3] This was Boone-San's second annual meeting with Koito's management, and if the first had gotten him nowhere, the second was even worse. Japanese shareholders' meetings, given the fact that non-*keiretsu* shareholders have little or no say in management, are not known for their democratic flavor. If most *keiretsu* managements had their way, they wouldn't be held at all. As it is, most are perfunctory and taken care of as quickly as possible. This time around, Koito's was another matter.

When Boone-San and his entourage walked into Koito's June meeting, they were cordoned off from Japanese shareholders, "protected" by 20 hotel and an additional 25 Koito-hired security guards, and then heckled for three hours by the *sokaiya*, professional extortionists who disrupt annual meetings in the hope of extracting a payoff from management but also are often hired by Japanese corporations to intimidate any disruptive, dissident shareholders. Boone-San's crew, for their part, were taunted with "Yankee go home"—"We've won the economic war"—"America lost because it's stupid"—"Remember Pearl Harbor." No subtlety there. After hours of harangues during which one of Pickens's interpreters, who left in tears, had to be replaced, Boone-San and his crew stomped out of the meeting in a high Texas twit. His saccharine video hadn't worked and exactly who was responsible for orchestrating the scene remains unclear.[4]

What is clear, though, is Pickens had run smack, right up against a wall constructed in the *zaibatsu* way. It's one reason why Boone-San's efforts to jostle the system at times took on farcical airs. First, there are the cross-shareholdings—the 3, 4 to 5 percent shareholdings, bricks mostly owned by friendly banks, insurance companies and *keiretsu* companies also tied together in a cat's cradle of cross-ownership. Then, there's the cement—the economic ties that hold a *keiretsu* together—the buyer-supplier, lender-borrower relationships that help give the *zaibatsu* wall its tensile strength and get the raw materials there just in time. Giving the structure a soul *(amae)* are the personal, group (batsu) ties—intertwining and binding from family, town, school and company. These are the ties—the manager to manager, chairman to chairman, worker to foreman rapport—that make dealing with a group member on any number of levels easier and frequently more productive than with the outside world. And finally there are the architects—some retired and some still very active who continue to give shape to the *zaibatsu* way—particularly those ministers at MITI and the Finance Ministry. It is their bold design that has given purpose to the structure. When Boone-San jumped into the Koito fray with both pistols blazing, he ran slambang into this wall. While Pickens's contretemps came chiefly on the shareholder level, many other Americans seeking to make a deal or do business in Japan have, and can expect to, run into the *zaibatsu* monolith on other levels in Japan. The Japanese, *keiretsu*-dominated distribution system is but one example of the group's exclusionary force in Japan. This force permeates almost all levels of business.

So far as Koito was concerned, it was just like any other 2,000 or so major Japanese corporations listed on the Tokyo Stock Exchange—60 to 70 percent of its shares were owned by friendly, long-term shareholders, whose shares were also held in stable, cross-shareholdings. Today, it is estimated that Japanese corporations own some 73 percent of Tokyo Stock Exchange shares while individuals hold about 23 percent, with foreigners having the remaining 4 percent.[5] By contrast, individuals owned nearly 60 percent of U.S. shares in 1988, a figure which doesn't include the enormous number of shares held as proxies for individuals in pension funds, mutual funds and insurers' accounts. As Robert Zielinski and Nigel Holloway point out in their recent book *Unequal Equities*, "the structure of share ownership in Japan has created two classes of shareholders, the 'outsiders' and the 'insiders.' The outsiders, who are individuals, foreigners, and speculative groups buy shares purely for investment and, in the issuer's view, contribute nothing to the growth of the company's business. . . . If individual investors are unreliable as far as Japanese firms are concerned, foreign investors are an outright threat."[6]

So not surprisingly, Japanese law demands that there must be a two-thirds majority—66 percent—shareholder vote on any major corporate issue, which in effect gives management and fellow friendly *keiretsu* shareholders virtual control of a company.[7] This share concentration is also one reason the share price-earnings multiples on the Tokyo Exchange are so high—only 30 to 35 percent of a company's shares and usually much less ever getting to market. Such a concentration of shareholdings in corporate hands did not come about by chance but evolved after the war as corporations consciously sought to have their shares placed in stable hands and reassembled the old *zaibatsu* ties that had been severed. The system has also proven to be a remarkably effective way for a company to raise new funds through stock sales to *keiretsu* members—a ready market and also a source of cheap funds since Japanese corporate managements do not feel it incumbent on them to pay investors high dividends, preferring to reinvest as much profits as possible. In brief, this is the system Boone-San came up against. Tough pickens.

Pickens's role, however, is more complicated and compromising in that he likes to cast himself as the savior ready to reveal, uproot and slay the *zaibatsu* way—the exclusionary *keiretsu* modus operandi—when in fact he's apparently become a consenting tool of the system's ugly underbelly. It's too bad because what Pickens has to say about the *zaibatsu* way and how foreign companies haven't got a chance of penetrating Japan's distinct group capitalism is right on the mark. He's the wrong person at the right time to try to open Tokyo's markets and create a reciprocity where foreign investors can have the same access in Japan they can find in America.

Early in April 1989, Pickens took the plunge, disclosing that he had bought a 20.2 percent interest in Koito Manufacturing Ltd., Japan's largest maker of automotive lighting equipment. While his stake was worth $1.12 billion at the time, Boone has consistently put its value at around $800 million. As the feisty Pickens soon learned, taking on Gulf Oil Co. as he had in 1984 and walking away with a $400-million profit or attacking Phillips Petroleum Co. or Unocal Corporation was child's play in comparison to getting his way with Koito, a key member of the Toyota group.[8] That Toyota owned 19 percent of Koito is only a small part of the picture. Remember Georgetown. The ties even bind tighter and run deeper here. Caveat emptor might be apt advice to investors coming from outside the group and seeking to make waves.

Pickens was also performing a first—a foreigner taking on a *keiretsu* firm in the homeland. No one without Pickens's ego would dare to make the leap. However, the tough Texan from

Amarillo with the hide of an armadillo could huff and puff and huff and puff—issue press release after press release as he did, but he couldn't blow the house of Toyota down. In effect, most of what Koito subsequently did to stave off Pickens was an unnecessary sham. They certainly didn't need six new directors as protection. Koito's defenses were in place, built on strong foundations—its entourage secure when Boone-San made his move in April.

Even in Tokyo's high-flying market where stocks often carry price-earnings multiples ten times greater than similar firms' shares traded in New York or London, where Koito's shares had recently sold for over two hundred times earnings and where speculation is rife, Pickens's announcement came as a real shocker and it wasn't just because Pickens was a foreigner. Initially, both Pickens and Koito were quite restrained about Pickens's Boone Co. becoming Koito's largest shareholder. No one was picking a fight. Pickens said Koito should expand in Europe, America and Asia—a rather curious statement since Koito already had several operations in the U.S. and Europe and that "as a major shareholder, we hope to provide a positive influence on the directions and policies of the company."[9] He also soon revealed he was seeking several seats—three or four—on Koito's board so that he could exercise his guiding hand. After all Toyota, which had a similar stake, had three hand-picked directors on Koito's board.[10] Koito, for its part, said it was talking with its lawyers and financial advisers, adding that "there is nothing to do right now but wait to see how [Boone Co.] will exercise [its] shareholder's rights" and that it was customary for a new shareholder to wait half a year or so before seeking a seat on the board.[11] Shareholder's rights?

Both sides were being disingenuous and to a degree, continue that way. Though Pickens has continued to enunciate lofty goals of exposing just how threatening the *keiretsu* system of interlocking shareholdings and supplier relations is and is very articulate on the subject, Koito is probably correct in alleging that Pickens's motive for investing in Koito and later increasing his stake to 26.4 percent was much more mundane—pure and simple greenmail or more exactly yenmail. In Japan's highly speculative stock markets greenmail is a time-honored Japanese practice where an unfriendly investor will corner a substantial block of a company's shares and then be bought out at a premium price by a fellow *keiretsu* company, since Japanese companies can not buy their own shares. As Keiji Yasuda, an analyst at New Japan Securities Co., said at the time: "This isn't a normal investment. . . . Many people believe Mr. Pickens is a greenmailer, a pure green-mailer."[12]

It took Koito a little longer to publicly enunciate a similar conclusion, though privately it soon inferred this after it learned the provenance of Pickens's stock. Discussing the matter sometime later in a *Wall Street Journal* op-ed piece entitled "Boone-San, Either Put Up or Shut Up," Koito president and former Toyota man Takao Matsuura said:

At first, we at Koito Manufacturing Ltd. were perplexed. Why would Mr. Pickens be interested in Koito's stock at a time when it was selling at a price-earnings multiple of about 170 to 1, as a result of a stock cornering scheme by an infamous Japanese greenmailer? Where did he get this block of shares? What was Mr. Pickens's objective? How was this related to the greenmail ploy we had been battling at Koito for months?

"Red flags went up at Koito as soon as we discovered that Mr. Pickens had obtained his stock from Kitaro Watanabe, the very man Koito had been battling. Mr. Watanabe, one of Japan's wealthiest men, has a history of speculation in stocks and real estate and is renowned for his attempts at greenmail. . . . He accumulated his block of Koito stock during an 18-month buying spree that had driven Koito's share price from about 700 yen to more than 5,000 yen. Mr. Watanabe twice approached Koito, looking for us to arrange a greenmail payoff. We refused. And we were aware that Mr. Watanabe was shopping his shares in an effort to unload his investment. . . .

The more we found out about Mr. Pickens, the more it became clear to us that putting a stockholder whom the American courts had labeled a greenmailer on our board would be highly irresponsible. Greenmailers—Japanese or American—are not welcome on Koito's board.

In this, Koito is no different from the American companies Mr. Pickens bought into. Not one of Mr. Pickens's American targets had given him or his representatives a seat on its board.[13]

So, given Pickens's investment record in the U.S., his murky dealings with Watanabe and Watanabe's alleged association with

Japanese organized crime—the *yakuza*, little wonder Koito didn't want Boone-San or any of his cohorts on its board.[14] And it's not too surprising that Koito added six new, friendly members to its board a month after learning about Boone-San's ways and connections,[15] or that it strengthened its anti-takeover provisions or that it hired Nomura Wasserstein Perella, the Japanese arm of the American merger and acquisitions gurus, to advise it before its mid-summer 1989 annual meeting. That's what American companies do all the time when confronted with an aggressive, hostile, unwelcome advance.

Moreover, considering their distaste for Boone-San, it's hardly shocking that Boone-San, their largest shareholder, was given little court at Koito's 1989 and 1990 annual meetings or that he'd storm out of the second meeting saying, ''It was a sham. An absolute farce. Koito showed the world what it's about. It's a closed system. They're against foreigners.'' Pickens is given to high theatrics in his shareholder fights and shareholder rights don't amount to much in Japan.

And then Boone-San was further discredited some months after the 1990 annual meeting when a change in Japan's disclosure regulations[16] forced Boone and other shareholders with stakes of 5 percent or more in listed companies to tell the Finance Ministry the details of their investment interests. The rule change created some of the openness Pickens had been fighting for, with the Finance Ministry receiving 4,474 disclosure filings in little over a week. But ironically, it also meant that he had to give more information regarding his dealings with billionaire, one-time Tokyo used-car dealer and $500-million Hawaii hotel owner, Watanabe. To a degree he'd been hoisted with his own petard.

Following months of speculation as to what sort of deal he'd cut with Watanabe after meeting with him ten different times over a four-month period, Pickens said, in effect, that Watanabe had financed his purchase of the 26.4 percent interest in Koito. More specifically, he told the Finance Ministry Boone Co. had pledged all of its Koito shares as collateral on a loan from Watanabe's Azabu Tatemono K.K. and that the loan was used to finance the purchase of the 42.4 million Koito shares, mostly from Watanabe.[17] At the time Pickens, however, refused to say if Watanabe's loan was interest free, as many suspected. If this were true Pickens apparently had nothing to lose if he stormed in and out of a Koito's meeting and might gain something, as yet to be disclosed. It's also hard to believe Pickens would have paid the expenses of 32 supporters traveling to Japan just on a lark but if it's the case, it would be in character with extravagant Texan gestures. Pickens's disclosure proved just what Koito had been saying all along. Said a gloating Koito: "It is clear that Boone Co.'s only investment was of its name as a cover for Watanabe's greenmail campaign."[18]

Still, Boone-San had every good reason to be enraged when he stomped out of the 1990 annual meeting. To say Koito's largest shareholder didn't get any respect would be an understatement. Some claimed Boone or Watanabe had actually staged the whole thing to put Koito in a bad light and give Boone good reason for quitting a losing situation. Koito's Matsuura, for his part, denied Boone's allegation that the company had organized the *sokaiya*. Matsuura, however, did nothing to quell the mob of hecklers or to defend Boone-San during the meeting. He did, at one point, admonish Boone-San to stick to the point while Boone-San spoke and was being heckled by the *sokaiya*.

So, assuming Boone-San had no part in orchestrating the vituperative proceedings, which seems a fair assumption, no wonder Boone-San was furious at being raucously stonewalled and made to look like an impotent fool—unable to get three directors elected to Koito's board and blathering on about how the *keiretsu* system of corporate families is a barrier to free markets. Boone-San, however, was absolutely right about how *keiretsu* work and how outsiders—be they Japanese outsiders or foreign nationals—are systematically ostracized from the group. That's precisely what happened at the meeting. Flamboyant Boone-San, the proverbial nail that sticks up, and his entourage were physically separated from the group—encircled and "protected" by a security force that more than outnumbered the Texans. Foreigners, and especially Americans, are frequently called *gaijins*, a derogatory abbreviation of *gaikokujin*, meaning "outside country person" or somebody outside of a group. The weight of the word's meaning is on someone being removed—not being a part which is a curse in Japan, so it easily becomes a prejudicial term. Since there is really no precedent for a foreign company buying a big chunk of a major Japanese company's stock and then asking for a position on the board, Koito and Toyota can say they would act differently under more benign circumstances but it's hard to believe. It's hard to believe that a Toyota would surrender any of its control over Koito to any foreign company.

The point is that Boone-San was a *gaijin* and even if he'd been the high-minded fellow, on a crusade as he likes to portray himself when he's testified before Congress about *keiretsu*, even if he'd never greenmailed a share of stock in his life, even if his criticisms of Koito had been totally justified, even if the provenance of his Koito shares had been as irreproachable as a Morgan Guaranty or a Goldman Sachs, he most probably wouldn't have gotten an inch further with Koito, though they would have been more polite.

Certainly the stock market knew this—knew that no *gaijin* was going to make a way with Koito. The week after Boone Co. let it be known it had bought up a fifth of Koito's shares and wanted a say in the way Koito was run, Koito's shares registered the biggest percentage drop of any major issue on the Tokyo Exchange, falling 12.8 percent. Puzzle—on most markets threats from a new major shareholder usually cause the object company's shares to levitate on speculative greed. But then another puzzle—in the prior week Koito's shares had risen 22.7 percent. This was the first of many puzzles Pickens would have to confront.[19]

Equally puzzling and still unclear is why Watanabe thought Pickens could do better than he had and why Pickens apparently also concurred in this view—his ego notwithstanding. Watanabe had begun hoarding Koito's shares in 1987, apparently believing Toyota would do for group company Koito as it had for Toyoda Automatic Loom, Toyota's forerunner.[20] When the Nihon Tochi greenmail group cornered a block of Toyoda Loom's shares in 1986, Toyota eventually acquiesced, buying back the stake. However, when Watanabe appeared on the scene with a similar scheme, Toyota, who looked like rich, easy pickings given that it had more than $20 billion in cash in the till, made it clear at least on two occasions through Koito that it had had enough. As it's turned out, Watanabe would probably have been better off unloading his Koito shares at the time rather than bringing Pickens in and continuing to badger Koito through him.

In April 1989, when Boone-San announced the purchase of the Koito block, its shares were selling at 4,830 yen. He later told the Japanese government he'd paid 3,395 yen a share for his first block.[21] Well, by the end of 1990 Koito's shares had been carried down in the market's undertow and were selling for 3,030 yen each. At such levels Watanabe may still have a profit but annual carrying costs of $80 or $90 million a year are bound to erase these profits pretty quickly. As Koito's Matsuura pointed out in his *Wall Street Journal* op-ed piece, "this 'investment' makes no financial sense . . ."[22]

However, Toyota's 19 percent stake in Koito makes perfect sense in the context of the *zaibatsu* way. Koito is a major member of the Toyota group, with Toyota buying up nearly half of Koito's annual production. And then there was Nissan Motor, Koito's second-largest customer, owning 6.6 percent of its shares and accounting for 14 percent of Koito's sales. Other major shareholders included Matsushita Electric Industrial with 5.9 percent, Nippon Life Insurance with 4.4 percent, Dai-Ichi Mutual Life Insurance with 3.6 percent and those with under 3 percent: Matsushita Real Estate, Japan Securities Finance, Mitsubishi Bank, Sumitomo Bank and Dai-Ichi Kangyo Bank. Just to underline the point about cross-shareholdings, Nippon Life and Sumitomo Bank are also major shareholders in Nissan and Matsushita Electric. Such relations go on and on and are just one manifestation of how power in Japan is concentrated in remarkably few hands.

There was no way Boone-San could expect to penetrate or elicit support from this group unless the group were so inclined, though if his stake grew to 33 percent he would have some veto power. Really Koito had little to fear and neither did Toyota. Koito was caught and protected, inviolate in the *zaibatsu* web of influence. It is also why an unfriendly takeover is virtually unheard of among the major *keiretsu* stock exchange-listed companies. It may be as easy as pie for Bridgestone to buy up Firestone on the NYSE or Sony to buy Columbia Pictures from Coca-Cola, but the same is not true in Japan. Japanese corporations awash in cheap dollars can globalize and buy into America at will as they change from a predominantly industrial society to a more service-oriented economy requiring less brawn and more brainpower in technology, telecommunications and finance. It is estimated, for example, that much of the funds Sony used to buy CBS Records and Columbia Pictures had an average cost of less than 1.5 percent, whereas an American firm embarking on such an acquisition binge would pay about ten times that for financing.[23] Japanese firms will continue their expansion abroad even though Japanese banks have become somewhat strapped by past standards and cannot lend at rates as advantageous as in prior years. The fact is that many Japanese companies are so awash in cash that they don't need much help from their bankers—rather the reverse. According to a recent tally Hanwa, a steel trading firm, had $17.2 billion in cash and securities, Mitsubishi, $15.2 billion and Sumitomo, $11.3 billion, just to give a few examples.[24] Money will pave the way. There is no such easy access for American firms in Japan, even those much less brash than Boone-San, and really no hope that there will be.

It wasn't just the Koito-Toyota ties that Boone-San was attacking. The *zaibatsu* way just represents an incredible concentration of impenetrable power for an outsider. It can be seen in the banks and securities firms as they continue to consolidate, in the Big Six *keiretsu* holding companies and the major corporations such as Toyota that mimic this way and in the government. Japan's four largest securities firms control an estimated 60 percent of the trading volume on the Tokyo exchange, benefit from a rich fixed-commission scale and have been known to cover rich trading customers' losses. In 1990 the latter practice triggered perhaps the largest stock market scandal in Japan's history, when the top four firms—Nomura, Nikko, Daiwa and Yamaichi Securities—revealed they'd paid their biggest customers hundreds of millions of dollars to make up for their trading losses. Though some American firms have been successful in making money in this environment, the Salomon Brothers and Morgan Stanley of the Tokyo exchange are the exception.

Such a concentration of power is also seen in the large institutional investors—the banks and the insurance companies—where a remarkably small number of firms hold dominant positions in key sectors of the economy. Moreover, they are in the process of further consolidation. The merger of Mitsui Bank with Taiyo Kobe Bank in 1989—the biggest bank combination ever—created the world's second-largest bank, with assets approaching $400 billion.[25] Such a merger is part of a movement to create so-called "universal banks," that would cluster a whole host of financial services at the top of Japan's six major financial groups—the ever-familiar Sanwa, Mitsubishi, Mitsui, DKB, Sumitomo, and Fuyo groups who already control an estimated 30 percent of Japan's economy. Each "universal bank" would have the regular banking and securities operations but would also encompass trust operations, regional banking, insurance, consumer finance, pension fund management and mergers and acquisitions. It is just this powerful concentration of assets that Koito was hooked into when Boone-San made his overtures.

Of course, Boone-San's expectations were that Toyota would come to the fore to buy him out, since not only the shareholdings but also the just-in-time supplier relationships were being sullied. As with other Toyota group companies, Toyota enjoyed the privilege of controlling the top jobs at Koito with its own chosen few. President Matsuura was a Toyota man and so too were others in top positions. Then suppliers such as Koito have frequently seen their profits cut to cushion Toyota's hard times and Toyota reputedly also gets parts discounts from Koito. The expectation was that Toyota would pay dearly to preserve this *droit du seigneur*.[26]

The futility of such expectations, however, was also apparent at the outset when the periphery *keiretsu* ranks fell into formation. In stepped the Ministry of Finance, which launched a number of investigations as to how Boone-San had obtained the Koito shares, when he disclosed his holdings. And then the Tokyo Stock Exchange initiated an inquiry into trading in Koito's shares to determine whether there'd been any insider trading, hidden dealings or stock manipulation. None of the investigations turned up any dirt, but they delayed Boone-San's dealings and helped set the tone for subsequent negotiations. There was no question whose side the ministries were on.

A shareholder democracy Japan is not. For the most part, Japanese shareholders not belonging to the group are given short shrift, having to content themselves with virtually no say in management and a dividend yield that averages less than 1 percent.[27] The Japanese are big on talking about the rights of the stakeholders as part of their form of unique capitalism. Their definition, though, of stakeholders encompasses an exclusive group—active and passive members of the *keiretsu*. As Boone-San's experience graphically underlines, outsiders beware. In early 1991, Boone-San got rid of his Koito stake.

But then, as Kazuo Nukazawa, head of the *Keidanren*, said, "Ours is not the rugged and brutal capitalism of the eighteenth and nineteenth century . . . " Perhaps Nukazawa should pay the Tokyo Stock Exchange a visit. It might change his views.

Welcome to twenty-first-century capitalism—the *zaibatsu* way.

10

America's Task: Returning to "Go," Getting Down to Basics

I think the U.S. and Japanese economies might be likened to Siamese twins fighting with each other. If one kills the other, the other also dies. No one wins.

—Naohiro Amaya, a prime architect
of the Japanese miracle[1]

Where does the money come from?
Most of it flows from Japanese companies, agricultural interests, and business associations, particularly the *Keidanren*. . . . The *Keidanren* alone gives the LDP nearly $100 million a year. Its member companies provide many times more. In the 1990 elections, the LDP raised more than $1 billion from the Keidanren and other business interests.

—Pat Choate, *Agents of Influence*[2]

By 2:15 the lines of black limousines that pile up here every lunch day are thinning out. Just beyond the *Keidanren's* ornamental pool, the cars of the remaining corporate elite wait idle—the big, clunky, cushy Nissan Cedrics and beefed-up Toyotas with pairs of shiny, rearview mirrors sprouting from their hoods, antennas spiking from the trunk, lots and lots of chrome, and white linen antimacassars decorating the headrests. As the somberly suited, economic samurai depart through the *Keidanren's* spare, modern lobby, a screen hanging from the ceiling answers a constant preoccupation here and throughout Japan—how many yen it takes to buy one dollar. This day 145 yen will do the job nicely and a year later all it will take is 130. Reassured, they pass two white-gloved porters and meet their chauffeurs standing ready to take them to offices here in the Otemachi or in the neighboring Marunouchi district—Mitsubishiville. It's a scene that's repeated at the *Keidanren* every Monday through Saturday except for the New Year's holiday and short of an earthquake, it's hard to envision what might alter this quotidian pattern and what it symbolizes in Japan's economy.

Make no mistake. This is no figurehead organization. The *Keidanren*, or Japanese Federation of Economic Organizations, is where Japan's corporate leaders gather to lunch, dine, drink, hold meetings and seminars and lobby when they've made it to the pinnacle of economic and, almost by definition, political power in the *zaibatsu* way. Its members include many of the key players in, and architects of, Zaibatsu America, the *keiretsu* system and the Japanese Miracle. As Chalmers Johnson has noted in his book "*MITI and the Japanese Miracle,* being president of the *Keidanren* is the most influential post in the country for making policy for the business sector."[3] Among the *Keidanren's* vice chairmen are Ryoichi Kawai, chairman of Komatsu Ltd., a wise-looking Shoichi Saba, adviser to Toshiba Corporation, and Takeshi Hijikata, chairman of Sumitomo Chemical Co. Ltd. There's Nobuya Hagura, an International Finance Committee chairman and adviser to Dai-Ichi Kangyo, Setsuya Tabuchi, chairman of Nomura Securities, who heads up the Economic Research Committee and Yohei Mimura, chairman of Mitsubishi Corporation, who's chief of the Committee on Foreign Relations. Then there are two old boys and across-the-street neighbors from Nagoya, Toyota Motor Corporation chairman Eiji Toyoda, and Sony Corporation founder and chairman, Akio Morita—one of few nails that's always stuck out and made it.

At last count, *Keidanren* members came from 932 corporations and 122 co-dependent associations representing virtually all branches of Japan's economic life. These are the graduates of Tokyo, Keio and Waseda universities, who've been trained since

214

childhood in the ways of the group. At four or five they learned that when the teacher asked a question it was meant for this or that group and not for little Gaishi or Masao. And they quickly caught on to the pervasive dictum about the nail that sticks out getting pounded down. As part of the entering corporate class of 1947 or '52 or '53 at Sumitomo Bank, or Mitsui & Co., or Mitsubishi Heavy Industries or one of the other top *keiretsu* companies, they've worked loyally and indefatigably for their chosen company, finally ascending to the presidency or chairmanship. Or they've taken the other tough route to the top. They're the former ministers who've descended from heaven—from MITI or the Finance Ministry—to spend their final days as an adviser to or at the top of some corporation.[4]

Though the *Keidanren* likes to claim that it's a free marketeer and independent from the government, the lines of communication and ties with Japan's powerful ministries and parliament, the Diet, run deep. Not only is it a major lobbier of the ministries, but it is also a prime supporter of the Liberal Democratic Party (LDP), Japan's ruling political clique. The *Keidanren* provides the LDP with a stipend of almost $100 million a year, while its member companies come through with many times more. Around election time the *Keidanren* and its members really pull out the checkbooks. During the 1990 elections, for example, the *Keidanren* and its *keiretsu* of business alliances poured more than $1 billion into the LDP's bottomless coffers.[5] Moreover, if it's a spot where high-ranking ministers preach when they've descended from heaven, it's also a place where young MITI officers can be found learning about another aspect of the "developmental state."[6] And it's a place, as might be expected in male-chauvinist Japan, where no woman holds a top position. In effect, the *Keidanren* is a living monument to the success of doing business in the *zaibatsu* way. As such—as the *keiretsu* of Japanese economic might, it is a vital symbol of what the United States would like to see changed in Japan's insular domestic economy so that American firms could compete and invest more successfully here. Good luck. There's little chance of changing the *zaibatsu* way, either here or in America.

Enter America's Iron Lady of World Commerce, Carla Hills, a Washington anti-trust lawyer and former secretary of Housing and Urban Development under the Ford administration, whom President Bush selected to get tough with America's trading partners—especially Japan. To figuratively give muscle to her role, President Bush handed Hills a crowbar at her February 1989 swearing in as United States Special Trade representative, saying he knew she'd use it "with finesse and strength."[7] Though her presidential title refers to trade, Hills's mandate is much broader—a chief mission being to use her crowbar to pry open Japan's airtight, vacuum-sealed group economy as embodied in the *Keidanren*, the pinnacle of the *zaibatsu* way, where all the *batsu* connections come into full play and where U.S. negotiators frequently come to try and persuade the Japanese to change their ways.

So there she is, soon after becoming America's crowbar-plenipotentiary, off in Tokyo, her right hand stretched out to shake *Keidanren* chairman, Eishiro Saito's hand, while standing between them doing the introducing is *Keidanren* vice chairman, Akio Morita of Sony, who looks as if he had a better time with Cyndi Lauper. Clutched in her left hand is a dark portfolio, papers sticking out. Her agenda: a revolutionary American strategy with the unfortunate, impossible-to-remember name of the Structural Impediments Initiative (SII), which as it's developed has designated Japan's *keiretsu* and all that's incorporated in the *Keidanren* as a prime target of U.S. concern. There's more than a bit of irony in the fact that Hills's host on this occasion is Morita, since he's already begun Sony's global expansion into a vertically integrated entertainment giant that will include the acquisition of CBS Records and Columbia Pictures and he will later say that building Sony into a giant *keiretsu* is a major goal for his company.[8] Then, the *Keidanren's* Saito and Morita are, in effect, two of the kingpins of the *zaibatsu* way. Moreover, taking a crowbar to pry open Japan's economic system is just the wrong metaphorical tool. Contrast it with Japan's more subtle approach to its investment in the U.S. which Fujitsu president, Takushin Yamamoto, characterized well at a *Keidanren* meeting concerning the matter when he advised "the strong should walk on tiptoes."[9] Remember, the samurai did battle with beautifully wrought, centuries-old swords, honed to the utmost perfection—not crowbars.

Launched in July 1989, the SII talks were set up so that never-ending trade friction between the U.S. and Japan might be minimized by focusing on underlying factors that helped create Japan's trade surplus. As a result of these talks it was agreed the following year that if America and Japan could get their respective houses more in order, America's trade imbalance with Japan would improve. The idea was that America should focus on correcting its low rate of savings and investment, its chronic budget deficit and deteriorating education system, while Japan would have to deal with the problems inherent in its non-productive use of land, its high savings rate, its archaic distribution system and its exclusionary business practices as exemplified in its *keiretsu* relationships.

In the best of all possible worlds, such a novel approach might have worked—and certainly it's commendable to try and root out the real causes of the problem, but in the real world the results have been unfortunately as forgettable as SII's name. Certainly, America has done little to get its house in order along SII lines, but then neither has Japan. Moreover, the idea that Japan might dramatically alter the *keiretsu* system is pure dreaming. As Congressional Research Service analyst Dick Nanto noted in his testimony at the Joint Economic Committee Hearings last year:

> The *"keiretsu"* are a fact of life in Japan and are not likely to change significantly in the near future. Over time, however, all such arrangements tend to weaken because member companies grow so large that company policies become difficult to enforce, subsidiaries become financially independent, and the product lines of member firms become so complicated that the parent company can no longer provide meaningful guidance for them. Obviously, however, U.S. firms attempting to enter the Japanese market cannot wait for this process to develop.[10]

Put very simply, why in the world would the Japanese want to change an economic system—the *zaibatsu* way—that has worked so well for them and been a major contributor to the Japanese miracle? As Chalmers Johnson recently pointed out, "there's no reason on earth for Japan to take advice from Americans on how to run their economy."[11]

While the SII talks will most probably prove to be an exercise in futility for the U.S. and Ambassador Hills's crowbar hardly worth its weight in gold, the talks do underscore two very critical factors in America's relations with Japan: the prime importance

217

to the Japanese economy of doing business in the *zaibatsu* way and how America should get its economic act together. These two factors have, in turn, been key to the swift creation of Zaibatsu America.

Of course, the Japanese should open their markets more to foreign competitors. Of course, American investors and companies should have the same access to Japanese markets as the Japanese have to America's. This is only fair and reasonable, if the Japanese want to continue buying and selling into America as they have. It's what's called reciprocity. But the point is it's not going to happen, or if it happens at all, it will only come over a very, very long time as the Japanese economy evolves into something closer to a Western, laissez-faire state of affairs. And of course, Japan should take a larger, more positive role in the geopolitical sphere, in light of its niggardly behavior during the Iraq War. Their $13-billion contribution to the war effort is all fine and dandy, but getting it out of Japan was like extracting teeth.

For the Japanese, talk is cheap. They can negotiate and negotiate and then change their economy and the way they trade as little as possible. They know very well, the more they delay, the more they have to gain. Time is on their side. For Americans, talk is becoming more and more expensive. At this point in the evolution of Zaibatsu America, time is of the essence for America and time is running out unless America takes an initiative to keep its economic body intact—to hang on to control of its vital economic parts.

Remember, it didn't take centuries for Japan to become the world's leading producer of semiconductors, displacing America by a wide margin. It took, at most, a decade. The same is true for the creation of Japan's Auto Alley, whose production, along with Japanese imports, could boost Japan's share of the U.S. market to 40 or even 50 percent in short order. Remember, Toyota's Georgetown and Mitsubishi's Diamond Star plants only began production in 1988, Mazda's Flat Rock, Michigan, facility in 1987, Nissan's Smyrna, Tennessee, operation in 1984, and Honda's Marysville, Ohio, factory in 1982—all less than 10 years ago. Moreover, it took Japanese investors little more than half a decade to become the single most important factor in Hawaii's economy, while Sony totally transformed itself with the purchase of CBS Records and Columbia Pictures into an entertainment giant during the same brief period. Ten years ago the Maddens of Hamburg Place wouldn't have thought of having "A Night on Fujiyama" and ten years ago the U.S. wasn't the world's largest debtor.

The creation of Zaibatsu America has come about very, very fast and to a large degree Americans have themselves to thank for the current troubling state of affairs. However, to slow or reverse the burgeoning of Zaibatsu America will take time and great effort on the part of the American economy. There is a momentum, a life of its own to the *zaibatsu* way, as Japanese companies flock to invest in the U.S. Unchecked or not confronted, Japanese firms will continue to gain larger footholds in America's key industries: in autos, steel, finance, consumer electronics, high-tech and information technologies, often gaining additional market share in times of economic weakness as has happened recently in the U.S. auto industry.

Moreover, what has been seen thus far is just the beginning. The scope and focus of Japanese investment in the U.S. will burgeon as Japanese firms go after a larger share of America's vital parts. Japan is already coming on very strong in computers and with their dominant position in laptops, they're going to offer an even more formidable threat to U.S. producers as they increase their production facilities in America. Also marked for an assault by Japanese investment in the U.S. are high definition television, the drug industry, biotechnology and aerospace—areas of great importance to the U.S. economy and ones in which the U.S. remains a world leader.

Just how important these industries are can be seen from the examples of drugs and aerospace. The U.S. pharmaceutical industry is not only very healthy and profitable but it is the world's largest, with shipments amounting to $55 billion last year compared to a world market estimated at $150 billion. America's aerospace industry is similarly endowed, having been the world leader since World War II, with $120 billion in shipments last year in a $200-billion world market.[12]

To date Japan has not had great success in either of these areas but it is persevering. Remember, not so long ago a number of experts said Japan could never be a major factor in the computer business and look at where they are today. As just another instance of Japan's persistence and broadening presence in the U.S., there's the example of the new Boeing B777 passenger plane. Boeing is developing the aircraft in a project that includes Mitsubishi Heavy Industry, Kawasaki Heavy Industry and Fuji

Heavy Industry. About half of its body will be built in Japan. Moreover, the Japanese will pay for 21 percent of the plane's $3.7-billion development cost, thus in effect buying into American aerospace production while also learning how such a plane is developed and built.[13]

Finally, what are the lessons from the Marunouchi, the Tokyo Stock Exchange and the *Keidanren*—that the *zaibatsu* way is an extremely powerful force that is deeply rooted in Japan's economy and its psyche and that it is a mode of operating that has been largely exported to the U.S? In this light it's worth remembering that General MacArthur had the *Keidanren* created as an antidote to the prewar *zaibatsu* which he assumed he'd eliminated and as a forum where Japan's economy could become more democratic. Look at what's happened. The same six industrial groups that controlled 30 percent or more of Japan's economy before World War II, currently enjoy a similar position now. And look at the *Keidanren*. It's hardly the pinnacle of the sort of democratic capitalism that General MacArthur envisioned. But then why should it be? The world has changed in the past half century since the time General MacArthur was trying to give a defeated, humbled nation some seemingly sensible institutions.

So what should America do when confronted with the force of the *zaibatsu* way—a force that's making vast inroads on its own turf? It has to get back to basics and put value on its own basic strengths—its ability to innovate and make products people want to buy, its ability to save and grow, to save enough to grow and its ability to lead, as wonderfully exemplified in the Gulf War.

The beauty of the *zaibatsu* way is that it is a mode of accumulating capital, a capitalist system that works for the Japanese and it has worked wonderfully for them, but it is not something that Americans could adapt to their own society or character. At the moment though, it puts America on unequal footing, especially since the force of the *zaibatsu* way is only just beginning to be comprehended in the U.S. There have been suggestions that American industry form a sort of high-tech *keiretsu* of U.S. companies that would be structured along the lines of an NEC or a Fujitsu. American high-tech companies should form more alliances such as Sematech, the consortium of U.S. semiconductor firms created in 1987 with the help of the Defense Department and a $100-million grant from Congress to better compete against foreign competition, but it is really doubtful whether an American

220

keiretsu, having say IBM, Xerox and AT&T joining forces with a number of other companies, would work.

There is, however, an urgency for America to face the *zaibatsu* monolith head-on with all the strength, money and talent it can muster. The *zaibatsu* way is a very powerful force that gains momentum in the U.S. every day. If America doesn't wake up and confront what's happening in its own backyard, it's bound to lose more control over its vital parts. By America, I mean business, government, the nation's educational institutions and its populace, who must deal with the issues of Zaibatsu America head-on.

America has to be tough in confronting the *zaibatsu* monolith and there are some obvious things it should do. America should increase its rate of saving so that there would be more money for research and development and investment, cut its energy-sapping budget deficit, and greatly improve its elementary and secondary education. These are the obvious deficiencies currently plaguing the U.S. that once ameliorated would greatly improve America's global competitiveness, its future position in Zaibatsu America and the way its citizens live. In effect, the SII prescription of what America should do to get its act together is for the most part right on the mark.

In dealing with the specifics of Zaibatsu America, and its own economic well-being, the United States must also put some less obvious matters on its agenda. America should get back to the basics of manufacturing, redefine national security in terms of broader economic and technological security which the Japanese have done all along, and look to changing its anti-trust laws so that American firms can more easily join forces as with Sematech and so that it can better deal with the sort of economic structure represented in the *keiretsu* and the *zaibatsu* way. Current anti-trust laws appear to be incapable of recognizing the sort of economic power created by Japan's cross-shareholdings and group dynamics.

Perhaps one of the most important things America can do in confronting Zaibatsu America is to get back to the business of manufacturing, realizing that manufacturing does count. The so-called service economy, where brains supposedly replace brawn, has the potential of being a lightweight economy which, if followed to its logical end, becomes an airhead economy. Remember, this is the economy of the Reagan years—the hollowed-out, leveraged-out America. Of course, brawn without brains isn't going to get you very far either. The two—service and manufacturing—have to interact in a felicitous relationship. Unfortunately, some in America have forgotten how technology drives manufacturing and how the reverse is also true. Moreover, what's the use of a service economy where no one knows how to service anything because they don't know how they're made? If you happen to think making cars and semiconductors is not important or is of equal economic value as baking bagels, then don't worry—be happy. But such thinking can have a devastating long-range impact on the U.S. economy.

As the Council on Competitiveness points out in its excellent report released in March 1991:

> Pioneering research and Nobel prizes are not enough. Leadership in technology is closely linked to leadership in commercial markets. Unless ideas can be pushed, pulled and cajoled from the laboratory to the marketplace and unless technological know-how meets the tests of markets, America's jobs, standard of living and ultimately, national security will be at risk. Our national technology priorities must address this marketplace reality. . . .
>
> Unless the United States shores up its technological strength, Americans will feel the pinch in a thousand ways. The good jobs they seek will always be out of reach. The mortgage payments they make will take a bigger bite out of their paychecks. The national security that they have become accustomed to will become more precarious. And the high standard of living that Americans once took for granted will be beyond the grasp of future generations. . . . Most important, by improving the quality of goods and services and the productivity of the workforce, technology is the driving force behind America's competitiveness.

And the Council adds: "Unfortunately, in turning over technology to its competitors, America is turning over the keys to economic growth and prosperity."[14]

Welcome to Zaibatsu America.

Notes

CHAPTER 1 *Welcome to Zaibatsu America*

1. Edward T. Hall and Mildred Reed Hall, *Hidden Differences* (Garden City, N.Y.: Anchor Press/Doubleday, 1987), p. 43.

2. Kevin Phillips, *The Politics of Rich and Poor* (New York: Random House, 1990), p. 123, from "The Selling of America (Cont'd)," *Fortune* (May 23, 1988), p. 64.

3. Division of Research & Planning, Kentucky Cabinet for Economic Development, Frankfort, Ky.

4. "Bluegrass Country of Kentucky Goes to Shopping Malls," *Wall Street Journal*, (April 5, 1989), p. 1; "Weeks of Parties, 2 Minutes of Race," *New York Times* (May 3, 1989), p. 15; and an interview with Anita Madden, December 1989.

5. Robert Zielinski and Nigel Holloway, *Unequal Equities* (Tokyo: Kodansha International, 1991), p. 24 and Chalmers Johnson, *MITI and the Japanese Miracle* (Tokyo: Charles E. Tuttle, 1986), p. 204.

6. William Raspberry, "Good Sense from Paul Tsongas," *Washington Post*, (March 18, 1991), p. A11.

7. Frank Gibney, *Miracle by Design* (New York: Times Books, 1982), pp. 42–43.

8. Chalmers Johnson in Clyde V. Prestowitz, Jr., Ronald A. Morse and Alan Tonelson, *Powernomics* (Lanham, Md.: Madison Books, 1991), p. 167 and *Industrial Groupings in Japan* (Tokyo: Dodwell Marketing Consultants, 8th edition 1988–89).

9. The Fair Trade Commission of Japan, *The Actual Conditions of Six Major Corporate Groups* (Tokyo: August 1989) and Zielinski and Holloway, *Unequal Equities*, chs. 2–3.

10. James Fallows, "Containing Japan," *Atlantic* (May 1989), p. 48.

11. Zielinski and Holloway, *Unequal Equities*, p. 150.

12. James K. Jackson, "Foreign Direct Investment in the United States," Congressional Research Service, Library of Congress (Feb. 8, 1991), p. 12.

13. Candace Howes, "Foreign Direct Investment in the Auto Industry," a study for the Economic Policy Institute and Project on Regional and Industrial Economics at Rutgers University (December 21, 1990).

14. Frank Gibney, *Miracle by Design;* see ch. 2.

15. Zielinski and Holloway, *Unequal Equities*, pp. 22–23.

16. Ibid., p. 24.

17. Chie Nakane, *Japanese Society* (Tokyo: Charles E. Tuttle, 1989), pp. 101–3.

18. Ibid., p. 24.

19. Johnson, *MITI and the Japanese Miracle*, p. 55.

20. Nakane, *Japanese Society*, p. 3.

21. Johnson, *MITI and the Japanese Miracle*, p. 57.

22. Nakane, *Japanese Society*, p. 11.

23. Fallows, "Containing Japan," pp. 40–54.

24. Pat Choate, *Agents of Influence* (New York: Alfred A. Knopf, 1990), p. xi.

25. Chalmers Johnson, Noon Lecture, Economic Strategy Institute, February 28, 1991.

26. Douglas P. Woodward, "Locational Determinants of Japanese Manufacturing Start-ups in the United States" (Columbia, S.C.: College of Business Administration, The University of South Carolina, 1990, unpublished); Howes, "Foreign Direct Investment."

27. Cited in Prestowitz, Morse and Tonelson, *Powernomics*, p. xii.

28. Ibid., p. 100 from Stephen S. Cohen and John Zysman, *"Manufacturing Matters* (New York: Basic Books, 1987).

29. Robert Reich, "The Real Economy," *Atlantic* (February 1991), pp. 35–52.

30. Ibid.

31. Robert J. Dowling, "Robert Reich's Feel-Good Globalism," *Business-Week* (March 18, 1991), pp. 14–15.

32. See ch. 3.

33. Prestowitz, Morse, and Tonelson, *Powernomics*, p. 106, from Cohen and Zysman, *Manufacturing Matters*.

34. Hall and Hall, *Hidden Differences*, p. 43.

35. Zielinski and Holloway, *Unequal Equities*, pp. 26–28.

36. Ibid., p. 31.

37. Ibid., p. 211.
38. The Fair Trade Commission of Japan, "Six Major Corporate Groups" and Zielinski and Holloway, *Unequal Equities*, chs. 2–3.
39. Clyde V. Prestowitz, Jr., *Trading Places* (New York: Basic Books, 1988), p. 157 and *Industrial Groupings in Japan*.
40. "Morgan's Version of the Fed is Revealed, 1912." *Wall Street Journal* (March 6, 1988), p. B1.
41. Cited in Jon Woronoff, *Japan: The Coming Economic Crisis* (Tokyo: Lotus Press Ltd., 1979), p. 98; James C. Abegglen, "The Economic Growth of Japan," *Scientific American*, March 1970.
42. "Japan's Centres of the Universals," *Economist* (March 25, 1989), p. 92.
43. Johnson, *MITI and the Japanese Miracle*, p. 20.
44. Stefan Wagstyl, "Japan: Economic Growth in 1988 at 15-year High," *Financial Times* (March 18, 1989).
45. *New York Times*, (March 20, 1991), p. D5.
46. Hall and Hall, *Hidden Differences*, p. 55.
47. Prestowitz, *Trading Places*, p. 160.
48. *Forbes* (November 28, 1988), p. 37.
49. See ch. 8.
50. Leonard Silk, "A New Warning on the Deficits," *New York Times* (May 5, 1989), p. 30.
51. Leonard Silk, "U.S. and Japan: Revising the Ties," *New York Times* (March 10, 1989), p. 28.
52. "Head of Crash Study Blames Japanese Selling of U.S. Bonds," Associated Press (April 22, 1988).
53. R. Taggart Murphy, "Power without Purpose: The Crisis of Japan's Global Financial Dominance," *Harvard Business Review* (March–April 1989), p. 72 and Silk, "U.S. and Japan: Revising the Ties," p. 28.
54. Murphy, "Power without Purpose," p. 72, and Silk, "U.S. and Japan: Revising the Ties," p. 28.
55. Robert Pear, "Confusion is the Operative Word in U.S. Policy toward Japan," *New York Times* (March 30, 1989), p. 1.
56. Martin and Susan Tolchin, *Buying into America* (New York: Times Books, 1988), ch. 3.
57. Council on Competitiveness, "Competitiveness Index 1990" (Washington, D.C.), p. 5.
58. *BusinessWeek* (May 29, 1989), p. 88.
59. Robert Z. Lawrence, "Do Keiretsu Reduce Japanese Imports?"

(Washington, DC.: Brookings Institution, December 14, 1990), p. 35.

60. Ibid., p. 19 and Paul Blustein, "A New Study Fuels the Clash over Keiretsu," *Washington Post* (April 26, 1991), p. F1.

CHAPTER 2 *Auto Alley Zaibatsu Style*

1. "Excerpts," *Fortune* (March 26, 1990), p. 194.

2. Toyota company literature.

3. Maryann Keller, "Ideas for the 1990's," *Fortune* (March 26, 1990), p. 36.

4. Paul Ingrassia, "Losing Control: Auto Industry in U.S. Is Sliding Relentlessly into Japanese Hands," *Wall Street Journal* (February 16, 1990), p. 1.

5. Candace Howes, "Foreign Direct Investment in the Auto Industry," a study for the Economic Policy Institute and Project on Regional and Industrial Economics at Rutgers University (December 21, 1990), p. 31.

6. Douglas P. Woodward, "Locational Determinants of Japanese Manufacturing Start-ups in the United States" (Columbia, S.C.: College of Business Administration, The University of South Carolina, 1990, unpublished) and Howes, "Foreign Direct Investment in the Auto Industry."

7. Howes, "Foreign Direct Investment," p. 35.

8. Paul C. Judge, "Risks in Ventures with the Japanese," *New York Times* (October 11, 1990), p. C2.

9. Robert Kearns, "Japan-America Inc.," *Chicago Tribune,* (April 5, 1987), Section 7, p. 1.

10. Interview with Michael Kane, December 1989.

11. Here and throughout *Zaibatsu America,* the data concerning the specifics of keiretsu interlocking shareholdings and their investments in the U.S. come primarily from Dodwell's invaluable *Industrial Groupings in Japan* (Dodwell Marketing Consultants 8th edition 1988–89); *The Structure of the Japanese Auto Parts Industry* (Tokyo: Dodwell Marketing Consultants, 3rd edition, 1986); *The Structure of the Japanese Electronics Industry* (Tokyo: Dodwell Marketing Consultants, 2nd edition, 1988); Toyo Keizai Inc.'s *Japan Company Handbook* sections 1 and 2 (Winter 1989); the Japan Economic Institute's survey of Japanese companies in the U.S., *Japan's Expanding U.S. Manufacturing Presence* (Washington, D.C., 1989); the Kentucky Cabinet for Economic Development; and various corporate publications.

226

12. Doron P. Levin, "New Japan Car War Weapon: A 'Little Engine That Could,'" *New York Times*, (November 26, 1989), p. 1.

13. Keller, "Ideas for the 1990's," p. 36.

14. Kozo Yamamura and Ulrike Wassmann, "Do Japanese Firms Behave Differently? The Effects of 'Keiretsu' in the United States," from *Japanese Investment in the United States: Should We Be Concerned?* (Seattle: Society for Japanese Studies, 1989), p. 135.

15. Howes, "Foreign Direct Investment," pp. 31–32.

16. Jonathan P. Hicks, "Talking Deals," *New York Times* (December 21, 1989), p. 34.

17. Nick Garnett, "World Steelmakers Forge New Cross-Border Links," *Financial Times* (January 24, 1990).

18. Robert Thomson,"NKK of Japan to Lift Holding in NSC, *Financial Times* (April 27, 1990).

19. Jonathan P. Hicks, "Talking Deals," p. 34; Merrill Goozner, "Inland to Sell 13% Stake to Nippon," *Chicago Tribune* (December 19, 1989), p. 1., Sect. 3.

20. Mordechai E. Kreinin, "How Closed Is Japan's Market? Additional Evidence," London, Trade Policy Research Centre, *The World Economy*, Volume 11, Number 4 (December 1988), pp. 529–42.

21. *Financial Times*, Special Survey (May 16, 1990), p. 1.

22. Michael E. Porter, "The New Japanese Challenge to the U.S. Auto Industry," from Peter J. Arnesen, editor, *The Japanese Competition: Phase 2* (Ann Arbor, Center for Japanese Studies, 1987), p. 7.

23. *Financial Times*, Special Survey (May 16, 1990), p. 1.

24. Pat Choate, *Agents of Influence* (New York: Alfred A. Knopf, 1990), p. 8.

25. Vladimir Pucik, "Joint Ventures as a Strategy for Competition," from Peter J. Arnesen, editor, *The Japanese Competition: Phase 2* (Ann Arbor, Center for Japanese Studies, 1987), p. 47.

26. *Wall Street Journal* (April 12, 1988), p. 6.

27. Porter, "The New Japanese Challenge," p. 19.

28. Boye De Mente, *Everything Japanese* (Lincolnwood, Ill., Passport Books, 1989), p. 285.

29. *Wall Street Journal* (April 24, 1990).

30. Ian Rodger, "Family Firmly in Control," *Financial Times*, World Car Industry Survey (September 13, 1989), p. 15.

31. *Fortune* (May 5, 1990) and Toyota company literature.

32. *The Structure of the Japanese Auto Parts Industry*, p. 32.

33. Chalmers Johnson, Noon Lecture, Economic Strategy Institute, February 28, 1991.

34. Joseph B. White, "GM Follows Ford by Boosting Car Prices, Creating Big Opportunity for Japanese," *Wall Street Journal* (August 15, 1990), p. B1; John Bussey, "Did U.S. Carmakers Err by Raising Prices When the Yen Rose?" *Wall Street Journal* (April 1, 1988), p. 1; Joseph B. White, "Despite Record Profits, Big Three Auto Firms Seek More Protection," *Wall Street Journal* (January 24, 1989), p. 1; "Detroit Under Siege," *Economist* (April 14, 1990), pp. 13–14.

35. H. Brinton Milward and Heidi Hosbach Newman, "State Incentive Packages and the Industrial Location Decision" (Lexington, Ky., The Center for Business and Economic Research, November 1987), p. 23.

36. H. Brinton Milward, "The Estimated Economic Impact of Toyota on the State's Economy" (Lexington, Ky., The Center for Business and Economic Research, December 1986).

37. Milward and Newman, "State Incentive Packages."

38. Division of Research & Planning, Kentucky Cabinet for Economic Development, Frankfort, Ky.

39. Robert Kearns, "Japan-America Inc.," section 7, p. 1.

40. Howes, "Foreign Direct Investment," p. 61.

41. Joseph B. White, "Stumbling Auto Makers Face Tough '91," *Wall Street Journal* (January 7, 1991), p. B1.

42. Ibid. and "Roger Smith Reflects on Role at GM," *Wall Street Journal* (July 31, 1990), p. B1.

43. Ingrassia, "Losing Control," p. 1.

44. Keller, "Ideas for the 1990's," p. 36.

45. Joseph B. White, "Toyota to Boost Plant Capacity in U.S., Canada," *Wall Street Journal* (October 12, 1989), p. A2.

46. David E. Sanger, "As U.S. Auto Makers Shut Plants, Toyota Is Expanding Aggressively," *New York Times* (January 1, 1991), p. 1.

47. "Detroit under Siege," *Economist* (April 14, 1990), p. 13.

48. Ingrassia, "Losing Control," p. 1.

49. Ibid.

50. "Detroit under Siege," p. 13.

51. Ingrassia, "Losing Control," p. 1.

CHAPTER 3 *Tinseltown and Tin Pan Alley*

1. David Sanger, *New York Times* (October 14, 1990), S4, p. 3.

2. Cited in John Huey, "America's Hottest Export: Pop Culture," *Fortune* (December 31, 1990), p. 51.

3. Peter J. Boyer, "Sony and CBS Records, What a Romance!" *New York Times Magazine* (September 18, 1988), pp. 35–49 and cover.

4. David E. Sanger, "Sony's Norio Ohga: Building Smaller, Buying Bigger," *New York Times Magazine* (February 18, 1990), pp. 23–70.

5. John Schwartz, "Japan Goes Hollywood," *Newsweek* (October 9, 1989), p. 66.

6. Neil Gross, "Japan's Hollywood: More Ominous Than It Seems," *BusinessWeek* (October 15, 1990), p. 115.

7. Lester Thurow, "An 'Investment Economics' for the Year 2000," white paper on America's future by Rebuild America (Washington, D.C., June 1988).

8. Huey, "America's Hottest Export," p. 50.

9. Richard Behar, "A Music King's Shattering Fall," *Time* (September 17, 1990), p. 64.

10. Boyer, "Sony and CBS Records," p. 36.

11. Akio Morita, *Made in Japan, Akio Morita and Sony* (New York: E. P. Dutton, 1986).

12. Behar, "A Music King's Shattering Fall," p. 64 and Boyer, "Sony and CBS Records," pp. 35–49.

13. Schwartz, "Japan Goes Hollywood," pp. 62–72.

14. Richard W. Stevenson, "Hollywood Entices the Japanese," *New York Times* (October 3, 1988), p. D1.

15. Richard W. Stevenson, "Japanese Put Up $100 Million to Back Films in Hollywood," *New York Times* (August 20, 1989), p. 1.

16. Ibid.

17. Robert Thomson, "JVC in Film Deal with U.S. Producer," *Financial Times* (August 22, 1989), p. 18.

18. Neil Gross and William Holstein, "Why Sony Is Plugging into Columbia," *BusinessWeek* (October 16, 1989), p. 56.

19. Ronald Grover, "Lights, Camera, Auction," *BusinessWeek* (December 10, 1990), p. 27.

20. Huey, "America's Hottest Export," p. 52.

21. Gross, "Japan's Hollywood," p. 115.

22. Richard W. Stevenson, "Disney Turns to Japanese for Future Film Financing," *New York Times* (October 23, 1990), p. C1 and *Wall Street Journal* (October 23, 1990), p. B1.

23. Stefan Wagstyl, "Chief of Sony Tells Why It Bought a Part of America's Soul," *Financial Times* (October 4, 1989), p. 7.

24. Schwartz, "Japan Goes Hollywood," pp. 62–72.

25. Paul Farhi, "Rerun War on Fast Forward," *Washington Post* (Febru-

ary 20, 1991), p. D1 and Clyde Prestowitz, "U.S. Rules, Not Japanese Money, Lost MCA," *Wall Street Journal* (December 3, 1990).

26. Grover, "Lights, Camera, Auction," p. 27.

27. Wagstyl, "Chief of Sony," p. 7.

28. Ibid.

29. *Chicago Tribune* (November 10, 1989), p. 11.

30. Gross and Holstein, "Why Sony Is Plugging into Columbia," p. 56.

31. Schwartz, "Japan Goes Hollywood," pp. 62–72.

32. See *The Structure of the Japanese Electronics Industry* (Tokyo: Dodwell Marketing Consultants, 2nd edition, December 1988).

33. Schwartz, "Japan Goes Hollywood," pp. 62–72.

34. Boyer, "Sony and CBS Records," pp. 35–49.

35. Huey, "America's Hottest Export," p. 51.

36. Ibid.

37. David E. Sanger, "The New TV Makes Debut in Japan," *New York Times,* (December 6, 1990), p. C1.

38. Ibid.

39. Edmund L. Andrews, "U.S. Makes Gains in Race to Develop Advanced TV," *New York Times* (December 21, 1990), p. 1.

40. Ibid.

41. Andrew Kupfer, "The U.S. Wins One in High-Tech TV," *Fortune* (April 8, 1991), p. 60 and *New York Times* (January 6, 1991), p. D4.

42. Interview with Michael Schulhof, December 1989; Sanger, "The New TV," p. C1.

43. Sanger, "Sony's Norio Ohga, pp. 23–70.

44. Gross and Holstein, "Why Sony Is Plugging into Columbia," p. 56.

45. Ibid.

CHAPTER 4 *Silicon Valley*

1. Cited in Jonathan B. Levine, "Is the U.S. Selling Its High-Tech Soul to Japan?" *BusinessWeek* (June 26, 1989), p. 117.

2. Charles H. Ferguson, "Computers and the Coming of the U.S. Keiretsu," *Harvard Business Review* (July–August 1990), pp. 55–70.

3. Brenton R. Schlender, "How Steve Jobs Linked Up with IBM," *Fortune* (October 9, 1989), p. 48 and Philip Elmer-Dewitt, "Soul of the Next Machine," *Time* (October 24, 1988), p. 80.

4. Schlender, "How Steve Jobs Linked Up."

5. Geoff Lewis, Neil Gross and Jonathan B. Levine, "Computers: Japan Comes on Strong," *BusinessWeek* (October 23, 1989), p. 104.

6. Gina Kolata, "Japanese Labs in U.S. Luring America's Computer Experts," *New York Times* (November 11, 1990), p. 1.

7. *New York Times* (May 10, 1990), Editorial.

8. Lewis, Gross and Levine, "Computers," p. 104.

9. Robert Hof and Neil Gross, "Silicon Valley Is Watching Its Worst Nightmare Unfold," *BusinessWeek* (September 4, 1989), p. 63.

10. "Japan's Chip Makers: Falling off the Learning Curve," *Economist* (February 23, 1991), p. 64 and Robert Kearns, "No Peace in Silicon Valley," *Chicago Tribune* (April 7, 1987), Section 3, p. 1.

11. Ferguson, "Computers and the Coming of the U.S. Keiretsu," pp. 55–70.

12. Thomas Hayes, "Compaq's Dramatic 'Notebooks,'" *New York Times* (October 16, 1989), p. 21.

13. Ferguson, "Computers and the Coming of the U.S. Keiretsu," pp. 55–70.

14. David E. Sanger, "Working Warily with the Japanese," *New York Times* (October 1, 1989), p. E22 and Levine, "Is the U.S. Selling?" p. 117.

15. Lindley H. Clark, Jr., and Alfred L. Malarbre, Jr., "Eroding R&D: Slow Rise in Outlays for Research Imperils U.S. Competitive Edge," *Wall Street Journal* (November 16, 1988), p. 1.

16. Cited in Kearns, "No Peace in Silicon Valley."

17. Ian Rodger and Awatola Kaletsky, "Nippon Mining Lured by Gould Marriage Prospects," *Financial Times* (September 1, 1988).

18. David E. Sanger, "U.S. Parts, Japanese Computer," *New York Times* (September 7, 1988), p. 27.

19. Levine, "Is the U.S. Selling?" p. 117.

20. Sanger, "U.S. Parts, Japanese Computer," p. 27.

21. Levine, "Is the U.S. Selling?" p. 117.

22. Andrew Pollack, "Kubota Is Put in Middle of an East-West Clash," *New York Times* (July 20, 1990), p. D1.

23. Sanger, "U.S. Parts, Japanese Computer," p. 27.

24. Charles Leadbeater, "Japan Gets to the Heart of ICL," *Financial Times* (July 19, 1990), p. 11.

25. Steven Prokesch, "Fujitsu to Buy ICL Stake," *New York Times* (July 31, 1990), p. D1 and David E. Sanger, "A New Fear of Japan," *New York Times* (July 31, 1990), p. D1.

26. Ian Rodger, "The Rise and Rise of a Computer Industry," *Financial Times* (July 27, 1990), p. 3.

27. Prokesch, "Fujitsu to Buy ICL Stake," p. D1 and Sanger, "A New Fear of Japan," p. D1.

28. Sanger, "A New Fear of Japan," p. D1.
29. Cited in Levine, "Is the U.S. Selling?" p. 117.
30. Lewis, Gross, and Levine, "Computers," p. 104.
31. Louise Kehoe, "Strapped in for a Bumpy Ride," *Financial Times* (April 27, 1990), p. 22.
32. Ferguson, "Computers and the Coming of the U.S. Keiretsu," pp. 55–70.
33. Editorial, *New York Times* (January 17, 1990).
34. Lewis, Gross and Levine, "Computers," p. 104.
35. Kevin L. Kearns, "Flat-Panel Case Acts as Paradigm," *San Jose Mercury News* (February 25, 1991).
36. Ferguson, "Computers and the Coming of the U.S. Keiretsu," p. 64.
37. Cited in Lewis, Gross and Levine, "Computers," p. 104.
38. *Wall Street Journal* (January 16, 1991), p. B5.
39. Todd Mason, "The Book That's Creating a Firestorm," *BusinessWeek*, (October 23, 1989), p. 78.

CHAPTER 5 *Boardwalk, Park Place*

1. *Hawaii Business*, Entire Issue on "The Japaning of Hawaii" (January 1990); Bill Wood, "Generosity's High Price?" *Hawaii Investor* (November 1989), p. 27; and *Forbes* (July 23, 1990), p. 170.
2. *Honolulu Advertiser* (November 27, 1989).
3. Lucy Jokiel, "A Teed-Off Public," *Hawaii Business* (January 1990), p. 74.
4. City and County of Honolulu, *Golf Course Development on Oahu* (Study issued July 1989).
5. Albert Scardino, "Japanese Forcing U.S. Realty Prices Up," *New York Times* (December 15, 1986), p. 1.
6. Jim Carlton, "Gloom on U.S. Market Hits Japanese Investors," *Wall Street Journal* (January 21, 1991), p. B1.
7. Jokiel, "A Teed-Off Public," p. 74.
8. City and County of Honolulu, *Golf Course Development on Oahu*.
9. Karen Lowry Miller, "The Stealth Who Snagged Pebble Beach," *BusinessWeek* (September 24, 1990), p. 124.
10. Andrew Pollack, "Anxiety under that Fabled Cypress," *New York Times* (September 8, 1990), p. D1.
11. James Sterngold, "Pebble Beach Glee Is Hard to Hide," *New York Times* (September 17, 1990), p. C1.

12. Michael Thompson-Noel, "Big Business and the Greening of the World," *Financial Times* (October 27–28, 1990), p. 22.

13. Gregory Pai and First Hawaiian Bank, "Japan's Importance to Hawaii," in *Economic Indicators* (March–April 1989), p. 1.

14. Michel McQueen, "Akaka and Saiki Fight for Hawaii Senate Seat with Some Hula Hoopla but Little Mudslinging," *Wall Street Journal* (October 1, 1990), p. A16.

15. Gregory Pai, "Japanese Investment in the United States and Hawaii: An Assessment of Magnitudes, Impacts, and Policies," Speech for the East-West Center (May 4, 1989).

16. Pai and First Hawaiian Bank, "Japan's Importance to Hawaii."

17. "Foreign Investment in Hawaii," a Survey from the Office of the Mayor, City and County of Honolulu (March 15, 1989).

18. *Hawaii Business*, "The Japaning of Hawaii;" Wood, "Generosity's High Price?" p. 27; and *Forbes* (July 23, 1990), p. 170.

19. "Foreign Investment in Hawaii."

20. McQueen, "Akaka and Saiki," p. A16.

21. Gregory Pai, "Outlook for the Hawaiian Economy in 1989 with Special Reference to Japanese Investment in Hawaii," Speech to the Building Owners and Managers Association (March 8, 1989).

22. "Foreign Investment in Hawaii" and Richard Saul Wurman, "Hawaii Access" (ACCESSPRESS Ltd., 1989).

23. "Foreign Investment in Hawaii."

24. Ibid.

25. Ibid.

26. Cited in Greg Wiles, "Horita: Ko Olina No Ka Oi (the Ko Olina resort is the best)," *Honolulu Advertiser* (November 30, 1989), p. A3 and company literature.

27. City and County of Honolulu, *Golf Course Development on Oahu.*

28. Bank of Hawaii, Business Trends, *Frustration Looking for a Scapegoat* (May–June 1988).

29. Ibid.

30. McQueen, "Akaka and Saiki," p. A16.

31. Jokiel, "A Teed-Off Public," p. 74.

CHAPTER 6 *Wall Street*

1. Cited in Bernard Wysocki, Jr., "Meeting Mr. Big Face, Japanese Have Many Words for Arrogance; Americans in Tokyo Are Learning Why," *Wall Street Journal Reports, Technology* (November 14, 1988), p. R10.

2. *Playboy* (January 1991); cited in ad in *New York Times* (December 3, 1990), p. C12.
3. Michael Quint, "Japan's Giant Banks on the March," *New York Times* (October 1, 1989), section 3, p. 1.
4. Cited in Robert Guenther and Michael R. Sesit, "Credit Siege: U.S. Banks Are Losing Business to Japanese at Home and Abroad," *Wall Street Journal* (October 12, 1989), p. 1.
5. Quint, "Japan's Giant Banks on the March," p. 1.
6. Robert S. Dohner, "Japanese Financial Deregulation and the Growth of Japanese International Bank Activity," Occasional Paper 89–05, Harvard University, Program on U.S.-Japan Relations, p. 10.
7. Michael Quint, "U.S. Banks Cut Global Business as Rivals Grow," *New York Times* (July 5, 1990), p. 1.
8. Stefan Wagstyl, "Full Steam Ahead, Keen Lookout Aloft," *Financial Times* (November 6, 1989), and *BusinessWeek* (October 23, 1989), p. 126.
9. Carla Rapoport, "Tough Times for Japan's Banks," *Fortune* (July 16, 1990), p. 66; Robert Guenther and Michael Sesit, "U.S. Banks Are Losing Business to Japanese," *Wall Street Journal* (October 12, 1989), p. 1.
10. Dohner, "Japanese Financial Deregulation," p. 38.
11. Quint, "Japan's Giant Banks on the March," p. 1.
12. Michael Quint, "Big Japanese Bank to Pay $1.4 Billion in a Hanover Deal," *New York Times* (September 19, 1989), p. 1.
13. Quint, "Japan's Giant Banks on the March," p. 1.
14. Ibid.
15. Ibid.
16. Ibid.
17. Gary Hector, "Why U.S. Banks Are in Retreat," *Fortune* (May 7, 1990), p. 95.
18. Louis S. Richman, "How Capital Costs Cripple America," *Fortune* (August 14, 1989), p. 50.
19. Council on Competitiveness, *Competitiveness Index 1990* (Washington, D.C.), p. 4.
20. Richman, "How Capital Costs Cripple America," p. 50.
21. Robert Guenther and Michael R. Sesit, "Credit Siege: U.S. Banks Are Losing Business to Japanese at Home and Abroad," *Wall Street Journal* (October 12, 1989), p. 1; and Wagstyl, "Full Steam Ahead;" and *BusinessWeek* (October 23, 1989), p. 126.
22. Howard Rudnitsky, "A Yen for U.S. Capital," *Forbes* (August 20, 1990), p. 46.

23. Richman, "How Capital Costs Cripple America," p. 50.
24. James Sterngold, "Japan's Washout on Wall Street," *New York Times* (June 11, 1989), p. F1; Michael Sesit, "Japan Securities Firms Stumble on Wall Street," *Wall Street Journal* (June 5, 1989), p. C1; William Glasgall, "Tokyo Brokers Beat a Retreat from the Street," *Business-Week*, (February 13, 1989), p. 42.; and Leah J. Nathans, "Japan's Waiting Game on Wall Street," *BusinessWeek* (February 19, 1990).
25. Cited in Norman J. Glickman and Douglas P. Woodward, *The New Competitors* (New York: Basic Books, 1989), p. 60.
26. Sterngold, "Japan's Washout on Wall Street," p. F1, and Michael Sesit, "Japan's Big Four Securities Firms Hit By Losses in U.S.," *Wall Street Journal* (January 20, 1989), p. C1.
27. Michael R. Sesit and James A. White, "Japanese Firms Have Yen for U.S. High-Tech Investment Skills," *Wall Street Journal* (July 11, 1989), p. C1 and Nathans, "Japan's Waiting Game."
28. Guenther and Sesit, "Credit Siege," p. 1.
29. "Bank Lending: Sobering Up," *Economist* (October 21, 1989), p. 91; James Sterngold, "Japan Banks Turn Cautious on Buyout Lending," *New York Times*, (October 20, 1989), p. D1; Stefan Wagstyl, "Japanese Banks Lose Their Passion for LBOs," *Financial Times* (October 16, 1989); and October 16, 1989 issues of *Wall Street Journal, New York Times* and *Financial Times*.

CHAPTER 7 *Welcome to Japan, Home of the Zaibatsu Way*

1. Cited in Chalmers Johnson, *MITI and the Japanese Miracle* (Tokyo: Charles E. Tuttle, 1986), p. 156.
2. Robert Neff and William J. Holstein, "Mighty Mitsubishi is on the Move," *BusinessWeek* (September 24, 1990), p. 101.
3. The Fair Trade Commission of Japan, "The Actual Conditions of Six Major Corporate Groups" (Tokyo: August 1989) and Robert Zielinski and Nigel Holloway, *Unequal Equities* (Tokyo: Kodansha International, 1991), chs. 2–3.
4. Ibid.
5. Mitsubishi company literature, as is much of the following account of Mitsubishi's history.
6. Chie Nakane, *Japanese Society* (Tokyo: Charles E. Tuttle, 1989), p. 72.
7. Ibid., p. 24.
8. Ibid., p. 44.
9. John David Morley, *Pictures from the Water Trade* (New York: Perennial Library, Harper and Row, 1985), p. 57.

10. Merry White, *The Japanese Educational Challenge* (New York: The Free Press, 1987), p. 42.

11. "Japan Eases Rule on Korean Aliens," *New York Times* (January 11, 1991), p. A3.

12. Karel van Wolferen, *The Enigma of Japanese Power* (New York: Alfred A. Knopf, 1989), p. 74.

13. Associated Press, "Racial Slur by Japanese Aide Rekindles Anger," *New York Times* (September 23, 1990).

14. *New York Times* (November 12, 1990).

15. See *Industrial Groupings in Japan* (Tokyo: Dodwell Marketing Consultants, 8th edition 1988–89).

16. Steven R. Weisman, "Foreigners Are Crying Foul over Japan Airport Contract," *New York Times* (November 23, 1990), p. C1.

17. Ibid.

18. See *Industrial Groupings in Japan*.

19. Above and following are from interviews in January 1990 with Naohiro Amaya, Masao Takemoto, and Takaysu Miyakawa; cited in Robert Neff and William J. Holstein, "Mighty Mitsubishi Is on the Move,"*BusinessWeek* (September 24, 1990), p. 98.

20. See *Industrial Groupings in Japan*, p. 9.

21. Ruedi Arnold, "The World of Mitsubishi," *BILANZ* (August 1989) p. 445.

22. Van Wolferen, *The Enigma of Japanese Power*, p. 42.

23. John G. Roberts, *Mitsui* (New York: Weatherhill Inc., 1989).

24. "A Door to the West," *Financial Times* (March 7, 1990); "Daimler-Benz and Mitsubishi: A Tokyo-Stuttgart Axis," *Economist* (March 10, 1990), p. 72; David E. Sanger, "An Uneasy Alliance Is Born for Mitsubishi and Daimler," *New York Times* (September 20, 1990), p. C1; and Stefan Wagstyl, "Daimler and Mitsubishi Unveil 11 Joint Ventures," *Financial Times* (September 20, 1990), p. 1.

25. Neff and Holstein, "Mighty Mitsubishi Is on the Move," *BusinessWeek* (September 24, 1990), p. 98.

26. *BusinessWeek* (September 24, 1990), p. 102.

27. Ibid.

28. Ibid.

29. Ibid.

CHAPTER 8 *MITI City*

1. Sheridan Tatsuno, *The Technopolis Strategy* (New York: Prentice-Hall, 1986), p. xiii.

2. Cited in Bernard Wysocki, Jr., "Meeting Mr. Big Face, Japanese Have Many Words for Arrogance; Americans in Tokyo are Learning Why," *Wall Street Journal Reports, Technology* (November 14, 1988), p. R10.

3. John Markoff, "Future of Big Computing: A Triumph for Lilliputians," *New York Times* (November 25, 1990), p. 1 and Lawrence M. Fisher, "New Fields for the Supercomputer," *New York Times* (June 28, 1989), p. C1.

4. Editorial, *New York Times* (May 10, 1990).

5. Neil Gross, "MITI: The Sugar Daddy to End All Sugar Daddies," *BusinessWeek* (October 23, 1989), p. 112.

6. Michael Rogers, "The Future Looks 'Fuzzy,'" *Newsweek* (May 28, 1990), p. 46; Larry Armstrong, "Why 'Fuzzy Logic' Beats Black-Or-White Thinking," *BusinessWeek* (May 21, 1990), p. 92; and Sheridan M. Tatsuno, *Created in Japan* (New York: Harper & Row, 1990), p. 189.

7. Karen Lowry Miller, "Japan Pours Big Bucks into Very Little Machines," *BusinessWeek* (August 27, 1990), p. 83.

8. Fisher, "New Fields for the Supercomputer," p. C1.

9. Markoff, "Future of Big Computing," p. 1.

10. Ibid.

11. Tatsuno, *The Technopolis Strategy*, pp. 84–91; MITI, *Outline and Present Status of the Technopolis Project* (Industrial Location and Environmental Protection Bureau, October 1989), p. 1.

12. Tatsuno, *The Technopolis Strategy*, p. 95.

13. Wysocki, "Showing Off," *Wall Street Journal Reports, Technology*, p. R26.

14. Tatsuno, *The Technopolis Strategy*, p. 103.

15. Wysocki, "Meeting Mr. Big Face," p. R26.

16. Della Bradshaw, "High Hopes in the Race for Ideas," *Financial Times* (April 4, 1990), p. 14.

17. Ibid.

18. Cited in ibid.

19. Tatsuno, *The Technopolis Strategy*, p. 52.

20. Neil Gross, "Supercomputers: Guess Who's Streaking Past Cray?" *BusinessWeek* (December 10, 1990), p. 212.

21. David Sanger, "A High-Tech Lead in Danger," *New York Times* (December 18, 1988), section 3, p. 1.

22. Neil Gross, "Where Are Computer Makers Thriving? Hint: It Starts with a 'J'" *BusinessWeek* (November 19, 1990), p. 62.

CHAPTER 9 *Slim Pickens*

1. Cited in Mark Ivey, "Boone Pickens, Samurai Warrior," *Business-Week* (May 8, 1989), p. 90.
2. "Japanese Shareholders' Rights, Back of the Queue, Please," *Economist*, (April 29, 1989), p. 82.
3. Kathryn Graven, "Pickens Is Set Again to Challenge Koito at Annual Meeting," *Wall Street Journal* (June 18, 1990), p. A5D.
4. *Wall Street Journal, Financial Times,* and *New York Times,* (June 29, 1990).
5. Robert Zielinski and Nigel Holloway, *Unequal Equities* (Tokyo: Kodansha International, 1991), p. 27.
6. Ibid., pp. 30 and 55.
7. "Japanese Shareholders' Rights," p. 82.
8. Marcus W. Brauchli and Masayoshi Kanabayashi, "Pickens Stuns Japanese by Buying Big Stake in Ally of Toyota," *Wall Street Journal* (April 4, 1989), p. C1 and Ivey, "Boone Pickens, Samurai Warrior," p. 90.
9. Brauchli and Kanabayashi, "Pickens Stuns Japanese by Buying Big Stake in Ally of Toyota," p. C1.
10. "Japanese Shareholders' Rights," p. 82.
11. Ibid.
12. Brauchli and Kanabayashi, "Pickens Stuns Japanese," p. C1.
13. Takao Matsuura, "Boone-San, Either Put Up or Shut Up," *Wall Street Journal* (April 18, 1990).
14. Stefan Wagstyl, "Koito Moves to Stave off Boone," *Financial Times* (May 12, 1989); "Koito Hits Back at Its Predators," *Financial Times* (June 29, 1989); and James Dooley, "Yakuza Connection Surfaces in Pickens Stock Fight," *Honolulu Advertiser* (July 2, 1989).
15. Wagstyl, "Koito Moves to Stave off Boone"; "Koito Hits Back at Its Predators"; and Dooley, "Yakuza Connection Surfaces."
16. Robert Thomson, "Japanese Speculators Reveal All," *Financial Times* (December 14, 1990), p. 23.
17. "Pickens's Koito Stake Was Used as Collateral for Watanabe Loan," *Wall Street Journal* (December 19, 1990) and "Pickens Adds Koito Shares," *New York Times* (December 5, 1990).
18. "Pickens; Koito Stake Was Used as Collateral for Watanabe Loan."
19. Marcus W. Brauchli and Masayoshi Kanabayashi, "Battle for Koito Has Unusual Twist: Its Stock Drops," *Wall Street Journal* (April 11, 1989).
20. Stefan Wagstyl, "Boone Pickens Goes East," *Financial Times* (April 17, 1989), p. 27.

21. Matsuura, "Boone-San."
22. Ibid.
23. Zielinski and Holloway, *Unequal Equities*, p. 210.
24. Tad Holden, "Japan Is Like a Kid in a Candy Store—A Rich Kid," *BusinessWeek* (December 4, 1989), p. 50.
25. "Merger of Taiyo Kobe Bank and Mitsui Bank Reflects Japanese Banking Changes," *Wall Street Journal* (August 30, 1989), p. A7.
26. Ivey, "Boone Pickens, Samurai Warrior"; Stefan Wagstyl, "Boone Pickens Goes East," *Financial Times* (April 17, 1989), p. 27.
27. Zielinski and Holloway, *Unequal Equities*, ch. 1.

CHAPTER 10 *America's Task: Returning to "Go," Getting Down to Basics*

1. In an interview, January, 1990.
2. Pat Choate, *Agents of Influence* (New York: Alfred A. Knopf, 1990), pp. 28–29.
3. Chalmers Johnson, *MITI and the Japanese Miracle* (Tokyo: Charles E. Tuttle, 1986), p. 118.
4. Ibid.
5. Choate, *Agents of Influence*, pp. 28–29.
6. Johnson, *MITI and the Japanese Miracle*, p. 312.
7. *New York Times*, Business World Special (June 10, 1990), p. 20.
8. Dick Nanto, "Japan's Industrial Groups, The Keiretsu," Congressional Research Service, The Library of Congress, "Testimony Prepared for the Joint Economic Committee Hearings on Japan's Economic Challenge" (October 16, 1990), p. 11.
9. Cited in Clyde V. Prestowitz, Jr., *Trading Places* (New York: Basic Books, 1988), p. 309.
10. Nanto, "Japan's Industrial Groups," p. 9.
11. Chalmers Johnson, Noon Lecture, Economic Strategy Institute, February 28, 1991.
12. Council on Competitiveness, "Gaining New Ground: Technology Priorities for America's Future" (Washington, D.C.: March 20, 1991).
13. "Half of Boeing's New Plane Body is 'Made in Japan'—The Customer May Also be Japanese?" *Ashahi Shinbun* (March 5, 1991).
14. Council on Competitiveness, "Gaining New Ground."

References

Abegglen, James C., and Stalk, George, Jr. *Kaisha: The Japanese Corporation*. New York: Basic Books Inc., 1985.

Alletzhauser, Albert J. *The House of Nomura: The Inside Story of the Legendary Japanese Financial Dynasty*. New York: Arcade Publishing, 1990.

Arima, Tatsuo, "The Inner Landscape of Japanese Culture: A Personal Reflection." Speech given at the Hoover Institution, Stanford University, 1988.

Arnesen, Peter J. *The Japanese Competition, Phase 2*. Ann Arbor: The University of Michigan, 1987.

——. *Is There Enough Business to Go Around? Overcapacity in the Auto Industry*. Ann Arbor: The University of Michigan, 1988.

——. *The Auto Industry Ahead: Who's Driving?* Ann Arbor: The University of Michigan, 1989.

Barnett, Donald F., and Schorsch, Louis. *Steel: Upheaval in a Basic Industry*. Cambridge, Mass.: Ballinger Publishing Co., 1983.

Benedict, Ruth. *The Chrysanthemum and the Sword*. Boston: Houghton Mifflin Co., 1989.

Bergsten, Fred C., and Cline, William R. *The United States–Japan Economic Problem*. Washington: Institute for International Economics, 1987.

Burstein, Daniel. *Yen: Japan's New Financial Empire and Its Threat to America*. New York: Simon & Schuster, 1988.

Choate, Pat. *Agents of Influence: How Japan's Lobbyists in the United States Manipulate America's Political and Economic System*. New York: Alfred A. Knopf, 1990.

Christopher, Robert C. *Second to None: American Companies in Japan*. New York: Crown Publishers, Inc., 1986.

Cleary, Thomas. *The Japanese Art of War: Understanding the Culture of Strategy*. Boston: Shambhala, 1991.

Cohen, Stephen S., and Zysman, John. *Manufacturing Matters: The Myth of the Post-Industrial Economy*. New York: Basic Books, 1987.

Czinkota, Michael R., and Woronoff, Jon. *Japan's Market: The Distribution System*. New York: Praeger, 1986.

De Mente, Boye. *Everything Japanese: The Authoritative Reference on Japan Today*. Lincolnwood, Ill.: Passport Books, 1989.

Dertouzos, Michael L.; Lester, Richard K.; and Solow, Robert M. *Made in America: Regaining the Productive Edge*. Cambridge, Mass.: The MIT Press, 1989.

Dodwell Marketing Consultants. *The Structure of the Japanese Auto Parts Industry*. 3rd edition. Tokyo: Dodwell, 1986.

——. *Industrial Groupings in Japan*, 8th edition, 1988/89. Tokyo: Dodwell, 1988.

——. *The Structure of the Japanese Electronics Industry*. 2nd edition. Tokyo: Dodwell, 1988.

Dougherty, Andrew. "Japan:2000." Draft prepared by the Rochester Institute of Technology, Rochester, N.Y., 1991.

Drucker, Peter F. *The New Realities: In Government and Politics, in Economics and Business, in Society and World View*. New York: Harper & Row, 1989.

Emmott, William. *The Sun Also Sets: The Limits to Japan's Economic Power*. New York: Times Books, 1989.

Endo, Shusaku. *The Samurai*. New York: Aventura, 1984.

Fallows, James. *More Like Us: Making America Great Again*. Boston: Houghton Mifflin Co., 1989.

Fields, George. *Gucci on the Ginza: Japan's New Consumer Generation*. Tokyo: Kodansha International, 1989.

Frantz, Douglas, and Collins, Catherine. *Selling Out*. Chicago: Contemporary Books, 1989.

Friedman, Benjamin M. *Day of Reckoning: The Consequences of American Economic Policy under Reagan and After*. New York: Random House, 1988.

Gelsanliter, David. *Jump Start: Japan Comes to the Heartland*. New York: Farrar Straus Giroux, 1990.

Gibney, Frank. *Miracle by Design: The Real Reasons Behind Japan's Economic Success*. New York: Times Books, 1982.

Glickman, Norman J., and Woodward, Douglas P. *The New Competitors: How Foreign Investors Are Changing the U.S. Economy*. New York: Basic Books Inc., 1989.

Graham, Edward M., and Krugman, Paul R. *Foreign Direct Investment in the United States*. Washington: Institute for International Economics, 1989.

Halberstam, David. *The Reckoning*. New York: William Morrow and Co., 1986.

Hall, Edward T., and Hall, Mildred Reed. *Hidden Differences: Doing Business with The Japanese*. Garden City: Anchor Press/Doubleday, 1987.

Halloran, Richard. *Japan: Images and Realities*. Tokyo: Charles E. Tuttle Co., 1970.

Heilbroner, Robert, and Bernstein, Peter. *The Debt and the Deficit: False Alarms/Real Possibilities*. New York: W. W. Norton & Co., 1989.

Hollingsworth, Kent. *The Wizard of the Turf: John E. Madden of Hamburg Place*. Lexington, Ky., 1965.

Inoguchi, Takashi, and Okimoto, Daniel I. *The Political Economy of Japan*, Vol. 2: *The Changing International Context*. Stanford: Stanford University Press, 1988.

Ishihara, Shintaro. *The Japan That Can Say No: Why Japan Will Be First Among Equals*. New York: Simon & Schuster, 1991.

Ishinomori, Shotaro. *Japan Inc.: An Introduction to Japanese Economics*. Berkeley: University of California Press, 1988.

Johnson, Chalmers. *MITI and the Japanese Miracle: The Growth of Industrial Policy, 1925–1975*. Tokyo: Charles E. Tuttle Co., 1986.

Kahn, Herman, and Pepper, Thomas. *The Japanese Challenge: The Success and Failure of Economic Success*. Tokyo: Charles E. Tuttle Co., 1980.

Kennedy, Paul. *The Rise and Fall of the Great Powers*. New York: Random House, 1987.

Kester, W. Carl. *Japanese Takeovers: The Global Contest for Corporate Control*. Boston: Harvard Business School Press, 1991.

Kodansha. *The Best of Japan: Innovations, Present and Future*. Tokyo: Kodansha Ltd., 1987.

Lincoln, Edward K. *Japan: Facing Economic Maturity*. Washington: The Brookings Institution, 1988.

MacKnight, Susan. *Japan's Expanding U.S. Manufacturing Presence: 1988 Update*. Washington: Japan Economic Institute, 1989.

McCraw, Thomas K. *America Versus Japan*. Boston: Harvard Business School Press, 1986.

Morgan, James C., and Morgan, J. Jeffrey. *Cracking the Japanese Market: Strategies for Success in the New Global Economy*. New York: The Free Press, 1991.

Morita, Akio; Reingold, Edwin M.; and Shimomura, Mitsuko. *MADE IN JAPAN: Akio Morita and Sony*. New York: E. P. Dutton, 1986.

243

Morley, John David. *Pictures from the Water Trade: Adventures of a Westerner in Japan.* New York: Atlantic Monthly Press, 1985.

Musashi, Miyamoto. *A Book of Five Rings: The Classic Guide to Strategy.* Woodstock, N.Y.: The Overlook Press, 1982.

Nakane, Chie. *Japanese Society.* Tokyo: Charles E. Tuttle Co., 1989.

Ohmae, Kenichi. *Beyond National Borders: Reflections on Japan and the World.* Homewood, Ill.: Dow Jones-Irwin, 1987.

——. *The Borderless World: Power and Strategy in the Interlinked Economy.* New York: Harper Business, 1990.

Passin, Herbert. *Society and Education in Japan.* Tokyo: Kodansha International Ltd., 1982.

Phillips, Kevin. *The Politics of Rich and Poor: Wealth and the American Electorate in the Reagan Aftermath.* New York: Random House, 1990.

Prestowitz, Clyde V., Jr. *Trading Places: How We Allowed Japan to Take the Lead.* New York: Basic Books Inc., 1988.

Prestowitz, Clyde V., Jr.; Morse, Ronald A.; and Alan Tonelson. *Powernomics, Economics and Strategy after the Cold War.* Lanham, Md.: Madison Books, 1991.

Reich, Robert B. *The Work of Nations: Preparing Ourselves for 21st Century Capitalism.* New York: Alfred A. Knopf, 1991.

Reischauer, Edwin O. *Japan, Past and Present.* Tokyo: Charles E. Tuttle Co., 1985.

Roberts, John G. *MITSUI: Three Centuries of Japanese Business.* New York: Weatherhill, 1989.

Sanders, Sol. *Honda: The Man and His Machines.* Tokyo: Charles E. Tuttle Co., 1977.

Servan-Schreiber, Jean-Jacques. *The American Challenge.* New York: Atheneum, 1968.

Tatsuno, Sheridan. *The Technopolis Strategy: Japan, High Technology and the Control of the Twenty-first Century.* New York: Prentice Hall Press, 1986.

——. *Created in Japan: From Imitators to World Class Competitors.* New York: Ballinger/Harper & Row, 1990.

Tolchin, Martin, and Tolchin, Susan. *Buying into America: How Foreign Money Is Changing the Face of Our Nation.* New York: Times Books, 1988.

Toyo Keizai, Inc. *Japan Company Handbook.* 1st and 2nd sections. Tokyo: Toyo Keizai, 1989.

Van Wolferen, Karel. *The Enigma of Japanese Power: People and Politics in a Stateless Nation.* New York: Alfred A. Knopf, 1989.

244

Wachtel, Howard M. *The Money Mandarins: The Making of a Supranational Economic Order.* New York: Pantheon Books, 1986.

White, Merry. *The Japanese Educational Challenge: A Commitment to Children.* New York: The Free Press, 1987.

Whiting, Robert. *The Chrysanthemum and the Bat: The Game Japanese Play.* Tokyo: The Permanent Press, 1977.

Winston, Clifford, and associates. *Blind Intersection? Policy and the Automobile Industry.* Washington: The Brookings Institution, 1987.

Womack, James P.; Jones, Daniel T.; and Roos, Daniel. *The Machine That Changed the World.* New York: Rawson Associates, 1990.

Woronoff, Jon. *Japan: The Coming Economic Crisis.* Tokyo: Lotus Press, 1979.

Yamamura, Kozo. *Japanese Investment in the United States: Should We Be Concerned?* Seattle: Society for Japanese Studies, University of Washington, 1989.

Yamamura, Kozo, and Yasuba, Yasukichi. *The Political Economy of Japan.* Vol. 1: *The Domestic Transformation.* Stanford: Stanford University Press, 1987.

Zielinski, Robert, and Holloway, Nigel. *Unequal Equities: Power and Risk in Japan's Stock Market.* Tokyo: Kodansha International, 1991.

Index

Manufacturing base, 3, 13–15, 41–42, 221–222
Manufacturing Matters: The Myth of the Post-Industrial Economy (Cohen and Zysman), 13–14
Marunouchi business district, 4, 153–159, 169, 185, 220
Marysville, Ohio, 53, 218
Massachusetts, 101
Materials Research Corporation, 102, 115–116
Matson Navigation Companies, 133
Matsushita Electric Industrial Company, 18, 80, 84–86, 93, 103, 116, 209
Matsushita Real Estate, 209
Matsuura, Takao, 205, 207, 209, 211
Maui, 134
Mazda, 7, 22, 74, 218
MCA Inc., 84–86
MCA Television, 84
McCurry, Robert B., 76
McDonald's, 164
McLuhan, Marshall, 80
McNealy, Scott, 118
Medical devices, 119
Meiji Dori Street, Tokyo, 161–162
Meiji Mutual Life, 158, 176, 177
Meiji restoration of 1868, 4, 157,158
Meitus Advertising, 134
MGM/UA Communications, Company, 84
Michels, Allen, 111, 112
Michigan, 7, 61, 74, 218
Microchips, 12–13, 101, 106, 115–116, 186
Microrobots, 187–189
Milken, Michael, 151
Military equipment, 54, 119, 179
Mimura, Yohei, 173, 214
Ministry of Education's High Energy Physics Laboratory, 191
Ministry of Finance, 4, 11, 20, 27, 31, 152, 154, 211
Ministry of International Trade and Industry (MITI), 4, 20, 24, 31, 154, 155, 186–189, 191–197
 Electrotechnical Laboratory, 189, 191
 Mechanical Engineering Laboratory, 192
Mini-supercomputers, 111, 112
MIPS Computer Systems, 111

Missouri, 61
MIT (Massachusetts Institute of Technology), 94, 150, 185, 189
MITI and the Japanese Miracle (Johnson), 9, 171, 214
Mitsubishi Atomic Power and Precision, 174
Mitsubishi Bank, 145, 158, 174, 176, 177, 180–182, 209
Mitsubishi Bank North America, 180
Mitsubishi Corporation, 174–176, 181–182
Mitsubishi Electric, 176, 180, 181
Mitsubishi Electronics, 91, 103, 116
Mitsubishi Estate, 2, 87, 123, 142, 156–158, 174, 176, 180, 182–183
Mitsubishi Foundation, 172
Mitsubishi Gas Chemical, 182
Mitsubishi group, 4, 7, 17, 87, 115, 122, 154, 156–160, 165, 169–182, 210
Mitsubishi Heavy Industries, 174, 176, 180, 219
Mitsubishi International, 180, 182
Mitsubishi Kasei, 182
Mitsubishi Metal, 176
Mitsubishi Motors, 7, 35, 41, 48, 70, 73, 74, 89, 180–182, 218
Mitsubishi Office Machinery, 174
Mitsubishi Oil, 176
Mitsubishi Petrochemical, 182
Mitsubishi Rayon, 182
Mitsubishi Semiconductor, 181
Mitsubishi Steel, 180
Mitsubishi Trust & Banking Company, 124, 158, 174, 176, 180, 182
Mitsui Bank, 47, 63, 67, 146, 210
Mitsui & Company, 123
Mitsui group, 4, 7, 17, 18, 63, 117, 122, 134, 156, 165, 169, 176, 183, 210
Mitsui Real Estate, 133
Mitsui Trust & Banking Company, 6
Miyakawa, Takaysu, 173–174
Mizoguchi, Tadaaki, 181
Mizuno, Takanori, 144
Mobil Corporation, 19
Monsanto, 19
Montana, 6
Morgan, J. Pierpont, 18, 19
Morgantown, Kentucky, 49